Daring the Doctorate

The Journey at Mid-Career

Ada Demb

D1294656

ROWMAN & LITTLEFIELD EDUCATION
A division of
ROWMAN & LITTLEFIELD PUBLISHERS, INC.
Lanham • New York • Toronto • Plymouth, UK

Published by Rowman & Littlefield Education
A division of Rowman & Littlefield Publishers, Inc.
A wholly owned subsidiary of The Rowman & Littlefield Publishing Group, Inc.
4501 Forbes Boulevard, Suite 200, Lanham, Maryland 20706
www.rowman.com

10 Thornbury Road, Plymouth PL6 7PP, United Kingdom

British Library Cataloguing in Publication Information Available

Library of Congress Cataloging-in-Publication Data

Demb, Ada.
Daring the doctorate : the journey at mid-career / Ada Demb.
p. cm.
Includes bibliographical references and index.
ISBN 978-1-61048-694-1 (pbk. : alk. paper) -- ISBN 978-1-61048-695-8 (electronic) (print)
1. Dissertations, Academic--Authorship. 2. Doctoral students. 3. Adult college students. 4. Mid-career. I. Title.
LB2369.D45 2012
808.02--dc23
2012034795

Printed in the United States of America

For my people—from whom I learned so much.

Table of Contents

List of Figures and Tables

FIGURES

TABLES

Foreword

Dennis Shirley, Professor of Education, Lynch School of Education, Boston College

One of the oddities of contemporary life is that educators have gathered astonishing compilations of data about student achievement but somehow seem to have overlooked its most important dimension: namely, how it is that students not only *experience*, but *actively construct* their own learning. It has become an increasingly pervasive and unquestioned assumption that educators should start with quantitative test score data and plan backwards to improve instruction and curriculum with the goal of improving results. The National Assessment for Educational Progress in the United States and the Program for International Student Assessment of Organization for Economic Cooperation and Development are just two of the most ambitious tracking and monitoring systems that are transforming education globally at the time of this writing. Such a mechanistic and managerial approach altogether eclipses a quietly insistent anterior question: How does the individual not only *passively receive*, but instead *actively engage* with the learning process?

To answer this question, Professor Ada Demb of Ohio State University offers a rich treasure trove of information for the curious reader and especially for those with interests in adult education. Professor Demb observes that even though we know a great deal about the structuring and organization of the doctoral student experience in our universities, we know relatively little about the human side of the enterprise. What emotional considerations, what strategic and practical concerns, and what ethical preoccupations enter into the lives of doctoral students and especially those at the mid-career level? How do they compensate for the loss of the status and income, and the sacrifices of family time that are entailed in returning to graduate student status? How do they overcome the many impediments to their own learning that can be thrown up in their way en route to a doctorate, and how do they acquire the necessary humility to advance through the devious and trying stages of formulating a research question, designing appropriate research methodologies, gathering information, and finally interpreting it so that it makes a lasting contribution to new knowledge?

The answers to these and other questions are explored in the pages that follow in *Daring the Doctorate*. Here are narratives of doctoral students who struggle with family health crises, financial debt, and existential anxiety as they question whether they are putting their self-interest in advancing their academic careers ahead of their loved ones. Here are stories of individuals who push themselves, sometimes mercilessly, to overcome all kinds of professional and economic obstacles in pursuit of personal excellence and the aspiration to make a lasting contribution to the advancement of knowledge. *Daring the Doctorate* reminds us just how much heroism is around us on a daily basis if we but open our eyes to the many daunting tasks that individuals take on as part of their own personal quests for mastery of a hitherto unexplored niche of new knowledge.

Many research studies provide information but leave us inwardly untouched, but *Daring the Doctorate* does not belong to that genre. It reminds us that however much we may construct the doctoral student experience as one marked by a course of studies, a submission of a dissertation proposal, and a successful defense, an abundance of parallel and often over-looked events are in many ways the determinative ones that matter for the individual and for the profession. In the language of Jürgen Habermas, beyond the *Strukturwelt* of the organization and the bureaucracy lies the *Lebenswelt* of a far messier, confusing, and inchoate reality. Our lives are regulated, steered, and sometimes compelled by the *Strukturwelt*, but it seems to be a part of our human condition that no matter how much we might push for its dominance and control—one thinks of the machinations of totalitarian regimes, whether fascist or com-munistic—the *Lebenswelt* of individual experience will force its way to the surface and force us to acknowledge that it also lays legitimate claims on our attention and on our research.

I personally am grateful for this small gem of a book because it has changed how I will encounter my own doctoral students. *Daring the Doctorate* has taught me that it would behoove university-level instructors to be more mindful of, and more empathic toward, the doctoral students we interact with on a daily basis. We need to wonder at and validate our students' struggles and challenges; we need to remember that we ourselves once thrashed about with research methodologies and questioned our motivations and aspirations; we need to be quiet and practice deep and open-minded listening to the stories about their experiences that our students share with us day by day, week by week, and year by year. If we can do so, we not only will help our students to navigate the tricky waters that lead to the completion of their doctoral degrees, but we also will reexperience the joy and fulfillment that our universities still continue to offer students, and that provide the very raison d'être for their perseverance and necessity in an age in which so many educational institutions are in a state of perilous disequilibrium.

Preface

Are you restless? After being out in the workforce for a few years, do you have the sense there is more that you can accomplish professionally—if only you had another degree? Are you mulling the possibility of a faculty position? Or would you rather think in terms of a more senior administrative position? Are these musings leading you to think about getting a doctorate? If so, this book is for you.

Or, are you puzzled? Perhaps you have been teaching for some years now and advising doctoral students. Perhaps you are the graduate studies chair for your department, or head of graduate student services. Or maybe, you're a new faculty member. You have seen many students finish the doctorate successfully. And, yet you've "lost" some students—more than you wished, students you thought fully capable of completing the degree program. They left. Some of these students had jobs and families, but you thought they had worked out those details. You're aware of the increased murmur nationally about doctoral completion rates, and wonder whether you or your program could be doing something differently. If so, this book is also for you.

Perhaps you have just completed your doctorate and are wondering if others experienced the angst, stress, and exhilaration that you felt. Or whether they believed the journey to be worth effort? And how long it took for life to return to normal? This book is for you, too.

The book grew out of my experience advising doctoral students beginning in the fall of 1994, when Carole and Kelly appeared in my office. Accomplished mid-career professionals both seemed a bit at sea with their new circumstances. At the time, so was I, having just relocated to the faculty from the senior administrative position that had brought me to the university. Yes, I had a doctorate from Harvard, and a lot of research and administrative experience, but they were my first two doctoral advisees. So, we all gulped and agreed to proceed in this new adventure. We felt a bit like pioneers setting off for California in their Conestoga wagons. We knew where we wanted to end up, but set off with only a basic set of directions and a lot of trepidation. Since that time, twenty of my doctoral advisees have graduated, all but one having started the program at mid-career.

The advisor-student relationship in a doctoral program is an intimate one. During the course of four to five years typically, and sometimes six or seven years, you interact at the best of times and the worst of times. We laughed together, hung in there through confusing conversations, struggled to explain concepts and theories, gave and swallowed unwelcome feedback about papers and chapters, and occasionally, cried. Mostly, we met in my office, sometimes went to lunch, and one Sunday each year in the fall gathered for a late afternoon potluck at my home with the faculty and other PhD students in the program.

No matter how private or how easily they shared personal stories, I became aware of family situations and experienced the ebbs and flows of energy. Children were involved in accidents; parents died; divorce claimed a year and half of life; pregnancy and babies framed our schedules and thrilled us; remarkable new jobs took some across the country and oceans just as they were analyzing dissertation data and writing chapters. Between express mail, e-mail and long telephone conversations, we made it work, and they finished.

Five years later, a different person emerges: stronger, more focused, thinking more clearly and more complexly, seeing the world through multiple lenses simultaneously, and appreciating the previously unseen facets of everyone and everything around them. Now you know how to frame questions, and where to go looking for answers.

Completing a doctorate is complicated. Doing it while maintaining a full- or part-time job, or with a partner, or children, or some combination of all three is a gargantuan undertaking. And, shifting into the role of student after having been a successful professional—assistant dean of students, head of financial aid, admissions vice president, professor—challenges a person's self-image and threatens your center of gravity.

My observations of these twenty folks, and the three who are still mid-process, led me to believe that the experience of the doctorate for the person at mid-career differs significantly from those who move directly from undergraduate to graduate school, through master's and PhD. As I interacted with more and different students, there seemed to be patterns that emerged as the students hit a wall and then figured out how to get through it, hit the next, and figured out that one, too. I gave the walls names, but was unsure whether my perceptions truly reflected student experience.

So I asked them. On a vacation in Michigan, I had lunch with Kelly in the summer of 2009, and asked her. "What do you mean?" she asked. So I explained again. "Oh," she said. And, ninety minutes later, we forced ourselves to stop talking because my husband was getting restless. Tina reacted the same way a few months later. Then the academic year started and as always, I was caught up in teaching and serving as section head and doing everything else that takes your time and attention. Then during the winter, Tina said, "So are you going to do something or not?" And I sent out an email to the sixteen of my advisees who had already completed by spring of 2010, asking their opinions and whether they would be willing to come together to talk about their experiences. All sixteen said yes.

In August 2010, thirteen of my former advisees came to town for a focused discussion that began at 8:30 AM on Saturday morning, and finished at noon on Sunday, including a dinner on Saturday. More precisely, twelve people came Saturday, and one more person (Carole) arrived for Sunday morning. Some were local; others traveled from Vermont, Michigan, Wisconsin, and Maryland. We video-conferenced one person in from Washington, D.C., and Stephanie was on audio-feed from Luxembourg—with a large photo of her taped to the video screen. In November, Carole, along with the two others who missed the August sessions, joined a three-hour video conference. In all, fifteen people participated, for thirteen hours of focus group conversation, yielding more than four hundred pages of transcript. Not only did they give the walls new names, but they described walls and tunnels and rivers and rapids that I had not anticipated. This book is a distillation of their experiences, blended with pertinent background from previous research and some theories about adult development.

When fifteen professionals tell me they are willing to give three days of their time to come talk with me about "my" idea, I needed to prepare. In May 2010, Alycia Keller answered a query I sent to our masters' students, asking for someone to help with a literature review and organize the logistics of the conference. Together, we found and read about eighty books and articles, many of which appear in the reference list at the end of this book. For the researchers among the readers, the structure of the conference focus group and analytic methodology are described in the appendix. The project was reviewed and approved for human subjects procedures by my university's institutional review board. All the participants were students at The Ohio State University, in the Higher Education and Student Affairs program, and all were my advisees.

The chapters are organized thematically, and are full of stories. This is not a "how to" book, but rather a "view from the inside out" book. The final chapters present a synthesis of their experiences in the form of a model about the dynamics of the mid-career transformation, and the insights to be gained by applying several well-known developmental theories to this context.

During the period these folks were my advisees, I "lost" four other students. After one year, a lawyer figured out he really didn't need the PhD, and accepted a fine new legal position. One person working full-time at a local institution disappeared from classes and simply stopped communicating after the first year; didn't respond to any e-mail or third-party inquiries. Another kept promising chapters to a faculty colleague and me and then cancelling appointments. And a fourth stalled out after completing coursework, and just couldn't seem to frame the draft of the dissertation research, which our program requires prior to the candidacy exam. In sum, four out of twenty failed to complete. Three more are still in process (all in dissertation), chugging along just fine.

National statistics show that more than half the individuals who begin doctoral work fail to finish. In our program overall, our best estimate is a 60–70 percent completion rate. So the perspectives presented here represent successful PhD students—completed, graduated, and employed. They are remarkable individuals—talented, intelligent, committed, incredibly hard-working and high energy. I learned a lot from them, and offer those insights to you with their permission.

Acknowledgments

I want to thank the fifteen amazing professionals who participated in this project. Without them, it simply could not have happened. Special thanks go to Tina, who kept asking "Well, are you going to do it or not?" and the five who took the time to review drafts of the manuscript and provide feedback.

Few projects of any magnitude can be accomplished alone. The wonderful Alycia Keller signed on as a research assistant to help with background research, review the literature, and handle the complicated logistics for the August and November video conferences. I want to recognize Nicholas Thompson who set up the technical protocols, and then spent a weekend facilitating the video recordings.

I also want to acknowledge my colleagues in the Higher Education and Student Affairs program. We served together on admissions committees, program committees, dissertation committees and spent long hours in candidacy and dissertation defenses. My thanks, too, to my friend, Dean Michael Gerald, who asked a key question one February weekend on the beach.

Professor Ray Calabrese set an example when he asked me to write a chapter for his book and a year later set up the phone call with Dr. Thomas F. Koerner, now vice president of Rowman & Littlefield Education. The telephone conversation with Tom Koerner was the turning point in the project, and ultimately gave me the confidence to write this book.

Finally, I am grateful to my husband, Bill, for his patience and encouragement. He thought the beach meant vacation, and six chapters later realized why we bought the new desks for the study.

Chapter One

Doctoral Students and Project Participants

Doctoral students past, present, and future (like Dickens's ghosts) are the main characters in this conversation. Who are they? Who enrolls in doctoral programs, and how many of them are mid career? Who participated in this project, and why? What makes the project authentic? Those are the questions this chapter will address.

WHO'S STUDYING FOR A DOCTORATE?

The path to the PhD is a long one, taking from three to five years, and engaging the student in a journey that transforms an individual with talent into an independent researcher (Lovitts, 2005) with skills and perspectives related to research methodology and critical research issues in their field. Graduates move on to roles as faculty and researchers in higher education, and into the many professions as researchers and administrators in industry and education.

According to a most recent report of the National Center for Education Statistics (Cataldi and Ho, 2010), there were 2.7 million enrolled graduate students in 2007–2008, of which 15 percent or 405,000, were in doctoral programs. Later in the text, the same report refers to 3 million graduate students, which rounds to 450,000 students and will be our working number. The authors use three categories of doctoral education: PhD (60 percent), education degrees (15 percent), and any other doctoral programs (26 percent).

About one-third of those students either began their doctoral work more than seven years after receiving their baccalaureate (Choy and Weko, 2011) or received their doctoral degrees over the age of thirty-six (Hoffer et al., 2006). If we define *mid-career* to include those who began doctoral work more than three years after their baccalaureate, that proportion grows to about 56 percent of doctoral students, or about 253,000 adults. Across the three categories there are large variations: 56 percent of PhD students and 56 percent students in other programs began three or more years after their baccalaureate, but 92 percent of education doctoral students began three or more years after their baccalaureate.

Slightly less than half the students overall (212,000) are enrolled part-time and again there is variation across categories: 40 percent of PhD, 75 percent of education, and 40 percent of other. About half are full-time working adults (220,000): 43 percent of PhD students, 72 percent in education, 42 percent of the other. Close to 40 percent are married. In PhD and other programs 16–18 percent of students are married without dependents and another 19 percent are married with dependents. However, in education, about 16 percent are married without dependents, and 43 percent are married with dependents. And, between 5 percent and

12 percent of students are unmarried with dependents. The unmarried students without dependents comprise between 20 percent and 60 percent of students depending upon degree program.

AND WHAT DO WE KNOW ABOUT THE PROCESS?

Attrition rates in doctoral programs can range from 20 percent to almost 70 percent, depending upon the field (Lovitts, 2001, 12). While research has focused on reasons for departure (Cumming, 2009; Suhre, Jansen, and Harskamp, 2007), the graduate student experience (Devenish, Dyer, Jefferson, Lord, van Leeuwen, and Fazakerly, 2009; Solem, Lee, and Schlempe, 2009), issues with writing the dissertation (Calabrese and Smith, 2010a, 2010b; Galvan, 2006), very few seem to have addressed the dynamics related to graduate study for these individuals who continue working full-time while engaged in doctoral programs, or those who have entered doctoral programs mid-career, having left responsible positions to begin doctoral work (Gardner, 2008; Thomson and Walker, 2010; Walker and Thompson, 2010; Watts, 2010). Many professionals, particularly in the fields of education, human ecology, social work, and law, begin again in the middle of their careers.

The purpose of my research was to explore and illuminate the dynamics of the mid-career doctoral experience. The results yield insights that can be used by individuals contemplating PhD work, faculty supervising doctoral students, program administrators, and staff advisors to improve their ability to assist these talented students, or by those midstream who are struggling with the emotional and practical aspects of making it through PhD programs.

I sought answers to these types of questions:

1. Why do people leave productive professional positions to come into doctoral programs?
2. What are the major concerns of mid-career doctoral students?
3. What factors enable or inhibit them as they seek to make progress in their doctoral studies?
4. What aspects of the doctoral program differ from what they had anticipated?
5. What was most difficult about their programs?
6. What was most rewarding about the programs?
7. In what ways do they feel they have changed as a result of their doctoral experiences?
8. How do they believe their experience differed from students coming more directly from master's or undergraduate school?
9. What theories will assist in understanding these experiences more systematically?

WHO PARTICIPATED IN THE STUDY: WHAT MAKES IT AUTHENTIC?

Answering these types of questions required a qualitative approach that could engage individuals with relevant experience in discussions to explore the topics. For purposes of this project, the individuals must have completed their doctoral program successfully. In order to minimize variation by type of program, and/or advisor, I invited students whom I advised through to completion of the doctoral program. By June 2010 that included sixteen individuals; fifteen agreed to participate. All were enrolled in a doctoral program in education, specifically, Higher Education and Student Affairs.

Because they were reconstructing memory of their experiences, I used two major forms of data collection: (a) a reflection paper written by the participants, a form of autoethnography (Ellis and Bochner, 2003; Jones, 2009), and (b) focus group discussions. Thirteen graduates joined a two-day retreat in August 2010 that ran all day Saturday through dinner, and again Sunday morning. Two who were unable to participate in August, and one other, who only participated on Sunday, joined in a video conference for three hours on a Sunday afternoon in November. The reflection papers were shared with the group prior to the conference, serving as "prompts" for the focus group discussions. All the discussions were video- and audiotaped for later analysis. In all, the thirteen hours of discussion produced about four hundred pages of transcript. (A full discussion of the research methodology appears in the appendix.)

In previous research, attrition and completion rates have varied by field of study, discipline, department, institution, and programs. Doctoral programs across fields of study share many similarities and display many differences. Most salient for our discussion is one particular dimension: the degree to which the program demands that the student function as an independent researcher who must originate and frame the dissertation research and method, collect the data him- or herself, and write an independent set of analyses, interpretation, and implications. Students asked to function independently face different challenges than students who join ongoing faculty projects, or research center grants.

Students joining ongoing research projects often find themselves in team situations where research questions have already been framed, and their role is primarily to either replicate a study in a different milieu or to collect data and generate analyses that represent a subset of a larger project. The scope and methodology for the research have already been (largely) defined (Yates, 2010). Often, these students, whether in the social, physical, or natural sciences, are grant supported. Typically, these circumstances result in more efficient and direct paths through dissertation research.

Students who are required to originate, frame, conduct, and analyze their own research face different challenges. With guidance, it is still up to them to identify an issue important to their field of study; frame the issue in terms of researchable questions; define epistemology, research design, and a valid methodology; secure access to data (whether physical or human subject); and figure out how to interpret findings. The path through the dissertation research can be slow going, as students learn about and then execute the full research process, step by step. The participants in this project experienced doctoral research as independent researchers.

Either situation can produce fine and competent professionals capable of good research. At some point, those who participate in ongoing projects will learn the same skills as the independent students for identifying and framing questions and methodologies. They may learn these skills during their work in the larger project through the tutelage of a senior researcher or they may learn them later, as they pursue their own research projects. Nonetheless, in reading this book, it is important that the reader bear in mind the nature of the research challenges presented by this doctoral program.

THE CAST

Like a playbill, this section introduces the people who participated in the "mid-career project" and shared their stories. Fifteen individuals, eleven women and four men, brought their experience, insights, and lives to the discussion. I will refer to them always by their first names; two requested the privacy of pseudonyms. Ranging in age from twenty-six to forty-seven when they began the program, thirteen were married or partnered, and among them mothered and fathered sixteen children, four of whom were born during the degree journey.

The Women

Carole came to the PhD program at forty-one. Married, with six children, ages ten to twenty-one, she had been working for some years as director of financial aid at a small, specialized institution of higher education. A year into the program her boss changed institutions, and so did Carole, assuming a thirty-nine-hour per week, part-time job as an academic advisor. She maintained this position throughout her program. She commuted to campus, a 170-mile round-trip, several days a week. She was one of my first two doctoral advisees.

Davida arrived on campus as a twenty-six-year-old single mother with a newborn son to begin the master's program. She came to the program after three years of student affairs experience at two different institutions and would complete that program on schedule with her cohort. She began the PhD program two years later. At the ceremony to mark her PhD graduation, we recognized her son, then seven years old. She carried full-time graduate assistantship responsibilities (twenty hours per week) throughout both degree programs, first teaching, then in administration.

Emily returned to the university after completing a master's program six years earlier, having left her position at a small, independent private college as vice president for enrollment management. At forty-one, she was married and the mother of two adolescents. During her PhD program, she would go through a divorce, accompany her children to visit and select colleges, and relocate to accept a senior administrative position at an institution in northern New England just after completing data collection for her dissertation. She began the program with a graduate assistantship that quickly turned into full-time employment at the university, until her move in the final year.

Jaime came directly to the program from her master's degree at a prestigious private institution. Having worked for a few years, she was single, twenty-six years old, and new to the university and the city when she arrived. During the program she held a graduate assistantship. She met her fiancé partway through the program, maintaining a long-distance relationship until their marriage shortly after her graduation four years later. Her initial advisor accepted a position at another institution as she began writing her dissertation proposal and was preparing for her candidacy exam, so she asked if I would be her chair.

Kathy married the week before beginning the doctoral program. In fact, she missed orientation because of her honeymoon. She had spent seven years in the pharmaceutical industry before deciding that a doctorate in higher education would be the most productive path toward her goal of improving pharmaceutical education. At age thirty-one when she began the program, she was working full-time in an administrative role. Her school created a graduate assistantship for her during the fourth year of her program, so that she could focus on the research and data collection for her dissertation. She returned to the college full-time as an assistant dean.

Kelly began the doctoral program at the age of thirty-five after serving as director of financial aid for a midsized private college. She and her partner purchased a small house near campus, and she held a full-time graduate assistantship during her program. The second, of my first two advisees, she graduated within five year, and was immediately offered a senior administrative position at major land-grant university—a position she has held since that time.

Laura was one of the younger members of the group when she began her PhD at age twenty-six. Married, with no children, she had been teaching for several years as an instructor at a midwestern university, in the allied health field. New accreditation guidelines were being readied for implementation in her professional field and she enrolled in a program in higher education to gain a better understanding of the impacts that impending change would mean, not only for curriculum, but also in terms of the number and types of institutions whose programs would survive that change. She accepted a faculty position at our institution right after her graduation and has since been promoted to the associate level. She completed the degree in three and three-quarter years.

Olivia was the youngest of the group to enter the program at age twenty-six. She came directly from a master's program in public administration. Not originally assigned as my advisee, she sought me out in her second year. Married and working full-time, Olivia gave birth to two sons during her degree program. The first was born six weeks before she took her candidacy exam; the second arrived the day after she turned in the final, defense-ready draft of her dissertation. She graduated on schedule, within the typical five-year time frame.

Polly is among the more experienced of the group. She began the program at forty-two, and maintained her responsibilities as chair of a department of nursing at another institution throughout her degree work. Married and mother of two teenagers when she began, she handled professional responsibilities that included accreditation visits, curricular reform, and writing major grant proposals, along with a serious accident one son suffered during the program. She completed in six years, after beginning her doctoral work in another section of the department, and with a different advisor.

Stephanie was single and twenty-eight years old when she began the master's program, having spent five years as coordinator of an overseas student program in Europe. She started with a graduate assistantship during the master's program and was hired full-time as she began the doctoral program. She met her fiancé during a professional trip to Europe. They married a year later and moved to Luxembourg the year she began writing her dissertation. She completed the program in five years, and a month after the "mid-career" focus group discussions, gave birth to her second daughter.

Tina had earned two master's degrees and was a successful faculty member at another institution for sixteen years when she began her doctoral work, at age forty-seven. She continued in this role throughout her program, taking courses as she could and using summers for more in-depth research and writing. Because her first advisor retired from the institution, she requested my help. She took eight years to complete the program.

The Men

Ben was twenty-nine years old and married when he began the master's program. He had spent several years working in Asia, teaching English prior to returning to graduate school. Finishing the master's in two years while working as a graduate assistant, he accepted a full-time position in the same office when he began the doctoral program. Within two years, prior to his candidacy exam and dissertation research, he accepted a senior administrative position at a local community college. He continues to work for that institution. One of his children was born two months before his candidacy exam, and the other as he began writing his dissertation. He took six years to complete the program.

Brad was thirty years old and married when he enrolled in the doctoral program, having taught English in China and earned a master's at a different university. He had been teaching full-time at our institution for two years before entering the program. At that point, he shifted into graduate assistantship roles, first in administration and then teaching. He accepted a senior administrative position at another land-grant university five hundred miles away just after completing the data collection for his dissertation. He took five years to complete the program.

Brian was twenty-eight, partnered, and working full-time at our institution as he began his doctoral studies. He continued to work full-time throughout the program. His advisor changed jobs and moved to another institution, so Brian sought me out in his third year, as he was beginning to write his dissertation proposal and prepare for the candidacy exam. He finished on schedule in four years and holds a senior administrative position at a southern institution.

Seth completed a master's degree at another institution and had been working in residence life and student affairs for seven years prior to enrolling in the PhD program at the age of thirty-one. Unmarried, from the South, he was new to the university and the city with its northern climate when he arrived. He completed the program, while working as a graduate teaching assistant, in four years. He met his fiancée during the final year of his program. The most recent graduate of the group he is now a visiting lecturer in Texas.

WHY PARTICIPATE IN THIS PROJECT?

Why would these busy individuals with their many professional and family responsibilities take the time, two days for most, three for some, to participate in these sessions? For those coming from significant distances, the project budget barely covered airfare and offered no reimbursement for hotel accommodations, and for Seth and Stephanie, participation meant long hours in front of computer screens, where Stephanie lacked visual input due to trans-Atlantic bandwith limitations from Luxembourg. Their responses to a direct question in the reflection paper exercise and in the first focus group session, and comments from the final morning fell into eight categories: because Ada asked, to give back, because the experience was so impactful, to be part of the research, to provide perspectives for others, to listen to the narratives, to reflect, and to reflect with others who understand.

As gratifying as it felt to hear more than half indicate that being responsive to my request was a large part of the reason they came, it was even more interesting to listen to them offer other reasons that carried important messages, sometimes related to their current administrative roles, sometimes aimed at offering perspectives to potential students, advisors, and faculty, and often, related to a desire to share and connect at the deep level that is only possible with folks who have traveled the same journey.

"Giving back" was a term used explicitly by about five of the participants. "I decided to come this weekend really as a way to perhaps give back," Emily stated. Olivia was more specific, "This is an amazing opportunity to perhaps help others negotiate some of the emotionally taxing experiences the PhD experience presents." And Brian elaborated, using as an example the impact his presence, as a knowledgeable colleague and sounding board, appeared to have made on his supervisor's twelve-year hiatus,

> It has been about three years since I finished. . . . I literally moved . . . the week after I graduated to start my new job here and it was honestly like the first year before I stopped and thought about what I had gone through and then also, having a lot of colleagues down here who are either thinking about going back to school—my own boss, he actually started his doctorate and stopped for twelve years . . . and went back to finishing it. Finished last year and part of that was he had the ability to talk to someone, supervise actually someone, who kind of just went through what he was about to finish and I sort of observed from him, in some ways, as in, a sounding board and . . . just someone to process with, someone who could identify with what it means to prepare for candidacy exams and what questions could be asked of you during your defense and how I prepared for that. Just things like that I think were helpful because he didn't really have anybody around him who had had that experience.

Several people, particularly Polly and Carole, felt that those contemplating the experience needed to understand the "impact" the experience could make on a person's life and the importance of the conversation as well. In the context of discussing her experience, and isolation as a result of the logistical demands of a long commute, Carole said, "Because I commuted to campus, much of my experience was singular and I did not share it with anyone, so this is an opportunity to talk about a pivotal and life-altering, career-changing event that was rich in personal meaning." She went on, "Because it was such a significant event and there's been so many ramifications and now it's like coming back to it and looking at it from a ten-year vantage point. For me that is just very impactful."

Polly focused on the unpredictable nature of personal journeys, and the role the PhD might play in that journey.

> The compelling part of this conversation for me is really about individual journeys. I believe it to be more true today than ever before, that people don't end up on their life journey were they started out to go. I graduated in 1975 with a bachelor of science degree in nursing, with no plans for graduate school. A PhD was not on the radar anywhere, and a career in higher education had never entered my mind. It was through a series of personal and professional growth experiences as well as some significant stressful life situations that led me to where I am today. Over my twenty-eight years in higher education, I have heard many stories following the same theme. All of these stories had the same unpredicted path. Many have had a new beginning mid-career and over forty years of age. So, I think there is a greater meaningful story to be told through these conversations and potentially through work yet to be done.

Being "part of the research" itself offered Jaime and Stephanie a possible route to "jump-starting" their own work again. Jaime captured the sentiment: "The positions I've been in since I've graduated have had little to no requirement for 'academic' components or research, and the appeal of connecting to research again was appealing—this project may jump-start some more of this type of work for me." And for Laura and Seth, the idea of being involved in turning "anecdotal tales" into something beyond a "first-person column," perhaps even a developmental framework for mid-career doctoral students, was very attractive.

Davida and Laura cautioned program personnel (faculty, advisors, and students) to "listen to the narratives" of project participants. Davida focused on the stages of the process.

> I decided to participate in this study because I think it is important for others, including potential PhD candidates, dissertation advisors, committee members, and graduate programs to hear narratives of students who have made it through the doctoral process. It is tough. There is a part of the process where you are excited, and say that "I made it, I am here." Then you enter the process, take the core requirements and commence the research end of the degree. You hit roadblocks, but you push past them. And, eventually you are done. Afterwards . . . you feel overwhelmed, glad you're done, and then I think there's a process of withdrawal, like you've been doing this for many, many years and then all of a sudden, your life switches.

Laura drew attention to the practical outcome of listening. "I would say that that's one of the reasons to do this project is that when people are looking to come back to school, it is so critical that part of what they select is not the school, but the mentor. But I think this is really key. If we're looking for a concrete reason to do this and there's tons of theoretical reasons, but concretely is the message of how to pick your doctoral program."

Just about everyone agreed that the main reason for participating was "to reflect." "I like the idea of the reflection. This is a great opportunity for self-reflection and hence, personal growth. I very much look forward to the opportunity of reflecting back on the experience of being a PhD student and working on and completing my dissertation while working full-time, as much of it seems a blur now," Stephanie commented. The opportunity to reflect more formally, "as opposed to reminiscing" was important for Tina and Laura. Having the time to reflect, to get into an intellectual dialogue was valued by Brian, Brad, and Jaime, all three now in administrative roles. Like Brian, who picked up and moved to a new job in a new university in a different state the week after he finished, Kelly missed having the "time to kind of let things sort of settle down." She continued,

> Then you know life happens, and stuff happens and you just kind of keep going on that roller coaster . . . thinking about the program, thinking about what it meant and what it's been for me and how I did it, all of those things. So that was my why.
>
> The closure, as well, when I finished the PhD I had a lot of life pieces to pick up, and I never really thought backwards at that time.
>
> So you know, there you go. I wanted to do this partly certainly because you asked, and because I was interested but what I said about closure—not entirely sure exactly what I meant but that was the word that popped into my head, so that's the word I used. I finished in August. I graduated in August. I moved to Michigan from Columbus right after finishing program. You know that included selling a house, packing up everything, moving, and I started a new job within like a week or two.

As Ben said, many felt they had "not had the time to do reflective research and intellectual activity that was so intensely exciting, challenging as the dissertation and just being in a room of like-minded people." Ben's comment highlights the importance of reflecting "with others who understand."

Time and again, people talked about the connection and comfort they experienced being in a room with others who had travelled the same road. At the most basic level, the setting seemed to offer the chance to hear other stories, which in some cases, echoed their own, and in others, revealed fascinating differences. In addition, the group gave each person tacit permission to voice questions and discuss reactions and feelings about their PhD experiences, many of which are as vital today as they were during the program, as participants confront new choices that will continue to shape their careers.

Their comments describing the importance of *sharing* the experience highlighted so many slightly different dimensions, that I have quoted a dozen here. From their comments, I learned that the cohort experience the faculty intentionally sought to create for them during their programs, "lasted" much longer and remained important long afterward. The value of the cross-cohort conversation that I encouraged among all my PhD advisees as their advisor, and sometimes specifically requested, is much greater than I anticipated, apparently because the journey is so demanding, and so (potentially) isolating. Here they ascribe their participation in the project associated with the cohort experience.

"I was part of a very strong cohort during the PhD program. I didn't realize in the beginning how meaningful, nor how much I valued, the opportunity to connect and dialogue about the PhD experience until those moments escaped me. . . . At that juncture I realized the value of sharing this experience with others. This is an amazing opportunity to perhaps help others negotiate some of the emotionally taxing experiences the PhD experience presents," Olivia said. And then continued, "It's been really interesting too, anecdotally, I feel like I know something about each of you because I feel like from most everyone in this room, I followed you in this journey, so there's times that I've heard of you or been on this journey with you. But to actually be able to learn more about you, I thought was really something I would value."

Carole felt, "The major impetus for participating in the mid-career PhD project is the opportunity to discuss one of the most impactful periods of my life with a group of like-minded individuals. A shared experience is powerful, and processing and talking about completing my PhD ten years post-defense and graduation brings a certain reflection and tempering of the intensity of the experience." And Davida saw the project as appealing because it would allow her "to be in the company of others who share (at least), two major characteristics: (1) we all have doctorates; and, (2) achieved them with the guidance and support of the same advisor. Further, as a professional who is still attempting to 'locate' and 'step on' the next rung of the career ladder, this project will encourage me to pause, reflect and meditate on where I 'have been' and where I 'need to go.'"

Kathy found it "appealing to explore the similarities and differences between people who decided to earn a PhD after having worked for a while." Laura "also thought it would be interesting to compare my feelings, perceptions, and experiences to others. There is always comfort in knowing that others experienced similar situations." For Kelly, the weekend offered a sense of closure.

> The opportunity to reflect on the experience with others, maybe the opportunity to put some closure on parts of it. And maybe what's most appealing is the opportunity to in some way relive that experience, albeit at a distance of ten years. It was an experience that was exciting, frustrating, exhilarating, and mind-numbingly boring at the same time. . . . Letting us carve out some time and meet some people whose names I've heard over the years. Because it's been great to put personalities with all of the dissertations I've read. [Laughter.]

Shortly before the focus group sessions in August, I had asked Carole if she would talk with a current PhD student whose dissertation topic about the career choices of female veterinary students seemed closely related to Carole's career consultancy business. With her agreement, I put them in contact, and the student felt they had a terrifically productive conversation. Carole found it equally stimulating:

> She's well into her program, and she called me . . . and we probably talked for an hour and a half with an incredible conversation. She left with just a whole different view, I think, of moving forward. I mean it was awesome for me on my side, because it was this very strong sense of giving back. She was obviously aware I was a [student] a long time ago, but 'I'm here to encourage you and here are the things that belong, here are the markers, etcetera.' I really enjoyed the conversation. . . . "Now," I said, "as you get further, let me know where you are." So now we are connected. I really enjoyed that conversation.

On Sunday morning, during the closing session, Ben offered this observation:

> Brad and I were talking yesterday I think about what an extraordinary opportunity this has been and it's so unique. Nobody ever gets the opportunity to come together almost as an entire group . . . with people who can truly understand this experience at a much deeper level than anyone else in our lives. To really get to sit in a room with folks and be able to relate at such a different level and a deeper level has been really fun.

The final insight that grew out of the question "Why did you agree to do this project?" relates to influence of time and life circumstances on the perspectives people brought to the conversations in August and November. Carole, who completed the program ten years earlier, offered a comment that contrasted with those Davida offered earlier, drawing our attention to the shift in perspective that occurred over the years. "I think my perspective is a little bit different because I am ten years post-defense. And I think if you were to ask me this three years post-defense, I would have a different response than I do ten years later because, you know, I understand the enormity actually of the experience and the impact of my decision to change careers that I wouldn't have had initially."

Ben began his program ten years ago, and made a startling observation about whether he thought he could do it again, now that his children are adolescents. His two daughters were born during his program.

> Since embarking on my doctoral program ten years ago almost to the day, I have had many conversations with fellow doctoral students, people holding PhDs, and those preparing to embark on the journey themselves. In the process, I have shared my own experiences and listened to others. I have also reassured many colleagues and peers that such a journey is "doable" if one is motivated and passionate about it. . . . I've never worked so hard in my life, but it was very rewarding and exciting intellectually. . . . I am very thankful I did it towards the start of my career, beginning at age twenty-nine and ending at age thirty-five, and that I did it straight out of my master's program. Riding that momentum and coming in with the study habits and way of living, helped tremendously. I can't imagine embarking on that journey now, as I approach forty and have elementary school–aged kids. That would have posed a totally different challenge.

Emily's choice to embark on a PhD meant stepping out of a successful career path, and ultimately affected her marriage so harshly that she and her husband divorced.

> My decision to participate in this project was driven by the fact that I believe I experienced the full range of reality in the pursuit of a degree, particularly at a time when most professionals were in the middle of their careers and thinking about upward mobility and I was making a conscious decision to take a step backwards (or at least a step sideways) in order to earn the degree. In addition, I was forty-one years old when I started. I was truly in the middle of my career. Because of the unique perspective that I have in this PhD experience, I decided to be involved in order for that perspective to be heard. This voice will be helpful to anyone who is making this decision, but it also will be helpful in the course of higher education career progression to validate that there are multiple ways for people to achieve a career track.

There was a common sentiment among all members of the group that the PhD program had been life-altering in so many dimensions that it was imperative to share the experience with others, particularly as there seemed to be a gap in the literature about the PhD experience. There were mixed feelings about whether anyone who read and thought about the group's comments seriously would be "scared away." Tina and Polly addressed those points on Sunday morning.

"The literature in our field contains little to nothing about mid-career professionals pursuing doctorates, a void that needs to be addressed. The mid-career professional's pursuit of an advanced degree represents another facet of adult learning, my primary research interest," Tina said. Polly followed with, "But I think that if the book concludes in some very pragmatic ways they can think about how to be successful, I think you don't scare them away. I think you give them some value to choose."

Daring, brave, focused, determined, tenacious, caring, fearful, uncertain, creative, responsible, distracted, strong, capable are some of the words that describe these individuals. And, yes, *smart, impressively intelligent*. All had been accepted into a top-ranked higher education doctoral program. They discovered the PhD required much more than the simple words coursework and a research dissertation could convey.

WHAT DID WE LEARN FROM THEIR EXPERIENCES?

We learn from their comments that the journey to the PhD is complicated, challenging, backbreaking, exhilarating, and life-changing. It is a process, encompassing a honeymoon period, later withdrawal, and adjustment back to a different life, and requiring reflection to fully internalize and appreciate the accomplishment.

Their experiences revealed a complex set of emotional and social dynamics that in turn, assaulted and supported them through their programs. Like athletes with the dream of competing in the Olympics, they had a dream and vision, and en route encountered challenges and setbacks, and found themselves embedded in relationships that created a level of complexity they never imagined or anticipated.

The dynamics, represented in figure 1.1, will be shared through the voices of these fifteen graduates in the chapters that follow. The diagram illustrates the key dynamics affecting their ability to make progress through both the steps of the doctoral program, and their own personal transformation through the feedback loops and their labels. It shows the impact of the advising relationship, their personal ability to balance competing demands, the peer group, and the ways they found to gain a sense of satisfaction along the way. The structure and climate of the department and program certainly contributed to the dynamics, but through the advising relationship. A robust advising situation could interpret or ameliorate program and departmental circumstances; a thin advising situation left the student more directly impacted, and responsible for his/her own interpretation of rules and requirements.

Figure 1.1 The Dynamic Gearing of the Doctorate

The chapters that follow will address these dynamics and are organized in four parts: Timing, The Emotional Reality, The Supporting Cast, and The Never-Ending Journey. While the research literature tends to focus on elements that may appear in The Supporting Cast, this book invites the reader to share the stress, tension, exhilaration, and determination that characterize the week-to-week, and month-to-month reality of climbing this mountain. For example, the group focused on the paradoxical role of family—central to the support needed, and a source of much guilt. Substantial comments are offered about the role of advisor, and a fine distinction drawn between an advisor and mentor.

Some of the participants left senior administrative positions, for example, financial aid director for a college, to begin the program, and accepted low-paying graduate assistantship positions; some maintained complex administrative responsibilities, such as chair of a department of nursing at a community college, during the program. Some used the PhD to move forward in a well-established career track; others wanted the PhD to create new options; and a few did not anticipate the scale of the personal and professional transformation that would occur. Married, single, with and without children, breadwinners all, ranging in age from twenty-six to forty-seven when they began doctoral studies, nonetheless their experiences converged on a set of emotions and people who were critical during their programs.

Part I

Timing

After twenty years of working with mid-career doctoral students, the very first question that I hoped to answer was why people left productive professional positions to enroll in a doctoral program. For those continuing to work I wondered why they would complicate their lives and the lives of family and employers by taking on this enormous challenge.

Certainly, the finances of enrolling represent a substantial cost. Either a person gives up a full-time salary and benefits for a poorly paid graduate assistantship or accepts the burden of paying for graduate tuition, fees, and books. Whether in terms of opportunity cost or direct outlay, the loss may represent a minimum of $15,000–$20,000 a year, for four or five years.

In addition, the logistics of doctoral education in a site-based institution must be taken into account. Travel time, class hours, group meetings, library work, and study time at home are just a few of the realities, particularly for the first two or three years when the majority of classroom work occurs.

The second question that drove this study was whether mid-career students truly differed from other students. For example, financial costs and logistical inconveniences apply to everyone. Even if the student is single and twenty-two, who really wants to live in student housing, subsisting on a stipend of $12,000 per year for five more years?

These are the questions addressed in chapters 2 and 3. Together we learned that the timing is meaningful, and there are specific reasons for embarking on this new path. Moreover, there were recognizable and important differences that characterize mid-career students and set them apart from their younger counterparts who progressed directly from bachelors and masters degrees.

Chapter Two

Why the Doctorate Now?

Despite fascinating differences in life journeys and circumstances, there was remarkable similarity in the reasons people gave for making the decision to pursue the PhD at that point in their lives. A combination of pragmatic and emotional considerations dominated the conversation and the recognition that each of them seemed to possess a predisposition to engage in more challenging roles or with more complex ideas. All held responsible and interesting jobs as teachers or administrators in colleges and universities. Yet, they felt the need to expand their capabilities. More pragmatically, they wanted to create more career options—by enlarging their knowledge base and gaining the credential. Brian recounted his thought process.

> I was at a [professional conference] session where they were talking about, "Should you get your PhD? Should you not get your PhD?" And one of the pieces of advice that really stuck with me is that someone on the panel said, "If you want to be a vice president or if you want to be a professor, if you want to do these things, you're going to need it someday, so start when it's a good time in your life." And so for me, you know, I knew it was going to be at least five years from whenever I started be it, year twenty-eight or thirty-four or whatever and I was in a good place personally and professionally and mentally and whatnot to start it and so I decided to.

Davida recalled a conversation with a supervisor before deciding to return to graduate school, and he told her that she wouldn't be successful without a master's degree and "certainly a PhD in higher education, there was no way." Jaime put it most succinctly: "In the end, it had always been a professional and personal goal that I knew I would regret if I didn't do it at this time in my life. What if down the road I was interested in a job or up for a promotion and not having the PhD prevented an opportunity?" And Ben

> did the PhD because I wanted to have the full gambit of options. I wanted to be able to do whatever I wanted to do in the field of higher education or administration or student affairs. . . . In my twelve years in the field I've been an advisor, I've been a coordinator, I've been assistant director, I've been a director, I've been a grants administrator, and I teach. At first I thought I was going to go into international education, and my career took a different turn. I thought I was going to keep moving from director up towards dean, but then I missed the students, and so I kind of made a difference change, but it gave me options and that was important.

Brad could have continued down his same path, but found it unappealing.

I actually had the opportunity to take my boss's job about halfway through, and decided not to despite some appeal of that for exactly the same reason. I clearly could have kept going down that path, and I would have been fine. . . . But I just wanted more options, and the way to get to the level of those options was through that credential. That wasn't the only reason I did it, but clearly that was among the—that was one of the components of the rationale.

Among the people within the group the degree of clarity about specific next career steps varied, but not the fundamental belief in its importance. Kelly offered this example:

When I started PhD, I didn't really know what I wanted to do. I knew that I needed to do it. Okay, I needed to be fairly pragmatic. I wanted to be able to take advantage of opportunities. I could not do that without a doctorate, and I wanted to be in a different school than I was, and I knew I was going to have a hard time doing that, and actually working at the level I wanted to work at if I didn't have that doctorate. My career goal was pretty nebulous. I was always, when asked what are you going to do with this, my answer was always pretty much, well you know the right job will come along at the right time.

For those, like Laura, who had more specific career goals, the doctorate represented a career "turbo boost." "The changes in the educational preparation of athletic trainers were what drove the need for me to obtain a PhD in Higher Education. I needed a more thorough understanding of accreditation and administrative issues that are involved with managing a higher education program." Stephanie also wanted "to get the PhD so that I could continue to do what I love at a different level. . . . I knew what I wanted to do. I knew where my area of focus was, and I knew that I needed and wanted the PhD in order to continue on in the field."

And two, in particular, who thought they were gaining turbo boost in the same career, found themselves catapulted in slightly different, albeit, very satisfying, directions. Kathy began her PhD in her home field of pharmacy, and describes the change:

I started on the journey to get a PhD in a different area, and then switched to higher education. So my initial intent was a turbo boost within the pharmaceutical industry, and then I got into higher education. Started working on a self-study for accreditation said, "Hmm, maybe I could do this?" So then it was—you know well maybe it was turbo boost but within two different career areas.

Had she pursued her original PhD she would likely have moved from a career carrying out research to a career designing research. And Polly, "left the core of nursing to go into a deanship in a broader area, many of which I didn't have background in, but I would still say that's a turbo boost."

By contrast, Olivia felt like her career was already in turbo mode, having been promoted from a coordinator to assistant director in three months. For her, the doctorate would create a parallel level of legitimacy. The other assistant director "probably had like twelve years of professional experience on me, so I felt like what I lacked in experience, I was gaining by doing the experience in theory, together by working full-time and working on the PhD."

As a whole the group was clear that while they could have had adequate careers without the PhD, options to move up, seek faculty positions, or broaden responsibility would have been denied them without the degree. All had some aspiration to achieve more interesting, powerful or different roles and almost all made a self-conscious choice to disrupt their current job situations to pursue the doctorate. They were a group of individuals also, who have a predisposition to work with ideas, to be intellectuals, and to widen their nets professionally. "So," I asked, "you do this just to create options? Surely, you don't put up with the nonsense to find options!" The responses came in a chorus of laughter, "Yes, you do. It sounds like we all did it! Sure you do, absolutely!"

How do we explain the "restlessness"? Participants, like Carole, were hard put to explain. "I mean, I absolutely could not explain to anyone rationally why. I was on the top of my game professionally, at a job that I loved, why I would subject myself to this experience. And I just kept saying, there's a bigger world out there and I, I've got to go there."

What is the source of the restlessness? On the one hand, it is no mystery. Human development researchers and theorists since Erikson's earliest models (1959, 1963) portray life journeys as a series of stages framed in terms of an innate drive toward development (Levinson, 1986; Sheehy, 1978). Sheehy used decades as the delimiter, while Levinson's longer time frames capture life in four "seasons." Most interesting for us here are the ways they describe the changes in perception that lead to transitions, and the length of transitions. Sheehy's earliest research proposed that changes in four areas of perception lead to transitions.

> One is the interior sense of self in relation to others. A second is the proportion of safeness to danger we feel in our lives. A third is our perception of time—do we have plenty of it, or are we beginning to feel that time is running out? Last, there will be some shift at the gut level in our sense of aliveness or stagnation. These are the hazy sensations that compose the background tone of living and shape the decisions on which we take action (1978, 4).

Similar to Sheehy, Levinson (1978) identified three domains for his male subjects: biological, psychological, and social. They and Erikson indicate that individuals become aware of entering a new phase of their lives quite gradually. The transitions between stages are lengthy; Levinson's estimate was quite specific and mirrors the span of a doctoral program. "The move from one era to the next is neither simple nor brief. . . . The transition between eras consistently takes four or five years—not less than three and rarely more than six. This transition is the work of a developmental period that links the eras and provides some continuity between them" (1986, 19).

And, does this comment resonate with you, the reader? More recently, researchers in the U.K. distilled a similar theme in their survey responses from eighty-nine doctoral graduates.

> A central theme . . . has been the continuing importance of intellectual and emotional growth in the benefits derived from the doctorate. In retrospect, and in the advice former students would give, pleasure is stressed—in study, satisfaction at completing an esteemed project, friendships, intellectual networks, and in developing skills in writing—and altruistic concerns: to make an original contribution to knowledge in their chosen field, to their community and to their profession. (Leonard, Becker, and Coate, 2005, 146)

Thus, the decision to embark on the doctorate may represent the mechanism for achieving a life transition that resolves deeper development needs. Transition theories, like Bridges's (1991) three-step model, help conceptualize the emotional and psychological aspects that might occur during Levinson's three- to five-year transition. At the heart of the process are the questions of how to deal with loss, move through confusion and find a new direction. And so for the mid-career professional departing a job to enroll in the doctoral program or adjusting concurrent job roles to enroll in the doctoral program, there may be a useful frame of reference.

On the other hand, considering the enormity of the disruption that a doctoral program represents, the decision to accept the "dare" that life presents comes from somewhere deep inside each and every individual. Carole attests to this.

Well, I often tell people that you need to have a burning in your belly and you need . . . it's the only way that you can quench the fire because this is going to be a really, really, really tough experience. A very demanding experience and if there's any other way that you can have that fulfilled in your life, I recommend doing it. But, if you come to the conclusion that the only way to quench that fire is to put your feet, you know, to the test and move into a doctoral program, it will be a life-changing event. But you've got to really, really want it really, really down deep in who and what you are.

Each time I meet individually with a prospective doctoral student, someone interested in applying to our program, and occasionally at the admissions interview with the faculty, the applicant asks the faculty to characterize their ideal doctoral student. Typically, after quick glances around the table at each other, my faculty colleagues and I come up with a variety of mundane comments. In truth, while it helps to have basic analytic talent, writing skill, and a sense of the key issues or questions that might serve as a dissertation project, the characteristic most valuable during this process is the hunger to grow, and willingness to persevere that Carole calls the "burning in the belly." Ben called it passion, saying "There's a passion to do this that has brought us to this table at this point. It may be passion coupled with ambition. It may be passion coupled with other things . . . because that's often I think maybe what undergirds the individual strength in many ways."

THE NEED FOR PASSIONATE COMMITMENT

As the participants talked that Saturday and Sunday, all of us realized there would be a serious risk in telling the truth about these experiences: that readers who might be considering a doctorate could be scared off. We talked of "fire in the belly," of "swallowing the wolf," intestinal fortitude, accidents, C-sections, and passion.

Davida arrived at Ohio State with a two-week-old baby, "certainly KJ came at an unplanned time but, hey, we moved, we rolled with the punches. . . . I wasn't going to advance any further without a higher degree and so I said, baby and all, I'm going there. I'm going to do what I have to. And . . . that first quarter was very difficult for me. I probably was experiencing postpartum but I didn't know that's what it was called."

Brian pointed out not only the level of personal investment and patience with administrative nonsense, but also the willingness to make the investment is directly related to whether a person's goals remain the same.

When people say, "Well, I'm thinking about getting a PhD" . . . you just don't think about it. You need to be fully invested into it and realize the ramifications of what that decision will have on you professionally and personally and I think that that passion needs to be there . . . obviously for learning but then I think some of the other things that I realized going through the program was that there's also a lot of—I don't want to call it, like maybe hoop jumping . . . like with the graduate school or other . . . rituals that are involved with completing the degree that in addition to learning new material and becoming an expert in a certain niche are equally as challenging to get through at times. . . . I think some of my classmates who still either haven't finished or never will finish, a lot of that was they no longer wanted to be the vice president of student affairs. They realized that three years into their requirement, and so for them, I guess going through the cost benefit analysis of whether or not to invest more time and finances in something that, at the end of the day, may or may not help them to attain their long-term goals, if they've shifted.

Yet some who succeeded, like Kelly and Tina, weren't at all sure about their goals when they began. By contrast, Laura's clarity about her goals, to understand the changes in the educational preparation of athletic trainers, kept her on track. Carole was even more pointed: "It can't be just something that you just take lightly and do on a whim. You've got to have perseverance and the willingness to make enormous personal sacrifices. My youngest child probably never remembers a time during his growing up years that I wasn't a student."

However, having clear rationale was not enough. According to Kathy, "It's how bad you wanted it and how much you were willing to work for it that really made the difference; not how smart you are. I mean certainly there has to be some baseline level obviously, but that's what the admissions process is for." Laura's translation of Kathy's sentiment was stronger, "It wasn't about how smart you were, it's just how much torture you were going to take. . . . How much was I going to tolerate? How badly did I want this?" Some classes assumed knowledge of theory that she did not have; some teachers were boring; and some PhD students from other programs were downright arrogant. It was not always a peak experience.

Irritants took different forms. Tina learned on a Tuesday about the two-day orientation program that would begin on Thursday. She was teaching full-time at another institution and extricated herself from classes and meetings to attend. By 10:00 PM Thursday evening it was still going strong, with yet one more exercise on the agenda. She said "I'm going home. I'm not doing this." So she left. "So the other six in the cohort were all buzzing, 'What's going to happen to me if I go home?' because we all figured out it was some kind of test by the faculty for endurance or something like that." When she asked the next day if the schedule had been intentional, she was told it simply the result of bad planning. Other irritants stemmed simply from the usual rhythm of an academic organization. Faculty leave for other jobs; temporary faculty take over courses and it's necessary to just "go along" with the flow.

WHAT DOES COMMITMENT LOOK LIKE?

Three stories capture the sense of commitment and personal sacrifice best. Olivia and Ben describe their strategies for accomplishing the studying and, particularly, dissertation writing in families with small children. And Polly recounts a nearly heartbreaking tale of her son's accident and her continuation in the doctoral program.

Olivia gave birth to two children during her program. The first child was due the first week of November in her third year, and so we set her candidacy exam and oral defense for the end of September/early October making sure there was at least a month before her due date. With both children she experienced wonderful pregnancies, full of health and practically turbocharged. The following comment reflected her activity several months before the birth of her second child, in August. The baby was due on the 29th, but the doctor felt the baby was too big and was going to induce labor on the 21st. She turned in the final draft of her dissertation to me on August 20th.

> I compare my PhD experience with an eating disorder of sorts. My strongest memories are sneaking out of bed at 3:30 or 4:00 AM, laptop in tow, hoping none of the other inhabitants of my household would awaken. I'd tip-toe downstairs to the kitchen—but not to indulge in anything more than my obsession to prove that *I could do it all*. I knew if I planned things just right I would be able to slip back into bed before anyone would know of my indulgence. I also knew when, and in what quantities, I would require coffee and diet coke to give me just the boost I would need to make it through the day at work or active in motherhood.

Ben, who had a full-time job, wife, and two young children, describes a lifestyle that he lived all through his doctoral program.

> My strongest memories are of the dissertation-writing process. At the time, I worked as the director of Advising Services at the Community College. I would work all day nine to ten hours, come home, have dinner with my family, help put my kid(s) to bed (we had my second the month after I completed data collection—phew), then I would head downstairs to my study, which I affectionately called "my cave," to work. Sometimes I wouldn't get down there until 9:30 or 10:30 PM and I would write until 12:30 AM or 1:00 AM. On weekends, I would write during naps, which would sometimes last two to four hours. I remember the routine of turning on an opera on the CD player, sitting down at the computer, pulling out tapes to transcribe or already-transcribed interviews to code.

Polly chaired the department of nursing at the same community college where Ben worked. She was the family breadwinner, for her husband and two sons.

> It was May of my first year in the program and I was deep into pondering my next steps, as well as continuing to learn my new administrative role at work when my world was suddenly turned up on end and I was reminded of what is really important life. I was headed home from OSU following a Monday evening class when I received a call from my husband saying that I needed to go directly to Children's Hospital, as our fourteen-year-old son had been in an accident and he did not know how badly he was hurt. Billy had sustained a severe head injury and we almost lost him that day. He was comatose and on a ventilator in the ICU for two weeks and when he regained consciousness, it was a long road back. He was in the hospital for two weeks on the neurological unit and another seven weeks in the rehabilitation unit followed by some outpatient therapy.
>
> I took my final exam for my second course in the qualitative research series the day that Billy moved from ICU to the neurological unit. It is totally amazing to me that I received a B in that course. I took an incomplete in my education course and actually enjoyed writing the final paper over the summer as I stayed at home to help my son recover. It was sort of a cathartic experience. I think there was a lot of emotion in that paper which is usually not my style. However, the professor seemed to enjoy the outcome.
>
> My son, miraculously enough, was able to return to school that autumn with some additional assistance, so I decided to take just one course for that quarter. People have asked me why I stayed in graduate school with all of this going on in my life. In the beginning of the quarter I don't think I knew the answer to that question, it just felt like the right thing to do. However, several weeks into the quarter, which was my first course with Dr. Demb, the answer became more clear. I connected with Ada and we had several conversations about research interests and where I thought this program was a fit for me. The more I could frame the fit of the program with my goals as an administrator in higher education, the more I felt that this was a really important part of my life that I should keep. Work at my college continued in a very challenging and busy manner and thus my time in graduate school was my only "me time" and I enjoyed the challenge.

WHAT CAREER STAGE OR AGE IS BEST? AND HOW DO YOU EXPLAIN YOURSELF?

From the age range in the participant groups, the clear answer to the first question is that each person makes a personal decision based on individual life circumstances, needs, and goals. The point, according to Ben, is to be clear that

> you're making a conscious decision as an adult that this is what I want to do. It's not coming straight out of college and going "Oh, God what am I going to do? Maybe I'll go to grad school." Like I have a buddy who went straight from college and got his PhD in anatomy, and now he's this highly accomplished full professor here, but it's funny because his wife was the one who said,

"You got to do something with this science degree." . . . He just kind of stumbled into it. Now it's become his passion, but it was something that he stumbled into at age twenty-one or twenty-two. For we who are coming at it as adults, there's more of a sense of I know I need to do this.

Ben's reflection about the timing of his own choice presented an ironic contrast for many in the room the weekend we held these discussions. He began the master's program mid-career and then moved directly into the doctoral program. "I can't imagine embarking on that journey now as I approach forty and have elementary school–aged kids. That would have posed a totally different challenge. My children have no memory of my doctoral work, in that I conducted my research and writing when they were sleeping as infants and toddlers. . . . Making that commitment in your forties when you have all these other things and other obligations, it's different."

Emily, whose marriage dissolved during the doctorate, explained the differences from her perspective.

It was obviously a pretty significant commitment to leave a full-time job and have, at that time, a husband who said, "Yes it's okay. You can go be a TA," even though I was primary financial bread winner at the time. . . . The other challenge was trying to help others understand my decision making. Did people believe that I was forced to leave my job? Why would I give up a good job? Was this a selfish act? Why would I do this to my family? Others understood totally and were supportive of the decision. Again, I believe doing this at age forty-one is very different had I chosen to do it even at thirty-five since, given my career progression to date, it seemed unnecessary for continued career advancement.

SCARY STORIES OR MOTIVATIONAL TESTIMONIALS?

Ambrose Redmoon (n.d.) said of courage, "Courage is not the absence of fear, but rather the judgment that something else is more important than fear." So, perhaps there's a new equation, "goals + fear = motivation" that works for some people.

For Olivia, Emily's sacrifices were a source of inspiration and motivation. "I went through the first year of courses, and that was fine. I felt like I was growing but even when I applied to the PhD program, I hadn't thought a long time about the commitment to having a PhD. I saw Emily doing it. Emily worked in my office. I admired Emily tremendously. She was a source of inspiration in the sense of saying, 'You can do this.' I watched the sacrifices that she had made to take that on, so that was a source of motivation." Carole overcame her fear by focusing on her other talents.

The bigger challenge for me involved fear of failure and fear of the unknown. I believed I was not smart enough to obtain a PhD; however, I was told that persistence was the most important trait I could bring to the experience. Because I tend to be hyper-responsible, overly conscientious, and incredibly diligent, I believed I could do it. I had a burning in my belly to explore new ideas, to broaden my view of the world. However, it felt like I was putting everything on the line by pursuing a PhD.

Davida recalls a different metaphor.

There was a great, sort of metaphor that a professor uses that you've got to be able . . . "to swallow the wolf." Because if not, you know, once you enter into it and you got the wolf down, it will eat you alive if you let it. And so, it really is a test of endurance. It is like, and I've never ran a marathon but I gather from what I know and from friends who've run them, I mean, it really is, you know, the starting, that adrenaline pumping, I'm here, I'm doing this. And then you get to the part of the race where you're all by yourself and you're looking around like, "Where—what happened to everybody?" And then you get to a point where you're like, "Am I going in the right direction? Am I doing what I'm supposed to be doing? Am I on the right path?" And then there's that part of the race where you've gotten through those examinations and you see that finish line off in the distance but then there's still more hills, those hoops that you have to jump through. Brian's right, with the graduate school, with the financial aid office. . . . And then you see that . . . finish line and it feels good. So it really is a test of personal endurance. You really do find out, I think, on the deepest and darkest night, again when you hit that wall, what you are really made of.

In the next chapters we will delve further into the emotional weather through which these folks navigated. Like the weather, the emotional reality was at times energizing and exhilarating, and at other times created feelings of fear, and guilt and isolation. Before moving into that discussion, chapter 3 will reveal more about the "real-life" meaning of mid-career through the eyes of the participants.

Chapter Three

What's So Different about "Mid-Career"?

The doctorate is a marathon for all doctoral students, but the special circumstances of mid-career folks differentiates them from others. While some differences are a matter of nuance, of degree, others look more like radically different realities. Three major differences between mid-career folks and those who go straight through stand out: both the risks and complexity associated with a dramatic change of roles, and the richness of experience brought to the new role.

THE RISKS

The group began focusing on risk very early in the discussion. Carole's first comments about her reaction to the reflection papers highlighted it.

> In terms of what struck me about the reflection papers, I just thought it was an incredible group of people that had so much courage who decided to wander off into something that was an unknown and really make themselves vulnerable; whether it's emotionally or psychologically or physically . . . but the whole idea of risk. Taking it on and getting into an experience that I think very few are willing to do. To make yourself that vulnerable, that open, and then to embrace an incredible experience that took each of us to a different place. That's what struck me about the reflection papers.

Risks come in different forms, and people perceive risks differently. Of the fifteen who participated in this study: ten including Jaime, Kelly, Davida, Ben, Brad, Laura, Emily, Stephanie, Seth, and ultimately Carole, as she explains below, were working professionals who left their previous positions to enroll in the PhD program, accepting graduate assistantship positions that paid tuition and about $1,100 a month in stipend. Comments about risk covered a variety of topics including shifting educational contexts, career, family, and finances. The sense of their comments varied by age, stage of career, and family status.

Jaime, who was very early in her career, focused on the shift in educational contexts. She did her undergraduate and master's studies at institutions much smaller than Ohio State. "I'm really glad I took a risk and went to a big research institution; not only for the resources it provided, but to also round out my resume. . . . It would have been very easy to stay at my master's institution, but the risk was worth it in the end (and at the time I wasn't married, nor did I have a family)."

For those who were more than ten or fifteen years into their careers, the focus was on career risks that, for most, loomed very large. Kelly, having left her job as director of financial aid, said simply, "The stakes are high. I mean I walked away from a full-time job." And for Carole, who had spent twenty years establishing herself in the field of financial aid, the professional risks seemed profound.

> Well, you know, it seems to me that a mid-careerist has a lot more on the line. If you're early in your career, by contrast with . . . somebody that's twenty years into their career. So it, I felt like I was putting everything on the line that I'd spent twenty years building and if this backfired . . . I'm thinking of Kelly and others who were at least twenty years into their careers and they resigned positions and moved to Columbus to pursue this. And that was a risk that I, I just would not be willing to take. So, I think the risk seems anyway, to be much bigger if you're doing it mid-career. . . . I had a couple in my cohort that . . . had done everything, boom, boom, boom, and really had not even established themselves professionally. They didn't have as much to lose as those that had twenty years that they had invested in their career to that point. So from my vantage point, it is different to be doing it in mid-career rather than earlier in your career.

Yet, for Stephanie, who also left a full-time job, but, like Jaime, was single and early in her career, the professional risk seemed manageable.

> I think for me there was less—there was a risk of course because you are leaving a full job. You're leaving something you love presumably, in my case, to do something—to get the PhD so that I could continue to do what I love at a different level. For me, there was less a risk because, as Ben said, I knew what I wanted to do. I knew where my area of focus was, and I knew that I needed and wanted the PhD in order to continue on in the field. So I think once that was clear to me, it didn't seem like a risk.

Carole later went on to articulate a spousal dimension that was operative for several members of our discussion group.

> I was also thinking that for my spouse, I think there was a lot of fear that I was going to grow away from him. This experience was going to take me away from him. I think probably one of the compelling reasons for him was that he doesn't have a college education, so here I am. First I went and got my master's and then some—I have this perpetual thing going, and I think his fear was I was going to leave him. I was going to grow away from him.

Laura's version was just as poignant. "I'm similar. He [her husband] quit school, and his family was telling him I was going to do that, so it made it worse. . . . We think there's risk for us. The risk for them is, because they're putting all this time, and they're giving of themselves and . . . in the end it could have been for nothing because we could find another PhD and ride happily into the sunset."

And Ben, too, worried about his wife's concerns, "I mean especially like in mentoring and professional programs, you know sometimes people, and particularly men, will—they'll have a spouse or partner who supports them through the process. They get their degree and off they are with the younger person."

These folks felt the risk for their spouses was enormous, largely, as Brad pointed out, because of the length of these relationships and the depth of commitment. When he was in his twenties, he said,

> I was admitted to a master's program, and at the time I had been dating the woman who is now my wife for a year, and it required us to move across country, and it came down to me saying, "I'm going. I would sure like you to join me." Right, and you know, luckily she came and it worked out.

But you know we were—I was in my late twenties, and at that point if she hadn't come, you know my life probably would have worked out as well. . . . I would have partnered somewhere along the way.

Had that conversation occurred more recently, say ten years into the relationship, as Emily pointed out, it would have been a very different conversation. When two people have five or ten years invested in a love relationship, if they are then in their mid-thirties and perhaps are contemplating children, there is much more incentive and pressure for them to figure out how to make it work. "Just starting over," as Brad implied he might have done in his twenties, is an option no one really wants to consider. So the negotiation is very real. The decision to enroll in the doctoral program is a family decision about jobs and relationships. And, as Tina pointed out, "not everybody is willing to risk. That's why there is this limited number of us."

WHAT'S IN A ROLE?

Roles encompass relationships and identity, and it can be hard to separate the two. As an administrator, as the director or chair, you are the boss and bear responsibility for supervising others, setting agendas, making decisions, and accepting accountability for performance outcomes within time frames and budgets. You have access to broader institutional agendas and data, and feel part of the "administrative loop." You might be a successful grant writer, or a project director who has initiated and maintained collaborative partnerships with other colleges, local hospitals, and businesses. You have probably responded to student crises and maintained institutional policies.

As a professor (for those already in faculty roles) you are the content expert, charged with designing learning environments, choosing pertinent content, evaluating student progress, coaching, advising, grading, dealing with faculty peers in admissions and search committees, and other settings. You have a good feel for recognizing students who are in difficulty, and perhaps the sensitivity to open conversations with international students whose language skills are imperfect and who are unaccustomed to the open interaction between faculty and students that characterize American university settings. You may know very well how to supervise interns and give the kind of critical feedback young professionals need to progress in those settings.

People come to you with questions, and you have answers. Which vendor has the best software? What will be the impact of changes in the Pell Grant program? Which text book do you prefer? How did you handle the student who never turned in the paper last term? How do you handle suspected academic misconduct, like plagiarism? How do you convince the faculty that the curriculum redesign will be worth their time? And that they can meet the outcomes-based accreditation requirements in a timely manner? Should we respond to the latest RFP from the department of education? How should we respond to the request from the state legislature for information?

You are a professional of some standing, with status, independence, respect, authority, and the power to influence others. You have a track record. You know the local lingo and you "belong" somewhere. Your professional identity is an important part of your personal identity. And, of course, your daily life is governed by the timetables of your work environment, the meetings, the classes, the deadlines.

You have an income that pays the rent, buys food and transportation, and maybe health insurance. Perhaps you are also the breadwinner in the family, or at least half of the partnership that puts bread on the table for you, your partner, or spouse and/or children. Perhaps you are a parent, and/or a son or daughter, or an active member of your local church. Your life has a rhythm, individual and shared, and seasonality. Recreation is a word that has meaning for you, although perhaps not as often as you might like. Going to movies, out to dinner, playing an instrument with a local quartet, hiking or traveling form your repertoire. Perhaps you have framed longer-term plans for both your family and your career.

And Then You Enroll in the Doctoral Program

In their reflection papers, participants responded to questions that asked them to describe the most exciting, and most difficult aspects of the doctoral experience. Kelly's response directly addressed the point we are discussing here.

> For me the most difficult and the most exciting were the same . . . the nature of my assistantships influenced this. . . . The thing I found the most frustrating was to go from being someone who made decisions; ran my own office; was responsible for over a million dollars in federal, state, and institutional funds to someone that no one really expected much from. It was hard to walk into a situation that I could have wanted to reorganize so that it ran more efficiently but couldn't do that because—well, I was just "the grad student" and so my opinion really didn't count much. My opinion was invited, but at the end of the day it was more of a "let's do lunch" thing than a sincere desire to hear that opinion.

Carole worked throughout her doctoral program, although not in the position she thought she would. Unexpectedly, she found herself confronting a decision to follow her previous boss, and took a job at a community college as an academic advisor for thirty-nine hours a week, that is, at a part-time salary, with no benefits.

> Within just a short period time, within weeks of starting my program I was given a choice: either I quit my job or I quit my doctoral program. And that was just like this mammoth crisis in my life because everything in me is all geared up. I'm pursuing my dream but yet you're telling me I either have to give up my job or my doctoral program and that was a mammoth crisis to have to give that up.
>
> So, consequently I did take a different position at a different college. However, I was leaving the job and the role that I was in, which was the whole impetus for pursuing my PhD. So what you were doing, I was forced to give up what was the, I don't know, the hoping that was fueling why I was going to get the doctorate. And so, that became a, just a really tough decision—I found it a very difficult, area to process and move through.

For those who walk away from their jobs, the shift in role is dramatic. Rather than "being in charge" they now must "follow the rules"; they shift from having a clear identity to feeling totally at sea, and the loss of status is palpable, especially the first year. Laura remembers

> struggling and resenting the lack of freedom I had in managing my time. In my full-time job as a college instructor I felt like I had complete control of my time. If I didn't want to grade tests over the weekend, I wouldn't grade tests. However, once a doctoral student, I couldn't choose not to complete my assigned readings unless I wanted to be unprepared for class. The change in authority in the classroom from being the teacher to being the student was challenging for me.

Carole minced no words, "If you are losing that identity at the same time that you are now embracing a doctoral experience, you've got multiple things going on all at the same time. You've got this whole identity thing that's being . . . turned upside down."

Rather than having the answers yourself, you will be seeking answers from others—faculty, peers, staff, administrators. "I mean we just did not have answers," Carole said. "You know, literally, how to do basic things on the campus, you know, figure out how to do it." Rather than evaluating and supervising others, others are evaluating and supervising you. No longer spending money from the institution's budget, you are now budgeting your own money. A salary has been traded, in many cases, for a graduate assistant stipend, and student health insurance and required substantial adjustment, as pointed out by Laura, Kathy, and Kelly.

Laura recalled that during her doctoral program, she was

> preoccupied with three major issues. One was finances. My salary from my GAA position was less than half of what I used to make. I felt like I couldn't spend money any longer because my husband was the only person "working." I hate feeling dependent upon others, and that was what I had become . . . dependent upon my husband. He never told me I couldn't spend money, but yet that is exactly how I felt.

Kathy remembers the workload. "As far as the workload goes, I am still amazed to this day how I managed to work full-time, attend class, and attend to a new marriage and home. Financially it was rough at times to make it all work (lots of budget meals, etc.). My husband picked up extra work to help out, too." And Kelly commented on the finances. "I mean you know that was five years where I wasn't contributing monetarily to the household or saving for retirement or you know any of those kinds of things, and we knew going in that—somehow we were sort of banking on what I'd get out of this, meaning worthwhile or not, to be able to make that up."

For those continuing in their current jobs, life takes on a schizophrenic aspect. In your "day" job, you remain all that you were. As a student, everything described above, except losing the salary, applies. The same paycheck still arrives, however, much of it is earmarked for tuition, fees and books.

In addition, rather than teaching others, you become the "learner," beginning with the business of learning how to be an intellectual. Olivia said, "You think you have professional socialization, and then you find a whole other network that's operating in the sense of on the intellectual side. So figure out some of the norms of that intellectual side of socialization." Polly described this as her "reorganization . . . getting organized back into the intellectual community and ways of thinking and ways of interacting and ways of talking about materials versus my professional piece which is in academia, but it's two different things, really compared."

The changes that accompany enrollment in the PhD program could be likened to those that accompany the start of a new job in a new city—disruptive, but not necessarily earthshaking. So I asked our folks about that. Kathy jumped in to spell out the difference, with Ben and Laura nodding energetically as she spoke.

> Maybe one thing that distinguishes it is that when it's more of a career move or a job move, yes, that is an important *part* of your life but when you're talking about a PhD and, in most cases, we were working or being GAs it's an *all consuming thing* in your life. . . . Because when you accept a job, in most cases, unless you're a medical resident, it doesn't consume your entire life. Right? And you still have that part of your life that is yours and your partner's. That part of your life that is your time and your spiritual time, so you've got your forty-plus hours of work, but it's not all of your time. I felt like with the PhD program, it was my life baby between work and school.

In other words, even though the first three to six months of a career move might create a big mess, it's a temporary mess that will sort itself out and the rest of your life is still there. So the biggest change is that your "job," which is now the doctoral program, takes over your life, practically, emotionally, and mentally. The keyword for Ben was "overwhelmed."

> Something I was thinking about having to negotiate also, because I was an administrator and having to say "I am absolutely overwhelmed. I've got to go in at 6:00 AM this morning. I need to stay until 7:00 PM tonight." She [his wife] was like, "But you've got writing to do. When are you going to get all these things done?" There's that—and it's "give me some time, too" which is totally reasonable, but then that's hard to negotiate. Try to figure out how are you going to get your work done? How are going to still be able to do what you need to do for your PhD, and how are you not going to completely burn yourself out and alienate your partner? That's whew . . .

The rhythm of daily life as a doctoral student particularly in the first two years, is dictated by class schedules, due dates for papers and exams, team meetings and university-mandated deadlines. Sometimes there is a need for an "attitude adjustment" when it appears a class or workshop is a waste of time. Coming from an environment where "Without sounding too smug about it," Brad said, "there's a value to my time. You know I have been compensated previously for my time and my ability to figure . . ." and Olivia finished his sentence, "Don't waste it!" Brad went on, "I'm not sure that someone who is younger—chronologically young-er or experientially younger, has yet gotten to the point where they can attach that value to their time . . . but I still felt as though I need to sit here for these three hours, and if I were doing something else . . . let's move along." Kelly was less diplomatic in her description, and also gives us a clue about the strengths the mid-career folks bring to handling these stresses and irritations.

> I remember writing in my reflection paper about how sometimes things were just sort of like . . . really boring, and that's it. I mean what you're describing is the same experience that I had (also might be with the same class), because the curriculum hasn't really changed all that much prob-ably. But I think one of the advantages is, yeah, you figure out ways to just kind of let it go, and then I just figured out how to use that time more productively. Nobody knew if I was writing or listening, or if I was jotting down notes for chapters or the next paper that I had to write. I mean you develop all kinds of coping mechanisms, right? Just because I'm sitting in someone's class and that—oh, I don't necessarily owe them anything more than my good manners.

Somehow that comment sounded inconsistent with the comment Brad made earlier about feeling irritated that his valuable time was being wasted and intellectually insulted. When asked about the apparent disconnect, Beth's response shifted the conversation from "what we gave up," to "what we brought to the party."

USING EXPERIENCE, AGE, AND MATURITY TO "PUSH THROUGH"

Experience can lead to the ability to recognize and shrug off life's less important irritations and save a lot of mental energy. Basically, Beth said she did, in fact, get irritated, but then she "let it go."

> What it is about a mid-career person, and this is a really sweeping generalization and really is not fair to people who may be going straight through, but I can only speak for myself how I may have handled that if I wouldn't have had other experiences. I think I would have either given up . . . "You know, I don't need this. Forget it, I'm going to go in a different direction," or would have—

and just gotten so frustrated with it that I would have obsessed over it. There was a point in which I could just let it go. I would process or what have you, and then just say, "I'm just not going to let it worry me anymore."

Brad, who originated that part of the conversation, let it go on the way home at night. "You know, I got an hour-long drive to my home from campus and so a lot got let go during that hour, you know. I came back the next day and started again."

Kelly followed and pointed out, "Yeah, you had to trade your battles." Knowing which battles were worth the effort came from experience."

"In the work-day world," Brad said matter-of-factly, "we all put up with things that are not satisfactory. You know, because that's just part of interacting with other people." And, after some group laughter, continued, "Right, so why should this be any different?"

Kelly's attitude evolved from her early frustration to a more savvy appreciation of the situation.

> I think . . . it's 'learning how to pick your battles.' There's a lot to fight in graduate school—some of it's just learning the new culture, figuring out where you fit in the new hierarchy of things, but some of it is also deciding how much energy to put toward any one thing, whether that's a class you already took, a boring assistantship, a problem with an advisor . . . what can you change, what do you just have to cope with.

"Maturity" is a word often applied to people with experience. It's a word that can take on different meanings, depending upon the context. In the course of the conversation, I asked whether some of the ability to "let things go" came from maturity. Emily picked up the term and put it in the context of a skill that is particularly important for doctoral students: learning to accept criticism and really listen to feedback.

These are invaluable skills, typically learned the hard way, that can mean the difference between success and failure in a doctoral program. Critical feedback is the sine qua non of the life of a student. Not only is feedback a regular part of coursework, in the form of comments on exams and papers, but constant feedback on drafts of dissertation proposals and chapters shapes the life of a doctoral student at that stage of the program. It is common to write four or five drafts of chapters or sections of chapters, based on the feedback of advisors and doctoral committee members. Maturity does play a role in this context, according to Emily.

> Going back to your question about maturity, I think part of the ability for us to accept the feedback is out of proved prior experience. We've seen the outcome of when things don't go well and when things do go well. With that comes a level of acceptance to say that if we get feedback that's difficult to hear, the reality is that we've had that experience to see times when adversity comes out okay. That's, I think, a bit of uniqueness around the timing of—when I think about those experiences that I had in the first five years of the job versus you know having to tackle this now is very different.

The confidence of knowing that critical feedback need not be the end of the world, "that you'll get through it," is achieved only through experience. Maybe the feedback was pretty direct, maybe the workshop really went poorly, but you didn't get fired, and were later assigned another workshop to run.

In addition to gaining this equilibrium, there is a certain bank of wisdom about organizations and systems that comes from having had a job and being of a certain age. At some point, that knowledge can be used to your advantage, and you can become your own advocates, while still knowing, as Kathy said, "that we're still not completely in charge of our own lives."

"You learn enough about the system to navigate your way through it . . . and are finally able to clue in, and go 'Oh, I've done this stuff before.' If I could figure it out in my job, why can't I figure it out now?"

So the system navigation appears to be a bit easier for the mid-career student, than for the student coming straight through. Having found your way around in a professional environment earlier, it's possible to treat this new environment like you would in any new job, and start the process of figuring out the system. However, prior experience can be a double-edged sword. On the one hand, because you've worked in other organizations, you recognize that there is an informal situation and a power structure. You understand the principle of politics. At the same time, you realize that students (you) are in a much lower position, and may feel pretty insecure, wondering what you got yourself into. Whom can you trust? At the same time, from previous experience, you have some confidence that you will be able to figure it out.

Before the conversation even began that weekend in August, Laura had written in her reflection paper that one of the most important topics to cover was

> having life experience to relate to theory. This is something that must be discussed. Having experience to relate to what you are learning is one of the most important issues determining success in a doctoral program. I regret my lack of research experience prior to and during my doctoral program. It did impact my ability to apply and use statistics. On the other hand, my teaching experiences and academic advising experiences were instrumental in understanding educational theory.

A key advantage for mid-career people is the self-confidence that they could navigate the new system, and cope with the ups and downs of the learning environment. Experience from professional environments also served as a basis for discerning the way doctoral-trained professionals considered a variety of issues. It sharpened their understanding of their own learning, and helped them stay motivated. They attributed the difference to the time and effort spent "learning how to think critically and to evaluate things, to really become an intellectual," as Kathy explained. "And this in no way is disrespectful to any of my colleagues, but there are definitely times when I can tell working with people those who had the opportunity to engage in this intellectual endeavor and those who haven't." Emily described the same realization in different words.

> Related to that is certainly the dissertation exercise was pretty key in that, but for me the impact was just as much the quality of people with whom I was in class. Certainly in my professional role up to that point, there was an awful lot of pretty strong dialogue professionally, but it was so different being in the classroom and having the conversations. I know I'm not articulating very well, but it—I think that was what I see as something different about being mid-career is that you have something to compare the quality of that dialogue with that I don't think I would have had if I would have been doing my dissertation directly out of school. It was—I think that was just an unexpected bonus.

Excitement grew as folks were able to relate the theories and research encountered in coursework to a "real-life" job, whether the job was current or previous. Intellectual explorations yielded new insights for the professional arena, as Olivia attested. "For me, continuing in my full-time position while pursuing doctoral studies was completely rewarding. It was rewarding in the sense that I felt it was easy to establish a continuum from work to school; one environment where I learned about theory and one where I would apply it."

For Davida, there was no question that the work experience enable her to be even more successful,

> Looking back, I'm not sure I would have been as successful to where I am at this point, had I come straight out of undergrad, went to the master's, and gotten the PhD with little to no real true work experience. . . . I don't think I would be where I am today had I come straight through and not worked in admissions, not worked in student activities because I found myself—even in the master's program but more so in the PhD program, having much richer and fuller discussions with the older students. . . . It's funny, I think about the master's program. We were all good friends. We were a cohort, but the people that I was really inspired by were the folks who had worked, who could give real life examples in class. And, you know, kudos to the PhD cohorts that came before me, and I was privileged to sit in classes with them. I oftentimes think about your class, Dr. Demb, academic affairs—if you recall, all those PhD students . . . they all sat in the front. I wanted to sit up front. I wanted to view the PhD students because, you know, me answering the question as a master's student said one thing but to listen to them was like, wow, these are the people that I want to be like. So again, I don't think I would have done quite as well had I come through, bam, bam, bam without having any rich work experience.

Becoming a student again gave busy administrators new freedom and rewards. Once she got over her frustration with the relatively straightforward demands of her assistantship, Kelly appreciated the freedom it gave her. "While that was frustrating at first, it became pretty freeing. . . . I didn't really have to think much—most of what I did was pretty rote, once I learned what I needed to do. I also learned that my supervisors didn't really expect all that much of me—come in, do my job. If it took two hours, great! I had two hours where I could just sit and do other things. Rather than fight it, I learned to use it to my advantage."

The "freedoms" according to Davida were quite specific: "the freedom to just be a student again; to come and go as he or she pleases; to read a book or study theory (uninterrupted) and really enjoy it; to be in a scholarly environment with scholars-in-training; to have the opportunity to listen to and be taught by 'seasoned' advisors/professors/scholars; to work in an area of interest (either through an assistantship or practicum); to set his or her own course of study." "But," she continued, "this freedom comes at a serious cost. And for me, it was not just about my needs, but also son's and family's."

Virtually everyone agreed with Carole's summation.

> Completing a PhD mid-career is unique because each individual often comes with a well-honed set of values and beliefs. There is a huge store of information, experiences, and wisdom to pull from when interacting with the material, making it both harder and easier to process. Ultimately I would argue that completing a PhD mid-career has greater potential for richness and reward because the foundation and life experience is deeper and more is at risk—the greater the risk, the greater the potential reward!

Those comments reflect the level of mental, logistical and emotional challenges that were an integral part of their journey. It's now time to turn to those matters.

Part II

The Emotional Reality

Understanding the play of emotion is an integral part of creating truly educational contexts and experiences.

—English and Stengel, 2010, 521

In research projects such as this personal experiences are used to shine light into a black box—a box in this case that represents the mid-career doctoral experience. The data are comprised of stories and comments, and the challenge for the researcher is to find themes and to weave those themes into a sensible framework. Numbers and statistics play a smaller role in this type of project. There are moments, however, where numbers can be revealing and the beginning of this chapter is an appropriate place for a short detour.

Participant reflection papers and the transcripts from the August focus group and November video conference yielded more than four hundred pages of stories and discussion. Reading and rereading those materials led to a first-round identification of seventy-one codes. Once identified and named, for example, "family," similar comments would be flagged each time they appeared in the conversation. The two codes that appeared most frequently, for example, were mentioned more than seventy times: "advisor role" and "personal changes." The next step for the researcher is to group those codes into themes. For this project, nine major themes resulted. Each theme consisted of a related group of codes. Listing the themes in descending order, beginning with the theme which had the greatest number of referenced codes, is revealing: emotions (331), mid-career itself (285), advisor-related (190), challenges (144), support (134), family (83), mechanics of dissertation (58), why participate (44) and models and theory (11).

Now, I caution the reader to view these numbers skeptically. Coding is a subjective process and an inexact science; some codes might fit into more than one theme. "Risk" for example, fit with both "mid-career itself" and "emotions." Nonetheless, the dramatic range of frequencies (along with the vivid stories and comments) leaves no doubt that this group of participants felt their doctoral journey was highly emotional, that their mid-career circumstances were tightly related to the way the journey unfolded, and that advising played a major role in mediating this experience. There were a lot of challenges, and an almost equal amount of support. Family, however, fit into a category other than support, and by far the mechanics of the dissertation were mentioned relatively infrequently in this discussion of the mid-career doctoral experience.

Eighteen codes were grouped to form the "emotion" theme. The top eight were (in descending order of mention): fear, the cohort, choices and decision-points, commitment to the doctorate, costs, guilt, isolation, and emotional intensity. In other words, within the group of top eight were five negative emotions: fear, choices, costs, guilt, and isolation. The next cluster included: exhilaration, most exciting, passion, selfishness, and courage. "Strength" was also identifiable as a code, but generally those comments were captured within other codes. The emotional reality of the mid-career experience, as described by Emily, is our focus in the next pages.

> It is challenging to summarize the strongest feelings around the doctoral experience. Perhaps attempting to group those feelings is the best approach. Isolation, complexity, self-reflection, failure, guilt, selfishness, perseverance, success are the strongest feelings that still are very strong as I think back on this experience. As for topics, I am happy to talk further about ones such as fear, role of the cohort, finding time to study, finding time to write, changes in identity.

As noted earlier, it is the responsibility of the researcher to craft a sensible framework and storyline. So, for example, comments (and codes) related to "mid-career itself" and about the nature of participant commitment to the doctoral program were presented in earlier chapters to frame the context for the book. We will focus on "the cohort" and "commitment to the doctorate" in later chapters; the role of the cohort will form a central element in the discussion of the support network in part III.

The emotional reality was intense and involved everything from out-and-out fear, to costs, guilt, and isolation. Emotion-laden situations involved logistics, the original admissions interview, course work, classmates, coworkers, family, the dissertation, deciding not to walk away and just plain personal doubts. Specific examples of their worries, joy and challenges fill the next two chapters.

Chapter Four

Fear, Costs, Guilt, Isolation

FEAR OF WHAT?

For me, the most compelling aspect of the PhD experience was about conquering fear—on multiple levels. . . . The first experience I recalled was related to the physical demands (risk) of being an OSU student. I was totally unprepared for walking many, many miles carrying massive amounts of books through all kinds of weather. Because many of my classes were in the evening, I often walked alone at night, including walking over the icy Olentangy [River] Bridge in the dead of winter and thinking that if I fell over, they wouldn't find my body until spring.

In fact, I almost quit the program when I came out of class very late one winter night in frigid temperatures only to discover that my car had been towed (all the cars on the entire street had been towed). My cell phone was dead, and I had walked a long way to get to my car which was parked off-campus. So, at 11:00 at night I found a house with lights on and knocked on the door. I had no clue who to call, how to find my car, and was at the mercy of a young woman who was babysitting small children who could not be left alone. After many calls to security and police departments, my car was tracked down and located almost thirty miles from campus in an unsafe and unfamiliar section of Columbus. My benevolent rescuer finally bundled up the children and drove me to the junk yard where my car was impounded.

By now it is midnight, there are large dogs patrolling the grounds, there are bars on the windows, and I'm yelling through an opening that I don't have seventy-five dollars in cash, but I do have a credit card. When I am finally authorized to get my car, I now have to walk through acres of cars in a dimly lit area to locate mine, all the while worrying about the dogs, and still carrying my heavy book bag.

When I finally drive away, I realize I have no idea where I am (this is pre-GPS) and hysteria is starting to take hold. I simply start turning onto any street that has traffic lights and looks like it may be headed to a business district. By the time I found Interstate 70 and was headed back to Dayton, I seriously questioned the sanity of putting myself at risk all in the name of obtaining a degree that most of my friends, colleagues, and family members questioned. (By the way, Kelly came to my rescue [later], researched commuter parking options, and I purchased a "commuter" parking pass which alleviated towing issues.) While the car towing experience sounds so trivial, in retrospect it really represented a bigger issue—pushing myself way out of my comfort zone, taking an enormous risk (psychologically, financially, professionally), and conquering my fears.

Carole's "car story" as it came to be known that weekend in August, was one of two that framed the meaning of fear and commitment. (The other was Polly's retelling of the specifics associated with her son's accident and subsequent hospitalization.) Polly asked Carole, "How did you find the courage just to go up to a strange house and knock on a door that night?" Her response seemed to serve as a metaphor for the whole group,

> It was so late, and my thought was if I walked all the way back to Ramseyer Hall on campus there would be nothing open. I was terrified, but decided to walk up to a house with the lights on and ring the doorbell, even though it was very late at night, and it was so cold. It was like if I walked all the way back, everything was closed up. I mean where would I find anybody, you know?

Whether it meant knocking on the door of a strange house in the middle of the night, or delving into a new set of theories, or methodology, or realizing that learning the tools needed to pursue the dissertation topic meant taking two or three additional courses, at some point the best and only choice was simply to move forward. "Going back" made no sense.

Carole went on to say, "The physical challenge aside, the bigger challenge for me involved fear of failure and fear of the unknown . . . fear of being ABD [all-but dissertation]." Seth echoed these very words, "'Fear of the unknown.' . . . Coming in as a full-time student versus working full-time. I did not know when I finished what I would be doing. What job would I be in? It's a little bit [of the] aspect of would it be worth it, but I just didn't know how things were going to turn out in the end for me anyways." Davida used similar words: "Fear of that, that ABD possibility and knowing that that's out there and that some people are okay with that and they go on with life. I think there's the fear of the unknown, meaning the external things that are happening with work/life balance, with family with the financial sacrifice. And for me, again, the fear of what's next?" Laura's version was equally stark.

> Fear—I feared that I had made a mistake. I feared that I wouldn't be able to find a job after completing my studies, too. I took a very nontraditional route. Most people in my profession do not obtain PhDs in higher education. Instead, most pursue doctorates in science-based programs such as biomechanics, exercise physiology, or kinesiology. I took a calculated risk that was based upon what I perceived as a need. For the record, now that I am employed . . . I have never regretted my decision.

Doubt is another form of fear, and half the group talked about feeling that they might not have the ability to succeed in the program. The anxiety began during the admissions interview with the faculty. The anxiety was an unintended consequence of a particular comment from faculty that was intended as a compliment. Kelly's reaction was among the biggest surprises of the Saturday discussion.

> Yeah. Yeah. I don't know what it was like for other people's cohorts. Okay, but when my cohort started, when we were there for the interview process, I remember very clearly and some of the other people who were in that group. We were very clearly told, "Look this is a highly competitive program. Not everybody's getting it. If you get in it, you know that you were among the best of the best."

Ben confirmed that he was also told that, and Kelly continued.

> Okay. That's a very powerful message to send to someone. So I get accepted into the program. I wasn't calm because I'm a very pragmatic person. This was a very theoretical program. I didn't even fit. It took someone on the phone to convince me that perhaps this was a situation in which other people might know me better than I knew myself. The only—that was sort of the tipping point. That was what made me make the decision to come to this program. So I'm already sort of feeling kind of on my own then, and yet I'm been given this message that you're among the best of the best.

And so I asked Kelly, "Is that a compliment? Or does that strike fear in your heart?" "Yes," Kelly said, amid group laughter. "Yes, I mean it is a compliment, right? But, boy, is that a high standard to live up to." Amy and Ben echoed Kelly's comments. In a phrase it became, "Am I good enough?" Laura said, "I think the first quarter following the interview, I had a fear of people figuring out I was stupid."

The admissions process in this doctoral program involves two steps, a written application review, and an in-person interview with a faculty group. Doctoral admissions decisions represent long-term commitments that can affect faculty careers as much as the student. So, faculty organized their schedules in February and March so that as many as possible (up to five professors) can be present for the interviews. We felt very fortunate that everyone (about five faculty) was available to attend the session for Laura's interview . . . having no idea how that impacted her.

> Kelly's story about the interview and coming in is so true. . . . I was scared shitless in my interview because every faculty member in that building came in for my interview, and they told me that. So I'm thinking, "what am I a leper? Do I have a third head? Why does everybody want to hear my interview?" . . . They said it was because I was different. I had no higher ed. background. I had a master's degree in biomechanics. I had no—I was a professor at the time, not in rank. I was only an instructor, but still it was a college professor, and that just scared me, and I thought, well, nobody's going to work with me.
>
> Then I was out in the interviews with potential cohort members, and everybody had this great background in higher ed. and had degrees in higher ed., and I thought, "What am I doing? I'm crazy. I'm absolutely nuts for doing this." Then I remember I asked the question in the interview, "Do I need to read something before I start because everybody here seems to know about Perry, and I don't know who Perry is."

Tina, who had been a faculty member at a local college for more than fifteen years remarked, "my fears revolved around . . . looking inadequate for doctoral work . . . the phrase emperor without his clothes." And, Kelly added, "When are they going to realize they made a big mistake?" Emily offered a very specific example of the "Am I smart enough?" question.

> I had a big fear of the academic content of the dissertation: the fear of theory—fear of theory, the fear of rigorousness of the research methodology. It relates a little bit to the fear of the unknown, but it was the fear of the actual academic content. Even though there's that freedom that goes with this is your own project, and you're responsible for creating the knowledge. There's an awful lot of rules though that go with it.

Polly refined the thought even further, "Would it be a fear of maybe your own thought about your ability to academically portray the content in such a way that's it's going to be good enough? I don't know."

The pressure to be "smart enough" or "good enough" impacted many students. Questioning whether you could simply "pull it off" in terms of the daily demands of job, family, and children was the special province of those with children, and especially those who welcomed new babies into the world during their program, like Ben and Olivia. Olivia's first child was born during her third year, a few weeks after her oral defense of her candidacy exam. In other words, she wrote the draft of her dissertation proposal and prepared for and took generals during her first pregnancy. She found herself pregnant again shortly after the web-survey she developed for her dissertation went live.

Perhaps another one of my most vivid memories was the arrival of the terrifying moment I realized my family would grow for the second time prior to my completion of the dissertation. It's hard to believe now the news of Miles [second son] would bring anything but joy to my life, but, for the first real time when I realized I was expecting another baby, I truly doubted my ability to weather the storm. And that's when I began to allow my obsession, of sorts, to more or less completely define my approach to daily life. For example, I would do as all expecting mothers of young children would do, to read, and to read daily. Yet, unlike those moms I would seemingly feel jealously toward, at COSI [science museum] or the park, the ones who apparently delighted in exhausting every ounce of their energy in mothering. While my children were very young (infants, or in the womb), there would be few tales of caterpillars or goodnight moons—rather, read-alouds of drafts of chapters three, one, and two.

Rather than disappearing as students moved past the first year and on into the program, fear and doubt became associated with coursework, the dissertation, and progress. The fear evolved from questioning whether you belong to whether your work is good enough. It became a shift for Brad from being "the student who is receiving and processing other's work to become a producer of original work." For Davida, it was

fighting off the "beast" called Doubt (I cannot speak for everyone, but I think there is one critical moment during the process where you have a good cleansing cry, meditate, and then pick yourself back up and "claim" the process—my moment happened about two months before graduation).

For me it was to finally slay the beast. That's what the dissertation had become the last couple of months. I kept referring to it as the beast and all I could imagine was myself with this mighty sword, like slashing it. And the claiming was saying, "I'm going to do away with this monster called Doubt. I'm not going to let him into my mind anymore, he's not going to creep around the corner and say, "Ha, ha, I don't know why you attempted this." And I had to really believe that. And I knew other people kept saying, "You can do this," but it was almost like conquering this sense of fear. Like the fear that this is—"I'm not going to walk [onto the stage and graduate], I'm not going to go get my gown and my cap." And like I said, in church, I don't know if it was a voice talking to me, but I just had to let it go. Let go of the fear and say, "I can do this." And from that moment on, I cranked it out. So that claiming, saying "I can do this" and you, it's in your mind, it's in your spirit, it's in your body, you make it happen.

Worry about organizational politics also came into the picture. In chapter 3 we saw briefly that coming into the program with organizational experience was a double-edged sword. Kelly describes the fearfulness of the blade as she encountered the power differential and feelings of dependence on the advisor. While Kelly and then, Laura were the most vocal during this discussion, you could hear everyone around the table muttering "Yeah, yeah" as they spoke.

I mean that's the way the system is set up. There are different parts to graduate school, and we've kind of been talking about the intellectual parts. There's a whole other realm of things you've got to negotiate. Many are people's egos. There's a hierarchy; there are all [the] politics, and there are advisers who will just let their students walk into a hotbed of a committee that, you know, people are fighting with each other, and this person is caught in the middle. There is still a power differential, and that's why—in some ways that's why I think that fear gets so big, because we know, having worked, having come into this as mid-career, it's not—I mean most of us can recognize we're more in the middle of a political landmine that we can't fix. So you really have to have somebody that you trust to kind of help you negotiate your way through that. It's not—you might know what it can do, but you may not always be able to do it.

Kelly had a senior administrative role in the college where she worked previously, while Laura had been in a faculty position, and was very familiar with that culture.

You're 100 percent at the mercy of faculty. Perhaps, maybe that was one of the things that heightened our anxiety in the first quarter, because we had worked previously, and we were very aware that some people have agendas, and their agendas are very self-centered. So until you figure that out, who in the faculty has an agenda where they want to use you to promote themselves versus a faculty that's truly invested in seeing someone live up to their potential, that was part of the fear in not knowing where to lay your trust, but you're smart enough to figure it out. It's just time has got to give you that opportunity to figure out who is your facilitator and who really just wants to use you to help their own agenda.

As an advisor, one of the biggest surprises for me through the years was hearing the level of anxiety experienced by these capable, experienced professionals.

Brad: "I think we're all accomplished people. You know we all have intellectual—clearly intellectual abilities. We have skills but . . . you still question 'can I do this?'"

Laura: "Daily."

Brad: "Holy cow, you clearly forgot how did I get into this, you know."

Laura: "Yeah."

Ben: "Well, and we're apprentices in many ways. We are scholar apprentices and so we're looking to a master to guide us through that apprenticeship so that we too can become masters. It really is—I keep likening it to the monastic life, but in many ways it's similar in that respect."

Seth's fear, by contrast, was,

never within the program, or among my peers or with the faculty at OSU. I think it was when I went to ASHE [Association for the Study of Higher Education research conference] my first time, and now I have other people outside of the program who are critiquing my work, and I am reflecting back as a doctoral student to our program. I think that was something, I think I was really fearful that first time I gave a presentation at a—at a respectable research conference. "Maybe I'm an academic fraud," I guess in the bigger context, and I wanted to see how people related to that; but fear of the outside of our program.

DEFINING THE COSTS

As we might anticipate, financial costs dominated the conversation, but psychological costs were just as real. And sometimes, the combination produced other consequences. For all, however, financial realities topped the list of concerns. Carole was very clear.

Well, I was making a significant financial investment in that whole little experiment. And I just wasn't really, I wasn't willing to risk losing my investment. It was, like, way too much money, and I was taking that away from impacting an entire family by that decision, so I felt an incredible sense of responsibility for finishing it, even simply on that side of it. Just on a monetary side. Absolutely, . . . it's kind of like, what's the ROI? I've got to be able to make at least as much as I'm making now and so . . . the practicality of it was very present for me.

During the program, while Carole still worked, her income as a thirty-nine-hours-per-week advisor was far less than her previous income, and no benefits accompanied her part-time status. Davida missed "the consistent and reliable pay, especially when the cost of living, including food, gas, child care, and health insurance increased!" Laura, saw the financial impact of having only one full-time income on a daily basis in her diet.

The most difficult change is the combination of reduced income and lack of control over your free time. It is difficult to eat peanut butter and jelly every day. When you are surviving on a GAA [graduate administrative assistantship] salary, you cannot afford to "eat out" every day on campus. . . . There is not a surplus of funds, so it is difficult to afford quality food. Fresh fruits and vegetables are expensive. Cereal and bologna are less expensive. As my diet got worse, my weight increased. My clothes didn't fit as well and I couldn't afford new clothes. It's an endless cycle. I would also say that I had less time for exercise, which contributed to the problem.

For Seth, Carole, Laura, and Emily there was a palpable loss of identity. Seth realized during the first two weeks when classes began that "he was just another student." Carole dealt with a double loss, "first my identity as a higher education professional, and second, my identity within a parochial education system." Laura, too, faced an identity crisis during her second quarter in the program.

I remember . . . that when I resigned my job at Urbana University, I was also providing clinical care to Urbana High School, and I loved the women's basketball team, and I . . . made an agreement with the coach there that I would come back, and I would provide care to his team only. All he would do is cover my gas money back and forth, because I just didn't want to lose my clinical skills. I was having the hardest time when winter came around for basketball to start with the realization I couldn't do it. Traffic would not cooperate to get back to Urbana in time, and I remember having the conversation with Ada, and she keeps telling me, "It's not going to work. I never like to tell you never, but this practically is not going to work." And it was. It's exactly what you said.

I quit fighting the identity, and who I was previous is not who I am now. If I'm going to be successful in this, I've got to change who I am and to change my identity. I'm not an athletic trainer anymore. I'm not a faculty member anymore. I'm a student, and I'm going to have to go to studying on weekends, all weekend long. That's just the way it is. So I think after ten weeks for me—I'm not saying money wasn't an issue and things, but the large struggles came to a head very quickly, and they were resolved very quickly.

Emily pointed out the costs for those "who took longer than normal to finish. It was the loss of mobility. That if you chose to pass other positions because you were tied to the institution, so it was—that could potentially have another financial [impact]." Seth also left a full-time job and accepted a graduate assistantship so that he could focus on his studies full-time. For him, there were three tangible costs.

Loss of income. Yes, I was grateful for the full tuition waiver and modest stipend, but it was painful. I was fortunate to have a nice tax return and a vacation buyout when I left my previous job to float me my first year. I led a pretty modest life before and planned well financially (i.e., no loans), but was disappointed upon learning that other comparable programs like ours paid their GAAs much more (e.g., Michigan), and provided more support for professional development, etcetera. I was stressed about this all the time, the financial insecurity.

Loss of status. I was very involved in ACPA[1] when I started my program and well-networked but I didn't know anyone working for OSU and didn't have the reputation or status I enjoyed before. I would get frustrated at times in some offices at OSU because I was just a student, not someone with status and responsibility. However, I rarely mentioned my previous career, unless asked, so that I would purposefully be treated like the other students. Pros and cons to this approach!

As a single person, the loss of income and status also adversely affected my dating life. Not too many potential mates were impressed with me being a full-time grad student in my thirties unless they were associated with a university themselves or worked in academia. However, if I was a medical or law student, there would be less of an issue here since these usually lead to very high-paying jobs immediately upon graduation. Also, some friends and family didn't think it was a good idea to leave a job where I was coming up for a promotion and near my family.

We might chuckle at Seth's referral to potential mates, but two of the single women also picked up on it, as did Davida, who named "placing marriage or partnerships on hold, and delaying mother- or fatherhood" as two of the sacrifices people faced. Men, no less than women, have a sense about biology, and for a man in his mid-thirties who wants to settle down and have a family, the commitment to doctoral work on a very tight budget has real consequences.

Laura summed up her sense of overall loss: "Obviously going to school displaces your time somewhere else and there was a large amount of guilt in recognizing that you weren't the person you were, and you couldn't give the energy to some of the things that you used to."

GUILT

Feelings of responsibility toward family and coworkers were the biggest source of guilt, and, like the colors of velvet fabric, shifted in subtle ways with the light. Each life consisted of a different web of relationships, and taken together they illustrate an underlying tension that affects every aspect of the program. Brian spelled out the consequences for him: "After arriving to work at 8:00 AM and leaving for classes at 4:30 PM, then back home at 8:00 PM to then read/write more and wake up the next day to do the same thing all over again wore me down to the point where I felt as though I wasn't able to give my best to my job, school, and relationships (partner, friends, family, etc.)." And Laura underscored it. Basically, "the reading assignments and writing demands were great as a doctoral student. These demands displaced time with family. This created guilt . . . a lot of guilt!" As Polly said, "There was guilt all through this. There was no map to the decision. It was reminders about the guilt." Laura describes a family situation that probably resonates with a lot of people, although for some the gender roles might be reversed. Imagine quitting a job to enroll in a doctoral program when you have responsibility for supporting your brother and mother, and then reflect on the impact on your spouse, who now works extra shifts in a tough job.

> I think the guilt doesn't have to be kids. . . . I don't have children, but I do come from a very poor family. My father died when I was in college, and so my mom was trying to raise my brother who was still in junior high, high school when I started. There was a significant age difference, and my mom's only job to that point had been third shift in a factory, and you can't really raise a teenage boy when you're not home at night. My family relied on me financially, so that's where a lot of my guilt came from is that I didn't feel like I was holding up my dad's wishes to take care of my mother and my brother. It wasn't kids, it was truly extended family.
>
> . . . The guilt for me was that I now was giving up my income and asking my husband to be the sole money provider; and then send money back to my family, and he was taking a lot of flak from his family for sending my family money. That was a very complicated situation. We actually did have that same conversation. 'We're doing this for us. This will put me in a better position and ultimately my career stability will help us.' We did have that, but I think I felt an incredible amount of guilt knowing that he was picking up extra shifts, that he was working sometimes eighty hours a week out-of-state on road construction.
>
> That was part of the guilt I had that—look at me. "I'm sitting here typing on a computer in an air conditioned room. Oh, woe is me. He's on three-hundred-degree asphalt in one-hundred-degree heat working his eightieth hour this week." That was a lot of the guilt for me in that he was making an enormous sacrifice for me, and I'm typing in air conditioning. I didn't think that was so rough compared to what he had.

Almost everyone who was married or had a partner felt something similar. Kelly describes the impact of the program and the student experience on her partner in stark detail. A professional couple, before Kelly enrolled in the PhD program they talked it all through, and decided the decision would benefit them both, and later they could switch out—as they did when Cynthia went back to school to get her RN [Nursing].

> A piece of it, we've talked about the support that we need from our partners or our family members, and we've been talking about the fact that this is a really self-centered sort of process. I mean it kind of has to be. You sort of have to be to some degree a selfish person for a while, but that does take a toll on the other person. Not necessarily just your relationship, but the other person in general.
>
> Because as smart as Cynthia is, and as much higher education as she's had, this is not an experience that she's had. So the emotional ups and downs, . . . the ups and downs are incredibly intense. One day you feel like you can do this and the next day you're sure you're the most clueless person sitting in that classroom. And that feeling of being so out of your element is going to pass (and somewhere, you know that's true)—but your partner or your support person doesn't know it because they're not experiencing it. All they know is their partner is in a bad place and they don't know how to help them. There's no real frame of reference for that. . . . She would sometimes get frustrated because she just felt so helpless. She did not know how to help in this sort of situation, and I didn't quite realize the extent to which partners have issues around this until we were sort of together with a group of people and some people were in the doctoral program, and their partners were there.
>
> They started joking about, "Yeah you know we're the ones that ought to get together on a regular basis and form our own support group because, let's face it, this is crazy." I don't know exactly where I'm going with this except that that is something to be kind of careful of, I guess.

After Brad's muttered concurrence, she continued,

> You sort of realize that it's—there's a toll there that's more than just who's going to do the grocery shopping and how is the laundry getting done and who's carting the kids back and forth or taking the dog to the vet or whatever. I got to see a little bit of that [when Cynthia] was in nursing school, because boy, there's a culture that is pretty different. [Laughter.] As much as I know about how you negotiate higher education, there were times when I would just feel like, 'I got nothing for you. I have no idea how to strategize this or negotiate this.'" That's when I got the sense of what it must have been like for her for five years, just having no frame of reference to help me through things.

And Ben continued, "It takes us away emotionally, physically, sometimes spiritually from that person who is important in our lives and it's hard to make sure—or it takes work to make sure—that you continue to grow with them. I mean Marla used to joke that she was a grad school widow."

"It's a shared experience, but it's not exactly the shared experience," Kelly concluded.

Not all participants shared these feelings of guilt about partner situations. Tina was in her forties when she began the program, with a husband and grown son. "Well," she said during the conversation, "I'm thinking about all this, and I don't remember guilt. This I don't. Well, I don't think I was. I had been back to school four times since my husband and I had been married, and so—he's a very independent person so that's fine with him. As long as he doesn't have to do any of it." While we might think Tina's perspective could be attributed to a long-standing marriage relationship, Kathy echoed her comments—and her wedding had been the weekend before the doctoral orientation the September when she began the program.

I want to thank you for saying that you didn't feel the guilt, because I'm feeling as a woman having made the choices to not have a family. I'm married, but I do not have children. I didn't feel guilt in my program, but I can say that I met my husband, and we got married right before I started the PhD program. I had been a student. I was in the College of Pharmacy as a student, so the entire time that we were dating and then got married, he only knew me as a student. He had never seen me as a professional, and so maybe that's part of why.

So I'm glad to know that in our life circumstances we're going through this, that may have impacted it because I didn't have other commitments, and he was perfectly willing to be a part of this relationship where I was committed to this other thing in my life besides our relationship too. So thank you.

Responsibility for children, however, did produce guilt. Sometimes, the rationale for the guilt was not always straightforward. For example, trying to follow Olivia's description of the frustration stemming from her responsibilities as a mother, and to her family is a bit like traveling Escher's Möbius strip.

The times I left most frustrated would be when others would hold what I felt were seemingly unrealistic expectations about what work I could accomplish or when I could get work done. Oftentimes, as a mother, I would put in what felt like a full day's work even before I showed up at my job. Then, I would leave my not-so-easy professional position to again manage a household. I was exhausted. When I was lucky, I would be able to squeeze in PhD work on the weekends. Perhaps I placed some of the feelings on myself, but more often than not I was tangled in a complex web of responsibility that never ended. How could I not put my family first? Well, wasn't part of putting my family first giving my all at the job that pays the bills and put a roof over all of our heads? How did the PhD work into that equation and why weren't others more perceptive of my dilemma?

Her feelings about her children were more painfully clear.

Well, and I think it's not always within your context, too, where the guilt comes from. Like, I placed the guilt. The guilt was self derived. . . . I would watch other people who take kids to play groups, and I'd watch other mothers so actively engaged in their childhood, and I'd be thinking about when they're going to go down for nap and how I was going to re-create [my writing]. My mind was consumed with these other thoughts, and I'd watch every other mother so like just intently, actively engaging in motherhood. I'd be like rewriting a chapter in my head, so as soon as they fell asleep I could get back and write it down.

Olivia's children—her babies, to be more accurate, were both born during her doctoral program. So, her comments reflect the real-time pain of a new mother. Does the guilt diminish over time? Not according to Davida and Carole. Listen to their words. Davida was speaking three years after completing her degree.

You know, I was fortunate to have KJ [her son] at OSU's daycare, so anytime I was on-campus and I need to sort of hedge that motherly guilt, I could go see him. But I know at nighttime putting him down early so I could hurry up and get back to reading or writing, it really did unnerve me at times. And now as he's gotten older and I've finished the program, I do find myself overcompensating for time lost. You know, trying to set aside my needs, immediate needs, so that on Saturday mornings I can be up for a soccer game because I didn't always have the opportunity to do that.

I remember during general examinations being torn—"Do I get up and write Saturday morning or go sit out at a soccer field for almost five hours?" and I chose the latter, but I'm sitting at the soccer game not focused at all on my child and the game. I'm sitting there processing in my mind, "I've got to make sure I cite this, I've got to make sure I do this." And you know again, I will probably go to the grave—you know, Lord willing, I have any more kids, I would just probably shower them now because I just know and I pray every day that my example will rub off on my son. I said that at the end of my dissertation that one day he, I'll get to sit and watch him walk across the stage multiple times. That this is all worth it because literally he has grown up on OSU's campus and Capital's campus.

Carole finished the program ten years earlier.

Yes, but I still feel guilty about my children and I think I always will because there was just so much of me they didn't have and, you know—and even now. I mean, it wasn't just that program, it was the twenty years that I had worked before and it's been the ten, or fifteen years since I've worked after. I think that I can only speak for myself as a woman, but even now, I feel that I don't have the time for my, even my adult children and now almost, nine grandchildren. . . . I don't have time. I still don't have the time that I really think my family deserves. So, that'll probably go to my grave.

While both the men and women expressed strong feelings of guilt resulting from the lack of time for partners, family, and children, Ben raised an interesting question about whether and how gender impacted these feelings. In our society, women are still viewed as the primary care-givers and nurturers. So, while men may be permitted a certain degree of selfishness, many in our society feel that women who behave in a similar manner are stretching or breaking the norms of acceptable behavior. Tacit, expressed or self-imposed judgments can create a double-whammy for the woman who fails to fully meet expectations for care giving or selflessness.

Fear and guilt are hard to separate when the issue is the "fear of letting down others," or "not meeting expectations." Others meant partners, parents, friends, cohort members, faculty, and employers. The coworker concern had a particular twist to it for Brad, Stephanie, and Olivia, who said, "I had a fear of like wanting to fly under the radar at work, that I knew I was getting special privileges . . . special opportunities at work either to be gone for classes or to participate in special projects based on the theme part of my professional development. I was scared other people were going to figure it out, and that there was going to be some kind of standardization." If that were to happen, she would lose those privileges.

Stephanie was not concerned so much about losing privileges, "because my boss was supportive, but it was the fear or the realization that people knew I was being treated different-ly so then they were treating me differently, not positive." Brad, too, focused on his fear of disappointing others, of letting them down. His comments refer to the decision to accept a full-time, senior administrative position in the northern part of Wisconsin, just as he was beginning to analyze his dissertation data. For most students, the months spent analyzing data and writing up the analysis and interpretation chapters of the dissertation are one of the two periods of the greatest intellectual effort and intensity. (The other period occurs earlier, in the months of writing the dissertation proposal and preparing for the general exam.)

At a very critical point, I opted to leave for a full-time job. One of the other trusted advisers that I had here on campus, you know, who had been supporting me in terms of an assistantship said, "Do not do this. We've given you this time. We've provided you these privileges and you're going to go and you're going to be so busy you're not—I—you know you can do it, but I think you won't finish." . . . It all worked out, but to me, that really hit me that people were rooting for me and creating paths for me, that even were very special, and the last thing I wanted to do was let any of those folks down, even though I didn't, but that that was present in their thinking this. Like I was possibly squandering—not wanting those folks who had been so good not only to this point, and fears from it.

ISOLATION

New city, new environment, new role, people moving away—all these contributed to a sense of isolation, especially the strain of maintaining friendships at a distance. Jaime, "left family, friends, partner at home. . . . For a while I could do things—it was kind of nice in some ways, too, because I could be selfish—stay out, study or go workout whenever I wanted to—those kind of things, but coming home sometimes to an empty apartment, especially when I didn't know anyone was tough, too." Jaime was in a long-distance relationship during her program, and thought a lot about her friends.

> I started thinking a lot . . . my friends that weren't in PhD programs, just college friends that didn't do any of this [i.e., weren't in school] that they were getting promotions, advances, and making more money at work and going on trips. . . . That kind of brought home to me some of those personal things that I hadn't thought of when I started the program. Even though I was making new friends who understood what we were all going through, it still bothered me that I just couldn't participate, and so that kind of contributed to some of that isolation.
>
> I had no connection to Ohio State or Columbus when I arrived—all of my family, friends, and partner were on the East Coast, and I had some real moments of doubt as I started the program— what was I doing? Added to that, my advisor, one of the reasons I came to OSU, left at the end of my first quarter, so I really questioned my place and ability to succeed in the program.

Davida found it difficult to "remain 'grounded' and relatable to family members and friends who may think that you have forgotten about them (i.e., do not return phone calls promptly or have not responded to their e-mails) or 'gotten too big' for them. The 'naysayers' would say things like, 'She thinks she is all that!'(If they only knew!)." She also lost friends along the way, "people that I thought were friends that, you know, again, I'm glad they—I learned that they weren't, or weren't in my corner and that's perfectly fine too. I wouldn't say family deserted me but I think some of my family members had a hard time understanding why I couldn't always come back home for a holiday or I didn't immediately return a phone call a day later because I didn't have time to return the call a day later."

Like other professionals, faculty change jobs and institutions. The author had three different advisors during her doctoral program. Brian's advisor moved to another institution just as he was beginning to frame his dissertation research; she had suggested that I become his advisor. Nonetheless, her departure created real anxiety for him. "I would say during the program, there were definitely moments where I did fear if I could make it all the way through. . . . And then, you know, my advisor left the university and so I was abandoned."

In this graduate program during the first year, the doctoral students typically take six courses together: three core doctoral courses along with their counterparts in educational administration, and three of the four required core higher education courses, along with the master's students. Historically in each group, one or more students will organize monthly lunches or dinners, which often continue well into the third year. By the third year, a combination of events results in less synchronous progress. Delays are common. Students enroll in extra courses related to methodology and dissertation topics; some accept new jobs or face unanticipated changes in job responsibilities; partnerships that form or dissolve and/or children who become ill or need help in school become the main focus of attention for a quarter or more. Over time, friends and colleagues leave the program.

Olivia pointed out that she "experienced real fear when every one of my cohorts started to leave [graduate], and Emily left [moved to her new job]. I was not certain what kind of peer support that I would have. That was a real piece for me, and I know some people said you didn't feel like you have strong peer support anyways, but . . ." Although he completed his program earlier, Ben picked up her comment, "But, it's back to that cohort relationship. That's really important." As Olivia continued, "Yeah, fear of being the last one."

The result for many was a strong sense of isolation. Emily saw the contrast with a naturally high level of interconnections that represent a large part of her admissions work.

> As an additional topic, I would like to address the topic of isolation. I think this was so salient for me on so many levels. It crosses many of the topics that you have listed. It may be a bit of an emotional topic, sometimes hard to express those feelings, but one that I think is very critical to understand for a mid-career person who by the nature of that point in their personal and professional lives is very connected and networked and the isolation is really powerful.

Olivia reflected further. "Somewhere, amidst the countless hours spent together in core courses and at coffee houses, I found myself somewhat alone: alone on campus, alone in Columbus, alone, negotiating feelings of misunderstanding about my time and priorities with family and friends, alone amidst a growing tower of papers and books and alone with rising levels of anxiety and isolation." Her comment prompted a discussion that as it progressed, revealed an inescapable aspect of the doctoral work: the extraordinary demands for time-consuming, individual effort to understand personal perspectives and biases, and to develop new strengths. Participants expressed their understanding of this profound reality through a conversation that had its own momentum. Ben described the isolation.

> Isolation. I see that theme both positive and negative; the negative feeling of isolation and loss of status and some feeling of not being understood by loved ones and friends. But then the positive side of the isolation, I think Tina talked about the ascetic experience of writing. I used to go to my cave and I thought—and I described the life of writing a dissertation or doing a doctoral program as kind of an asset. . . . One thing I saw in the isolation piece is that there's a positive and a negative aspect to it, and sometimes you have to work through the negative to get to the positive. Maybe I'm seeing in the product that comes out of our conversation this also acting as a guide of sorts to mid-career professionals, to say it's natural to have that feeling of isolation. "Here is what has worked for people to move through that process."

And Kelly reframed it somewhat.

> This idea of isolation, . . . I don't know that I ever felt isolated, but I thought maybe we could have a brief chat about reframing isolation into the personal journey. I think maybe going into doctoral work, I didn't realize how individual it is; how personal it is, and so maybe that isolation is an outcropping or it's a symptom, or it's something associated with this very individual nature of the work that is working towards a PhD. But the term isolation to me has a very negative connotation versus a personal journey where the individual nature of this. . . . and I can honestly say that I was shocked at how much time I had to spend as an individual pondering things and working through things. I didn't anticipate that, but I don't know that I felt a sense of isolation. Maybe it was that, but I don't know that I felt it that way. I can tell you that Myers Briggs-wise, I started out as an extreme extrovert and at the end of this journey, I had become much more centered between introversion and extroversion, so I had that ability to work within myself and work through problems. I think I developed that other side of me. Now was it solely because of the PhD, or was it because I was getting more mature? I don't know, but that's just my observation.

The new circumstances that accompanied the shift from having been a working professional to functioning as a student heightened and compounded the feeling of isolation. Laura explains the impact of the two coming together, even for a natural "introvert."

> There were two distinct things I remember. One, you talked about the isolation. I told you I wasn't isolated. I fought isolation. I'm an introvert. I like being isolated, but what I hated was being isolated because . . . I was being told I had to. Being isolated in my room because I had to read for eight hours, now I hated that. I fought it the first quarter, and I fought having to dedicate that time to studying, but there came a point in time where I say, 'Okay quit fighting this. You chose this. This is what it's going to be. Okay you're not going to a cookout this weekend, you're staying home and you're reading papers. That's what you're doing.'

The isolation for some stemmed from the inconsistency between a personal style and the rhythms demanded by the doctoral program, from marital (or partner) status for others, and for Davida, from being the only African American women in her master's cohort. Single students, like Seth and Stephanie, were free of the constraints of responsibility and schedules that are a natural part of partnered life. They were free to use their time as they wished. At the same time, Seth noted that "I know for a lot of single PhD students, ours were a lot different in terms of isolation sometimes. There was no one to go home to and talk to outside of your personal supports." Stephanie and Ben often compared notes, and she marveled at how he could do the program with a wife and baby at home. "The only thing the program was affecting was my dating record, which wasn't so stellar," she joked. So the situation cut both ways. Partners meant support and responsibility, and no partner, meant flexibility and freedom, but maybe isolation and not support.

Davida's feelings about her situation are a caution to all of us about the importance of campus centers and organizations that provide a "place" where students of color, or other less common identities, can find a community. When she began the program, her son was an infant, creating an even more complex challenge.

> My postpartum was channeling those very depressing energies into work, into school, and so I was very connected to my coursework, very emotional, and that sense of loneliness that I've expressed to you and that sense of isolation, being the only woman of color in the master's program and not really having anywhere to turn. I think what saved me was that thesis research in connecting to the Hale Center on campus, because finally I had found a place where there were other people who looked like me.

Davida's master's thesis and dissertation both focused on the identities and roles of African-American women (the thesis on undergraduates, and dissertation on presidents). We self-consciously crafted a strategy that included finding the most productive connections to these communities to enable her to be successful. Her comments about isolation on campus as a master's student reminded me of a similar comment from a previous African American master's advisee of mine, perhaps eight years earlier. That young woman had been president of her senior class in college and exhibited all the social skills of a natural leader. During her second quarter in the program, she seemed subdued in our conversations, and when asked about it, she said, "You have no idea how hard it is to be a woman of color on this campus. It is so lonely." She later helped form the minority student graduate council on the campus, and has since completed her doctorate at another institution.

The sense of isolation imposed by the transformative nature of the journey has not been discussed in the literature with which I am familiar. Intuitively, it resonates with stories we hear about athletes, performers, and others in situations where the effort required to achieve a difficult goal requires reaching deeply into personal reserves to find the strength to continue. The phrase "dig deep" was born of those efforts. The flip side of digging deep is gaining the satisfaction of having accomplished something truly worthwhile and perhaps, getting the recognition for it. For newly minted doctorates moving into work situations where most of the professionals around them also have doctorates, the sense of satisfaction, of having accomplished "something special" can be elusive. Kelly described this odd phenomenon in the context of explaining her reason for taking the time to come to the August meeting—to gain some closure.

> Finishing a PhD is a critical experience but it's also a pretty sort of private one and kind of isolated. Right? Because I remember when I finished my generals and had a conversation with somebody else who had just sort of finished hers pretty recently, and the sense of we're walking around campus and nobody has any idea what we just accomplished and you can't just go up to random strangers and say, "Hey I just finished my generals." They're going to think you're nuts.
>
> But it's sort of the same thing when you actually walk across that stage. You have this doctorate. You have done some amazing thing and now you're going back to work, and you're probably in a place where 95 percent of your colleagues have the doctorate. It's no longer any big deal. All right? It's expected. So there's no way to really kind of put closure on that. If that is making any sense at all? . . . But it just sort of—it ends abruptly I guess. Then you just start off doing your own thing.

Fear, doubt, and discomfort seem to be essential to all learning "insofar as learning necessarily involves encounters with the new, unfamiliar, different and strange" (English and Stengel, 2010, 523). Fear can either impede or prompt learning, after all, learning typically results from discomfort. However, as we saw from this chapter, each person lives a different version of fear, and I agree with English and Stengel's observation.

> It is impossible to know for certain and in advance the set of circumstances that shift feelings of discomfort from energizing to paralyzing for each and every student. However, experienced educators can anticipate potential pitfalls based on past students' prior knowledge, patterns of misunderstanding, and typical interactions. Relying on one's professional judgment informed by the "wisdom of practice" may not seem like much, but it is all we have, and it is enriched significantly by the educator's willingness to consider affect as a key variable in the teaching and learning equation. (2010, 541)

The more we can anticipate some of the specific forms fear can take, the better able "doctorate hopefuls" and advisors may be to manage situations that could provoke these strong emotions, to turn them into opportunities for growth and development. By contributing the experiences of these doctoral students here, my hope is that the cumulative effect will allow faculty and advisors to broaden the knowledge base that constitutes their "wisdom of practice" by fifteen more students without the sixty "person years" of additional advising. In the following chapter we learn more about the factors that enabled these students to be successful.

NOTE

1. The American College Personnel Association, a national, professional association for members of the student affairs profession.

Chapter Five

Challenges and Exhilaration

MORE CHALLENGES

The complex and daunting emotional dynamics presented in chapter 4 were revealed through the focus group discussions illustrated colorfully through participant stories and comments. They included fear, risk, guilt, isolation, family and partner responsibilities, worry about finances, and coworker expectations. More challenges were revealed through responses to two questions first posed in the guidelines for the reflection papers, "What was most difficult about the PhD experience?" and "What were the critical moments?" Six more topics emerged: maintaining balance among priorities; time management and, especially, time to write; the intellectual challenge; expectations; choosing to stay in the program; and reentry after the doctorate. Balancing priorities with a job and time management/time to write were mentioned most frequently. Some of the more strident comments related to the intellectual challenge, gender roles, and reentry after the doctorate. In this chapter we will explore the first five, and save the reentry discussion for chapter 9.

Balancing Priorities and the Job

In some ways Carole's situation was unique, "with commuting from Dayton, which was a 170-mile round-trip every time and working full-time and having all the children still at home." But many identified with this aspect of her life: "I drove like a crazy maniac to get to class, go to class, and you know, jump back in my car and drive home to get home by about 10:30 or 11:00 at night." Whether the commute was 170, 17 or 1.7 miles, people with children, and/or partners and full-time jobs had very little time to have an "on-campus" experience beyond actual coursework. Olivia, Ben, Davida, Emily, and Brian were always in motion moving between school, work, and home.

Olivia and others constantly struggled with the question, "How could I not put my family first?" We heard about Davida's dilemma during the middle weekend of her general examination, which was a take-home format that involved writing responses to four questions over a two-week period: should she attend her son's soccer game on Saturday morning or get up and write. She chose the latter but her mind was elsewhere. On her list of most difficult was "Sacrificing quality time with loved ones. For about a year and a half, I loved my computer just as much as my son; but he was understanding and would get his toy computer and write his own dissertation!"

Without the drama of the heart-rending choices Polly faced when her son suffered the accident that put him a coma, Polly added other sports to Davida's soccer example, "Family obligations, of course, are the most important balance to consider. This means, in many cases, creative times for reading and writing such as swim meets, baseball games, and late-night sessions after all in the house are in bed."

The stress of these family matters sometimes generated more motivation. Olivia redoubled her efforts when she realized she was having another baby. "And that's when I began to allow my obsession, of sorts, to more or less completely define my approach to daily life," she said. Guilt about the changes and sacrifices her husband was making kept Laura from quitting during the first year when she was trying to overcome her lack of theoretical background. Even as she continued in the program, Laura found it "difficult to balance my studies with family time." Seth found one of the most difficult challenges arose during his final year as a consequence of his job search, "trying to balance a long-distance relationship, my dissertation defense and final submission, moving, graduation, and transitioning out from OSU."

While family concerns certainly created challenging trade-offs with class work, so did full-time work. Responding to the question "what was most difficult about the PhD experience?" Ben, Polly and others used nearly the same words: "Maintaining a career, and for me [Polly] a new career as I worked through the doctoral program was a challenge." "Developing balance is the most difficult challenge," according to Ben. Kathy's "strongest memories are of forming lasting friendships, balancing work, school and home and making ends meet financially. The most difficult was the workload. I had very little life balance during the PhD years. Work, school and taking care of a home, that was it." And Kelly "seemed to spend a lot of time writing grocery lists and 'things to do' lists in some of my classes." On Tina's list, "As difficult as it may be, make time and save energy for your family and for yourself."

Brian remembered the impact of his work schedule on his ability to participate in class-related group projects.

> There were a couple of my classmates who also worked full-time and the majority of us didn't, though. They had graduate assistantships. And, particularly in that first year . . . which is when I chose to do my residency requirement, carrying those classes on top of my job . . . which is particularly challenging and, several of my colleagues were also working, forty-plus hours a week and doing that as opposed to carrying, a twenty-hour-per-week graduate assistantship, which certainly impacted our dynamic in terms of group projects. Whereas a lot of my classmates would want to meet after lunch or a couple of hours before class at 4:00 PM that really wasn't an option for me. And so in some ways that drew lines within the cohort by default . . . based on our ability to hang out more and volunteer to do group projects with the entire group.

Carole told us, "The first turbulent waters involved making an unexpected career change at the very beginning of my program. . . . I took the gamble and submitted my resignation and accepted an academic counselor position at a community college, a decision that would haunt me later." She described the "drill" she had figured out during her master's program; balancing it all depended on being really, really organized.

> Certainly, balancing the demands of full-time work and a 170-mile round-trip commute to class with the demands of active parenting and involvement in my community of faith was challenging. However, I had just completed my master's degree and had the work/study drill down. With six children, a spouse, and a live-in elderly mother-in-law, I had to be extremely organized (i.e., had a six-week rotating menu), multi-tasked intentionally (i.e., sitting at a Little League game and studying on the sidelines). I also observed a twenty-four-hour Sabbath throughout my entire program, and believe the "rest" from work and school was critical and essential for restoration, renewal, and the successful completion of my program.

Time Management/Time to Write

Balancing priorities and time management seem to be two sides of the same coin. Emily nailed it when she said, "The time to write was a manifestation of priorities, choices, circumstances." And Davida called it "knowing how to set priorities. Yes—you can't do it all, and you have to constantly ask yourself, 'Okay, what needs to be accomplished first and what can wait?'" Ranking priorities means allocating time to those at the top, which in turn determines a balance (or imbalance). Stephanie's dilemma captured the essence, "Being pulled in two different full-time directions all the time. . . . As I loved my job, I would spend more hours working than I should, especially during the busy seasons and I would then have to remember that I was also a full-time PhD student. Always being busy!" For Laura, time to study present-ed the dilemma, "It wasn't a matter of finding time. It was more a matter of not having enough time. The first two years I felt as if no one could possibly finish all the readings that were assigned to us."

Brian summarized the most difficult, in "two words . . . time management." Earlier we learned about his daily schedule: the 8:00 AM–4:30 PM workdays, leaving for class, going home to read and write, going to bed and getting up the next day to do it all over again. The biggest surprise for him came *after* coursework, however.

> Once residency was over I thought that the rest would be easier to manage (fewer classes per quarter). While that was the case through the end of my coursework, when it came time for "independent" work—writing the proposal, prepare for candidacy exams, the entire dissertation process—this was the hardest time to manage. I soon realized that I was no longer on the professor's schedule, but now rather my own. If I didn't set goals, deadlines, etc., with my advisor (who is really good at these things), then it would take me longer to finish. I didn't want to be the eternal ABD candidate, but I also didn't want to feel guilty if I didn't spend every moment of my free time on school. . . . You know, when you're in classes you have deadlines and you have breaks, you have exams and down time. But, once you're done with the courses, you always have a dissertation to write and so you have to sort of come up with a structure that works for you in terms of chunking it into little manageable roles.

Almost all the participants wanted to comment about managing time and specifically, finding time to write. Writing, both analytic and reflective, is a big part of doctoral work (Thompson and Kamler, 2010). Most courses—certainly two or three each quarter, require substantial research papers. Coursework is followed by the candidacy exam, which in this program is typically structured as four questions, each posed by a professor on the student's committee. The exams are commonly handled in a take-home format, where students spend two and a half days writing for each question, for example, Monday morning through Wednesday noon, or noon on Wednesday through Friday afternoon. The exam format limits responses to twenty-five pages, including references. However, students usually write to the limit, drafting one hundred pages, synthesizing literature and theory during a ten-day period. And, of course, the dissertation itself is a massive exercise in critical thinking and writing.

In addition, prior to taking the candidacy exam this doctoral program requires that a draft of the dissertation proposal be completed. Proposals are comprised of the first three chapters of the dissertation: introduction, literature review, and methodology. While introductory chap-ters can run anywhere from ten to thirty pages, literature reviews tend to be extensive, and discussions of methodology are comprehensive. Those drafts can total another hundred pages. The major difference between the proposal draft and the candidacy exam is the amount of effort put into developing the dissertation proposal.

The proposal is the blueprint for the ensuing dissertation research and as such, must provide a meticulous justification for and description of the question/s, background, research, and analysis process. As a result, students often turn in as many as four or five successive drafts of each chapter to the advisor. It is an intense and interactive process. The candidacy exam, by contrast, is a one-off exercise. Drafts of dissertation proposals and the candidacy exam are typically written during the third year of a student's program, so there is often a six- to eight-month period after coursework has been completed when a student's primary activity is researching, analyzing, synthesizing, critiquing and writing about the dissertation topic, and related content areas, such as methodology. As an advisor, having been on the receiving end of drafts, and the "giving" end of commentary, I had anticipated some of the comments about writing, but not others. Substantial excerpts from the discussion are presented here because so many of the students I met initially felt they could fit dissertation writing "around the edges" of work and family obligations, and only weeks or months later, after frustrating efforts to write drafts of the first chapter, came to realize the need for large blocks of time.

> Literally, finding the time to write, and the discipline required to keep writing (endlessly), was challenging. However, my position at the community college allowed for downtime, and I was able to complete a significant amount of writing and editing during work hours. When I was near the end, and had to complete the final edits and pull my dissertation apart and rewrite (again!), I knew I was close to the limit of my sanity. I had endured a computer crash and had numerous versions of the chapters, and finally called on my calm and gifted mother who came from out-of-state, and provided the needed support to complete the final edits. Carole

> Finding the time to write meaningfully. Hitting a writer's block was always the toughest—the block could last for an hour, day, week, or even a month; but, also knowing that the block could be broken at 3:00 in the morning, 12:00 noon right when I was about to meet with a student, or at 6:00 PM, when I needed to get dinner on the table, lunch packed and clothes ironed for school. Davida

> Having an advisor who thought about things very differently than I did was very helpful. I remember some of our review sessions where I'd hand in a chapter and you'd [the author] go over it and I thought I wrote about it in the most salient and transparent and clear way and you'd be like, "I don't get this. Why is this important?" . . . and it would cause me to take a step back and say, okay, maybe there is a better way to say this. And, I've never had my writing so scrutinized in my entire life. I actually, still to this day, one of the things I learned was that I overused the word "these" and every time I write something I always read the sentence with "these" and without "these" and I always go without "these." Brian

> Finding time to write—I think this should be called "making time to write" . . . it is like exercise, there are always a million other things that need to be done and distractions to keep you too busy to write, family, jobs, etc. . . . so, you have to just make the time and do it. Being committed to it is key. Stephanie

Making time to write for Kathy and Polly meant renegotiating work situations. Kathy gave up her full-time time position, after negotiating with her college to turn the position into a graduate assistantship, reducing work obligations to twenty hours per week.

> Finding time to study was easier than finding time to write. Projects or assignments for class were defined and finite (e.g., you had six weeks to work on a paper on "X"). The dissertation was quite another animal in terms of writing. I am not sure that I could have done it without going to a 50 percent appointment. I cannot write in small blocks of time for a serious project like the dissertation. To this day serious writing like book chapters or articles takes dedicated half days for me at least. I cannot just drop in and out. . . . If I had not made the career choice that I made to go to a 50

percent position, I don't think I'd be sitting here today because I don't think, for me, I would have been able to finish without having taken my work requirements to a more manageable level so I had the intellectual time to write.

Polly took substantial time away from her position as chair of a department.

> Finding time to read and study was a little easier than finding time to write. I could read and jot down ideas anywhere, and I still do this. Finding time to write is another issue for me. I need concentrated, quiet, and uninterrupted time to write, as it is not my strength. For me, this often involved taking some days off from work when my children were at school. . . . It sounds like all of us in our own little way kind of figured that piece out. I mean I had to take some built-up vacation/ personal time, all that kind of stuff. I stored it up and then used that to take a month or probably almost two months spread out off to do this dissertation already. You had to do that because you can't just—I couldn't just sit and write for a couple of hours and go to work and come back and write for a few hours and go to work. I mean I had to find a way to do the concentrated time. . . . I have two sons and a husband that was working at the time. I packed up my computer and what-have-you and up I went to my mother's lake home.

While everyone agreed that blocks were needed in order to accomplish the type of writing required for the dissertation, Stephanie found herself in a rare situation that actually "saved" her from her tendency to overcommit to work. Her fiancé, whom she met while guiding a study abroad trip for students, lived in Luxembourg and she wanted to move to Luxembourg to be with him prior to their marriage. She asked my "permission" in the context of her program.

> When I asked your permission to move to Luxemburg . . . you said that . . . "if you're going to quit your full-time job and write full time, then yes, I support you 100 percent." In my case, because we moved to a foreign country and I wasn't allowed to work, because I wasn't married yet for the legal reason, I was able to write full time, and I absolutely agree that if I hadn't had that time, I probably would still be . . . working on my dissertation.

Synthetic work, writing that depends on integrating previous research, theory and analysis with new data, requires "stewing time." First drafts are essential and inevitably inadequate. The discipline of writing forces more systematic thought and reviewing earlier drafts often yields new and creative insights that result in the complete restructuring of a presentation or idea. (Producing an adequate working draft of this chapter, for example, took four complete drafts over two weeks.) Blocks of time leave the space to work through a full writing cycle: time to think, write, read, review, stew, and rewrite. It's often necessary to literally "throw away" previous drafts in order to begin again with a fresh idea. When writing time is cobbled together from a few evenings or parts of weekends, it can seem so limited that each draft produced is viewed as "precious" and the student/writer becomes reluctant to entertain creative new ideas that might mean having to "go back" and redo something because the time is simply not available. Only after major concepts and the storyline have been crafted can smaller pieces be identified and written piecemeal.

Carving out those larger blocks of time meant planning ahead with supervisors about schedules, using vacation time, and working things out with partners, spouses and children for quiet time, or time away. Brad's comment about the process leads to his advice to those considering doctoral study.

So there's a little intentionality that you say that "Finally I'm going to push through and do this," and however we arranged it in our personal lives we all did that. We all did that in some way. I think about [my advisor], in my case, saying, "Yeah, you can do this." Basically all I needed was her to sort of pat me on the back and say, "Yeah you can do it. Make it work for yourself, but I believe that you can take this next step." We negotiated that for ourselves in our lives in our own ways, but it clearly is that we chose sacrifices. We chose to put parts of our lives in abeyance so that we would carve this—I'll call it selfish—and did call it selfish—this very selfish time for ourselves. I think someone coming on the front end, something that's important to tell those folks is that you are—how are you going to map this out for yourself?

Intellectual Challenge

In the first chapter, I made a distinction about a student's doctoral experience based on the degree to which the program demands that the student function as an independent researcher. That difference is the key to understanding participant comments about the intellectual challenge. These participants were required to originate and frame the topic of their dissertation, the research questions and method/s, collect the data themselves, and independently develop and write analyses, interpretation, and implications. Their dissertation experience differs substantially from students whose dissertations are part of larger, ongoing (team-based) research projects.

Keep in mind that these fifteen individuals had been admitted to this highly ranked doctoral program because they had already demonstrated an exceptional level of intellectual ability and through at least two years of coursework had broadened their knowledge and learned new inquiry skills. Yet, structuring and conducting dissertation research in this setting challenged them to use every bit of their talent and knowledge. For all researchers, framing research questions accurately to focus on the information sought, and framing them so that they can be researched and will generate good data takes careful thought and creativity; for the neophyte it can be a trying exercise. Polly was not the only one who struggled with her questions, but she captured the sentiment for everyone at the table with these words:

> You can't imagine how stupid I felt when I couldn't get a question written. I'm going, "My God, this has got to be simple. All I've got to do is write this question." [Laughter.] But what you're thinking, you do all this massive amount of writing. You figure, "Okay, all I've got to do is come up with two or three questions. Why can't I get it there?" They don't understand how much goes into those questions and how important those questions are going to be when you run through all the data and everything else, but it's—[At this point, I interjected with a comment about a current student who took eight months to get her questions, and Polly, it turns out, knew her.] I know; we had several questions about that. We had several lunches over her questions.

As Ben testified, "You can get through the intellectual challenge, but if there were not that trust and [advisor] relationship, that intellectual challenge would push you right over the edge." Years earlier, Carole had a similar experience. "The research and dissertation process was challenging, starting with the first step—identifying my topic and narrowing it down to an identifiable and defined concept/area. Even developing my research questions was a painful process. It really was agonizing to discuss and explore my interests, and then to continue to experience a dense fog."

Fog can obscure research progress at any point in the process. Emily struggled to find a framework that would capture all the different dimensions of presidential leadership that she wanted to explore. After weeks of her trying, one afternoon in my office she and I together concocted a simple diagram. She took that home and reworked it into something quite different that belonged to her and presented her logic. Davida spoke about her meltdown two months before graduation as she was writing her findings chapter. And Ben had a similar experience, as he tried to find patterns within his qualitative data. "There was one point in the dissertation where I couldn't explain this phenomenon that I was trying to see, and Ada is like, 'Try using Senge's systems approach [1990].' I'm like, huh? So we started mapping it out, and I went home afterwards. I'm looking at this mess and trying to go, 'Okay. How am I going to do this?' Well, it ended up being the central part of my findings."

Sometimes the analytic strengths that serve very well in one context are insufficient and students and researchers need a completely different perspective. Polly, a nurse by training, was the first of three of my doctoral advisees who were practicing nurses. (The other two are working on their dissertations as this is being written.) Their wonderful ability to observe detail and use information sequentially enhances their effectiveness in health care settings. In educational research contexts, however, processing multiple dimensions simultaneously is often required. And for Ben, Emily, and Polly (quoted below) it meant shifting their thinking into new dimensions.

> As we started to work through writing, of course, my style is very linear logistic, and you had to break me out of this several times so that I could get—and that's my nursing background—to get me on the right [track], similar to Ben when you said, "Well you know you can frame it this way. You can match your concepts across in a grid," and then that gave me the framework to say, "Aha, now I can write about these. I get how they're—how it's coming out of the data and emerging, and the pieces are flowing together." Until I could see that framework, because that's the way I think, it was hard for me to get there.

Dealing with Expectations

Virtually everyone in contact with a doctoral student has expectations—husbands, wives, partners, "significant others," friends, supervisors, coworkers, advisors, faculty, and of course, the student, himself or herself. Expectations could be frustrating, worrying, or helpful.

As a mother, working full time, Olivia fretted, "The times I left most frustrated would be when others would hold what I felt were seemingly unrealistic expectations about what work I could accomplish or when I could get work done." Stephanie was concerned about the "jealousy of coworkers at my full-time job . . . as my boss was extremely supportive of my PhD. He had completed his while working full-time, and he was flexible in my working hours/ schedule. I was able to conduct any research I asked to on our students, so I had access to him and our student populations and some 'colleagues' complained that I got special treatment."

By contrast, faculty expectations gave Polly a boost. She recalled Kelly and Laura's dramatic and worried reactions when faculty told them they were special during their admissions interviews. Laura had thought, "Well nobody's going to work with me." While Polly always felt her work in a community college nursing program was valuable, she said, "There is a stigma related to people coming out of a community college and doing work at a university. For me it's such important work, but then to have that work valued and coming to the PhD program saying, "You know, you really—you can do scholarly work here, and it is at the level of Ohio State PhD level." I mean that was an 'Aha' for me." Her Dean's expectations were particularly helpful as she made choices.

> Knowing how to set priorities . . . is a key concept for me. I was fortunate enough that I had a dean at the time who understood this and knew that there were things that I purposely did not take leadership roles in because of my graduate studies. There were also other personal opportunities that I did not engage in during these years because I needed to keep the balance between family,

studies, and work. When the plate is full, something is going to fall off if you do not make the choice to move something off. Absent the choice to remove something, the wrong thing may fall off.

The impact of gender and role expectations came up several times during the conversation. Ben raised it the first day, as a result of a conversation he and Brad were having during the coffee break.

> That gender role and gender expectations and experience of being a wife or a mother or a partner or what have you is different for woman than for a man. It can also be based on the expectations within one's personal circle. . . . That was a lot of what you were trying to negotiate towards. You know expectations were different from what the movement you were making, so you had to go up against that wall. That was never something I had to confront.

In fact, all the messages he was getting were positive—that the move was ambitious and intellectually exciting. Laura picked up on his comment immediately, "Well, that is so key. You hit it. That's the difference in the gender. Women, we're not allowed to be self-absorbed. 'Shame on you for going to school.'" It was at this point that Olivia helped us realize that sometimes "the guilt was self-derived."

From opposite vantage points, Seth and Brad reminded us of the confounding dynamics that partnership brought. Seth, a younger single male, really had much the same experience during the program as one of his female friend in his cohort, also single and younger. If anything, the lack of a partner left each without the kind of emotional support others with partners might have. Brad took it one step further.

> It just seems to me that it would be [useful] to delve a little bit more deeply and consider the negotiations that occur with the important people in your life, whoever they are. You know the kind of immediate community that you belong to. In my case, my wife was living in Boston, been doing a master's degree, and I was here teaching at OSU. Then when she finished, that was my green light to start my doctoral program so that she could come here and work and then kind of swap incomes as it were. But again, I was very fortunate that we were willing to negotiate that, but the flip side of that was I took care of the house, and I took care of the cooking and I did—but that's okay. I had the time, and I had that to spare.
>
> Afterwards, now, we've reverted to slightly more typical roles, but there is still this sense in our household that "You took those five years out, and so you owe me X number of years of this." I mean that's okay, that's how we approached the problem. That may not be right for every couple, you know, every partnership broadly defined, but there is that call it reciprocity or sense of negotiation that I think helps folks to be thinking about that and how they might negotiate that in their important relationships.

Choosing to Stay, Not "Walking Away"

As Davida said, doctoral study is a marathon and every runner knows that when you see that finish line, it feels good. The high level of attrition in doctoral programs is apparent from the national data. It was certainly not a foregone conclusion that, once begun, all these students would complete the doctoral program, no matter how careful the admissions process. Getting to the finish line takes courage and strength. Every one of these participants hit a wall at one time or another. As I listened to the anxiety and doubts that permeated their lives, I thought surely some must have questioned whether they would continue. In fact, Kelly made just this point in an unexpected comment about the explicit decisions people made at various times during their years of study to continue with the program.

> The other thing that struck me in reading them [reflection papers] is . . . all of the decision points along the way—the things that happened—and folks came back to picking up their experience. . . . It just sort of seems to me that one of the things I think we all probably did in some way was always keep this experience as not just one decision that we had made and therefore we're trapped in it, but, for me anyway, it was a choice. It was like I made the choice over and over again. As long as I understood that it was my clear choice and that I could indeed walk away from it at any time I wanted to, in some way that gave the power back to me.

Did folks truly want to quit? And did they actually feel they could have "walked away" from the program, midstream? At what point did these "decisions" occur? I asked the group, "Who could have walked away?" Clear, affirmative answers came from almost half the participants: Polly, Kelly, Kathy, Jaime, Seth, Olivia, Carole, and Davida.

Jaime's reasons related directly to her advisor's departure.

> It was hard, for me. Did I have the conversation and entertain would I walk away? I seriously entertained it. I thought I could have left here, but would have gone somewhere else for my circumstances. Maybe others. I know Brian had the same—we both came in with [name] as our advisor, and she left that first—I guess it was our first year, and I really thought, "Do I follow her to Maryland where my partner that I'm now married to was in Virginia?" and that would have been an easy way to move. Go to Maryland, continue on and then at the same time he'd been offered a job across the country that he was entertaining. Do I move there and start another program there? . . . I would have left Ohio State and gone somewhere else thinking, you know, I would still finish, but it was leaving this program.

Seth, on the other hand, just focused on fit. "I could easily walk—I think I thought about that my first year. Was the program the right fit for me? And could I have gone somewhere else? And then, I think I could have. I was not locked in at all." By contrast, Stephanie, who was working full-time at the university, never considered leaving. "I suppose, yes, if an interesting job overseas happened, I would have potentially left both my job and PhD. But there was no other commitment keeping me to the program other than the one to be in the program."

The timing of the decisions to "recommit" varied, occurring at different times during participant experiences, for some in the first or second years, for others just before generals, or during the dissertation. For each person some crisis of confidence prompted an explicit choice. Kelly's comment had opened an emotional part of the conversation that elicited reactions from Laura, Kathy, Polly, Tina, Seth, and Ben. For Laura and Kathy, who came into the program with science backgrounds that were uncommon for higher education doctoral students, a critical decision point occurred during the first year, which was particularly trying. While both were strong intellectually, neither had previously studied some of the basic theories that master's students in higher education and student affairs typically encounter. Faculty created individualized reading lists to assist them in getting up to speed, but the initial gap in knowledge created an almost unmanageable sense of isolation and barrier for Laura.

> She's [Kathy] coming from a pharmacy background; I was in sport medicine background, and we're sitting in classes that first quarter, and I don't understand anything. I think it's what—I mean this is Swahili that I'm listening to. I remember I had moments where I cried, and I told my husband I was done. I'm quitting. I can't do this. I feel like the dumbest person on earth. I don't understand anything that's going on in a classroom. I think the moment was he's like, "We've made too many changes in our life, you're not quitting."

So there was a ton of guilt, but the guilt almost then became a motivating factor. . . . He's changed his job. He's taken on more responsibilities. He's working overtime, and so, yeah, I've asked everybody to make—it's not just me that's made changes. Everybody has made changes for me to do this. Once again, put the backpack on and let's go on Valdez. Take the donkey and let's move. We got to climb this mountain. [1]

In answer to a direct question about how she could come back to coursework and the program after her son's accident, Polly responded.

I found a comfort here. I know that that sounds weird, but there was a comfort in being able to step a little bit out of that role of mother, out of that role of department chair person and being able to immerse myself in something that was important to me to look into and study, get my arms around. This was—I think I wrote in my paper that this was my A time.

Tina talked about the pressure she felt at her home institution, and how that affected her.

It put me somewhat in jeopardy in a small liberal arts college where everybody knows everybody and that kind of thing. It made me uneasy that somebody thinks I was after her job when I finished this. Clearly I wasn't going to pick up and move to another part of the country where I was in life.

Those were some of the unsettling kinds of feelings that I had. I know there was a point, when I came to terms with that and just sort of had an emotional meltdown, and realized that what had happened to me was that I had lost my courage, and that was not like me at all. So I worked through that after a good cry. I remembered my courage, and I said, "Everything be damned. This is what I want to do." So this is how I interpreted your comment about making choices and having to recommit along the way. That was one way.

Well, getting over that was my Dolly Parton phase, when I took her life story that I just happened upon and decided that Dolly wanted to so much to be a star when she was seventeen or eighteen and endured all that she endured to do that, how much did I want this PhD? Then that was a turning point because I said, "Yes I want to do it." I sat down and I wrote—might have been when I wrote the three chapters . . . ; the first three chapters that summer. I had summer blocks. So I would just not offer to teach or do anything. I had a nine-month contract, so I didn't have to do that. Those were the kinds of years and opportunities to either move forward or drop out.

Carole's crisis came after she completed her coursework, and she began work on her dissertation proposal. At that point, she was already trying to look ahead to her future job situation.

Well, my passion was higher education and I had no plans to leave higher education. But, as you know, through a series of events that changed at the college and universities that I worked at, I made a decision to actually move to a different college and university right as I started my program. And then at the end, there really wasn't going to be a place for me. And I started realizing that I could not relocate from Dayton. There were only two or three institutions in Dayton, Ohio, and my, it was going to be very limiting to me professionally.

So when I decided to start working with a career consultant to figure out what I was going to do with the rest of my life when I grew up. I was actually—it was my last year of writing my dissertation, I was ready to walk, just to bail, leave the whole thing. It's like, "I don't know what the hell am I doing this for. I've spent all these years into this. I thought I was going to be vice president of student services." That was not going to be a reality so I had to do a lot of soul-searching . . .

. . . It took me three years to do coursework and two years to do my research. So I was, I had completed my coursework, I was a year into my, you know, into my research and that's where I kind of hit the wall and it was like, "I don't see any reason to go on because I don't see a future in higher education administration and I can't leave." Either I leave my husband, which, actually, I had a lot of angst around that, and six children. Do I take off so I can pursue my dream? It has to be out of Dayton, Ohio, and so that's when the whole thing kind of blew up and it was like, "Oh my goodness, do I just forge ahead and finish anyway?"

Seth, who had graduated two months prior to the conference, focused on taking responsibility for his own choices. "No, I thought Kelly's last point was really good about the—you know it was my decision to be in the program, and I think taking responsibility for myself definitely put things in perspective over the four years." And Davida faced her choice point in the midst of her dissertation.

> Well, yeah, I think there's a point during the process where, as Carole had said, you sort of hit the wall. I don't think I ever thought that I would not finish, it was just a matter of the time and when and my hitting of the wall actually happened about two months before graduation. I said it in the reflection paper; it's the moment of crisis I think you have where you just fall out and cry and scream and curse, and, actually, mine happened in church. It was Easter Sunday. I didn't curse in church but I sure did a lot of crying, probably a good cleansing cry. And I remember going out for dinner afterwards and getting home and I just, I said, "I've got to do this and for the next month and a half." I mean, I literally lived in front of the computer at work, at home. It was so bad, my son, I don't even know if he knew he had a mom anymore. But you do, you have this moment where it all falls apart and then you have a choice. Do you claim this process and move forward? And thankfully, I did.

Ben captured the sense of recommitment, of "claiming" the process in a very apt analogy.

> I'm hearing a theme of sorts that definitely resonates with my own experience with that idea of the personal choice. There's almost a recommitment that we have to make at certain key points. I think about relationships and our various partnerships very much the same way. You have your deep infatuation that then turns into love, and then it deepens but then it also cools. Right? And then you have to make that recommitment and work through those difficult times. But there's always a relevance, a passion and a sense of fulfillment in our relationships with people, but I'm also thinking in our relationship with this experience. For me personally, what I'm hearing seems to be that theme in some of our stories, this idea of relevance, passion, and fulfillment.

Brian could not participate in the August meeting, and therefore, had not heard Ben's comment. In November, he independently observed that the passion was somehow associated with a person's goals and many of the students he saw who did not complete the doctorate, failed to complete because their goals changed. And when goals change, they no longer have enough passion to overcome the challenges of the work. He mused, "No matter what you do as an advisor to help them, you know, sort of focus and . . . buckle down to write the dissertation, the passion and the goal has changed, and you know, so it's sort of external . . . to the actual process of writing the dissertation itself."

Brian's observation is consistent with findings that have shown up in research. "Most doctoral students enter graduate school fired up with enthusiasm and idealism. Along the way, this passion often seems to disappear. The positive side of this is that the romantic ideals of academic life are replaced by more realistic goals. The negative side is that the zeal with which many begin their studies is unnecessarily eroded" (Golde, Bueschel, Jones, and Walker, 2009, 64). One of the most important challenges for an advisor is figuring out how to help students maintain momentum and some sense of excitement as they shift perspectives.

Fear Becomes Exhilaration

Where did they find the strength to go on? After listening to the conversation about fears and doubts and guilt and costs, that was the main question on my mind. It was the same question that Emily had asked earlier. "What caused each of us to move past that feeling, . . . the guilty feeling? What was it that made us push past that and complete the process?" All of the participants in the focus group completed the program and were awarded doctorates. Each and every one of them finished. So that meant the "angst" did not overwhelm them in the end. Why not? How did they overcome the fears? Part of the answer relates very much to the initial commitment, and sense of purpose that drew them to the program in the first place. They made choices to continue; they "owned" the fear, and claimed the process. Polly ascribed it to maintaining balance.

> And maybe that relates to the strength and fear sort of teeter-totter, because to me this is all one big kind of balancing act. You can't ever let that teeter-totter get too far one way or the other. So I don't know, maybe that—maybe coming to that place and being able to make a conscious choice and recognizing that that's what you're doing. Owning it is a way to answer some of the fear questions.

Tina felt strength and fear were related.

> I would put strength and fear together, perhaps, that I heard a lot of people just talking about this. There was something that gave us this strength of fear, a strength to excel, a strength to—and perhaps with that came fear about choices. The choices also relates to the phenomenon you were describing earlier, Ada, the whole process of hitting a wall, and there was something that caused a curtain to be unveiled to then go to the next step until the next wall was hit. What I'm thinking about, I don't know which comes first. Is it the choices that reveal the next steps, or is it the next step then motivates choice? You know I don't know. It's just messy to me.

And for Emily, the fear evolved from one kind to another.

> My twist as I try to pick apart the kind of the feelings—I found my fear changing from the fear of not being able to do it to the fear in the end being willing because it was worth it. So there was a transition point in the fear that said, "Yeah I really can probably do this, but there's—it's so insurmountable that I don't know if it's worth doing—worth finishing." And that transition point for me came probably after general exams. General exams kind of was the solidifying point to say, "Okay I think I can intellectually do this, but I'm not sure what you have go through, to finish the dissertation is worth it."

As the journey continued and folks engaged with the demands of the program and recognized the gains that could accompany the personal changes they were experiencing, fear slowly transformed into excitement. Assessing the value of the change, Laura said,

> The most exciting change is the opportunity to improve yourself. I was a good teacher/educator prior to entering the doctoral program, but the theories and tools that I learned and acquired while in the program made me an excellent teacher/educator. There is not one day that goes by in my current career as the director of clinical education and associate professor that I do not use something that I learned in my doctoral program.

Carole experienced it as mind blowing, during her course work.

I began the program certainly would be considered midlife, and I felt very grounded when I started the program and I had a very naive assumption that I would only, that I really wasn't going to be particularly impacted by the experience. I was just going to go in, take bunch of more classes, and I'm good at taking classes and I was going to go on my merry way. What I underestimated was that I was actually personally going to be impacted. My master's did not remotely, I can't even think of one course in my master's program that even evoked me even having to look seriously at my own belief system. So when I got into the doctoral-level work . . . all of sudden it was like, "Oh my goodness, you want me to read this book and tell you what I think about it?" So, all of a sudden, having to learn the whole process of how you deconstruct and what does it mean to really look deeply, was a skill set I had never—or an experience I had never encountered before. So to be immersed in that for three years was, it was wonderful, it was awful, it was mind blowing, it was invigorating, it was exciting, and all of the above. And I really had to totally unpack my entire belief system.

Tina confronted possibilities as she wrote her dissertation.

In midlife, the fear was what I would have to give up in order to follow the path that the PhD opened up to me—as in surrendering a tenured faculty position. Roles that were opened up to me by the dissertation research or finishing the PhD. I had fellow faculty members who did not know how to talk to me about this, and they were just—they didn't understand it at all. That they did not know—they didn't see it coming, and they didn't know how to talk to me about it. But there was a fear, but then there was also a fear/exhilaration because it made me feel really excited, and it made me feel really young again. [Laughter.]

Brad describes the progression as he experienced it.

You know we all chose this and we managed to balance it in our own ways, but part of the process is being in over your head from time to time, and then sort of struggling through and you talk about development of continuum, if you want to play that game. You know there—it is truly a two-side—also two sides of the coin. We're afraid of it. I'm not sure we're going to do this. As we made those steps, and we made those hard accomplishments along the way, again—I'll stop saying "we." As time went on, I had a greater sense that I was going to finish this. Early on, there was a little bit of doubt, but it's structured in such a way, at least it was for me, that it became apparent at some point that this—I will finish this project. So that's where the exhilaration comes in I think.

Olivia, who also began the program with a different advisor, recommitted after seeing the excitement her research could produce.

I wasn't one who found Ada or who was originally assigned to Ada. I think that's interesting. But for me that was a point of re-committal. . . . I went through the first year of courses and that was fine. I felt like I was growing, but even when I applied to the PhD program, I hadn't thought a long time about the commitment to having a PhD.

. . . For me, that re-committal had happened a lot of times through working, through the advisor relationship. . . . There were times when just in the advisor relationship, where there was such a sense of you would be so excited about the work that we were doing, and just to know that the work that's something that I could do would produce enthusiasm. . . .

The fact that it could be something that . . . would really stimulate other people along the way I think was really important to me. So I just wanted—I thought that was a good time to tie in that recommitment for me had a lot to do with placing you in the role of advisor, and there were times along the way that the recommittal came through your enthusiasm.

Kelly connected the dots for everyone with her horror film analogy.

Yeah, the normal side of this sort of juxtaposition between the fear and the exhilaration, because I think there's something there. I mean, yes, this process was really scary, and there were times when it was just all scary. I mean, especially at the beginning, you know, "Can I really do this?" But there's a point at which we wean away those questions, "Can I do this? Have I gotten myself in over my head?" and they become tempered with the initial "Oh, God can I even do this?" Immediately followed by a "Huh, wonder if I can do this." Okay, where it becomes less fear and more of a challenge. I have a friend who loves horror films. All right, I hate horror films. He loves horror films. They terrify him, and he likes to be scared. I mean there's a fear [laughing], but there's an exhilaration there, right? There's something there, and there's something in the fear, too, that is almost a motive. There was a point at which it felt like somebody threw down a gauntlet, and there was no way I could not pick it up.

The excitement kept them going. Kelly marveled,

It was the most exciting, exhilarating, selfish—yeah, in a good way—kind of time that I ever had. Because there was never ever going to be another space in time where I would have the freedom to indulge in being the student thing. I'm being able to think about things in some ways kind of as long as I wanted to. . . . And maybe that's what made the rest of it worthwhile. I don't know, but it was an exciting time.

Seth called it having the time to be "in the academic climate and feel "scholarly"—the ability to pursue your research passions and even passing interests. Interacting with other like-minded people." Polly chimed in, "I would agree with exhilaration. I think it's pushing yourself just enough to be uncomfortable that you're learning and developing. Because I can honestly say the most rewarding things in my life have been the times when I pushed myself to be outside my comfort zone, just a little bit. Not enough to be terrified to have that growth. Yeah."

Jaime and Ben enjoyed the research process. Jaime "loved the qualitative research process, and learning the methods by which I would conduct my research—thank you Patti Lather! I enjoyed the interactions and interviews with my students, the involvement and engagement with the program I researched, and the outcome of the narratives the students told me." Ben relished the process of analyzing his dissertation data. "I remember the excitement of discovery as my analysis of data moved from simple coding to the development of theory and the creation of the systems diagram that grew out of an exciting meeting one lunch time. Those are some of my fondest memories, and most exciting intellectually."

For Carole, along with Kathy, Stephanie, Ben, and Olivia, "bringing together the theoretical and the practical . . . was enlightening, challenging and fun. It's akin to have a live laboratory to try on new approaches and new ideas with the opportunity to reflect and challenge my ingrained methodology." Ben added, "The key is to always relate what you are learning to your work and vice versa. They feed each other and excite in both contexts." Kathy said simply, "The most exciting part for me was all of the new knowledge gained that was immediately applicable (e.g., admissions law, student development, service learning). School projects were also an opportunity to bring in new ideas to my work environment."

Olivia experienced the combination as an accelerated growth curve which she carefully fostered.

I was growing (and advancing) faster than my peers, in part because I challenged myself to use the analytic skills I began developing in my studies in other arenas of life. I thought carefully about how to make school projects align with my professional obligations, which ultimately enabled me to succeed in both realms simultaneously. I'm not sure I would have been as intentional about the application of what I learned if I had done it retrospectively (applied my knowledge from the PhD experience to a job at the conclusion of my studies). For me, it worked.

Polly took the whole notion of symbiosis one step further.

> Once I was settled and working toward my research area, what I was reading and studying correlated with the new administrative job role I was growing into at work. Because there was no orientation of any kind for my job, the pieces I was lacking were knowledge about leadership, organizational change, higher education legal issues, decision making, etc. I knew my academic department well, as I had been a faculty member prior to moving to the chairperson role for fourteen years. I needed to know how to be an academic leader and this marriage of study and work was making that happen for me.

Kelly spoke about the sheer "fun of sitting with a group of doctoral students and talking about intellectual and theoretical stuff—the luxury of having the time and space to do that, to actually have time to 'think.' . . . most of the time, it was fun. Being able to live it, breath it, eat it, sleep it was a carved out space in time that most people don't get a chance to have. I was lucky." Brad called it a "gift."

> And if I may, to be in a room where there's a bunch of folks who are smart and we're thinking about the same problem in our own ways and personally, for me, to kind of watch that process and . . . a great gift that was. You know . . . I look at problems, I believe I look at them much more with greater complexity for having been exposed to those approaches. Sort of have to put up or shut up with your thoughts, but also have to unpack what others thought, or others are giving to whatever the solution for attacking the problem.

CALIBRATING THE CHALLENGES

Tina's strongest memories of her doctoral experience "swirl around . . . the amount of determination it took to persist in the effort for eight years, part-time, not knowing where the completion would lead once it was accomplished." "Fire in the belly," Carole called it. "In looking back, I believe it took a certain amount of moxie to leave a subculture I had spent forty-one years in and start on a five-year transformation odyssey." Whether the subculture involved parochial education, admissions work, teaching English to international students, residence life, or financial aid, each individual left an environment where he/she was productive, had developed skills, and was a respected member of a community—to enter an unfamiliar environment, where folks spoke a different language and danced to a different tune.

Ben expanded on the meaning of "passion."

> I think what drives some mid-career—and I saw this in all of our writing, and I wrote it down last night. I'd been writing it down throughout the day today, and all of the different things—is passion. There's a passion there to do this that has brought us to this table at this point. It may be passion coupled with ambition. It may be passion coupled with other things, but they're—because that's often I think maybe what undergirds the individual strength in many ways.
>
> I mean each of us persevered through those walls, and there's got to be a passion there that we took. So whenever I'm talking to somebody who's saying, "I'm thinking about doing a doctoral program." You got the desire and, if you want it, you'll do it. But if you don't—if you're pursuing it for the wrong reasons, it could be a miserable experience, absolutely miserable.

So whatever it was called, passion was fundamental to success. But there were other elements as well. Passion is a necessary, but not sufficient component of the equation. And what does the equation look like? And how would we even construct an equation? A well-known tool helps enormously to visualize the key factors in this journey. It's called a "force-field" analysis and was developed by Kurt Lewin almost forty years ago (1975). A simple and powerful analytic tool (one of my favorites), it can be applied to any setting; change is the goal. We use it here to help us sum up the challenges faced by mid-career students.

Figure 5.1 shows the most basic elements of the analysis—a diagram illustrating a desired path from Point A to Point B. The vertical line represents the current position of the person on the path from A to B. The objective is to identify the factors or forces that are hindering forward progress and those that are enabling, or supporting progress. The factors are depicted as arrows, pointing to the right and left. The relative size of an arrow can be used to indicate the relative strength of the factor.

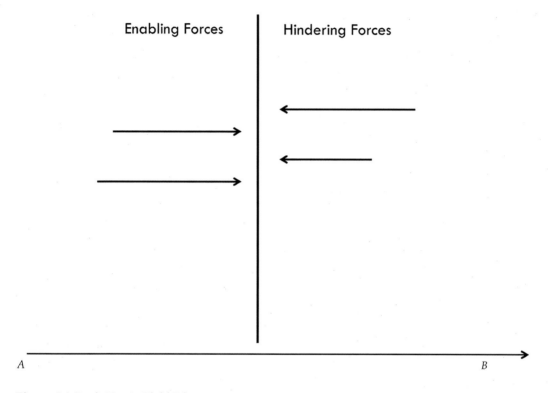

Figure 5.1 Basic Force-Field Diagram

The first valuable outcome of the analysis is a systematic identification of the forces creating the dynamics of a situation. For either a person or a group trying to make change in an organization, the discussion surrounding the creation of the diagram can be very revealing. The second outcome is the strategy or plan that can be derived from the diagram. At first glance, most people think that strengthening one or more of the enabling arrows will lead to progress. But, herein lies one subtle beauty of this tool. For it is, after all, a tool for analyzing factors related to human behavior in a change process.

Consider two people, standing face to face, with hands up in front of them in patty-cake mode, pushing on each other. What happens if one pushes harder? Typically, the other digs in his/her heels and stiffens to resist more strongly, possibly even pushing back. So, strategies that focus solely on enabling forces may backfire. With this in mind, a different option becomes apparent: removing or reducing the strength of one or more of the inhibiting forces allows progress toward the objective, by simply moving obstacles out of the way of the naturally enabling forces.

Figure 5.2 uses a force-field analysis to depict the dynamics of the journey toward the doctorate. The hindering forces revealed through participant discussions have been relabeled, "Challenges" and appear on the right. The relative strength of each challenge is suggested by the different lengths of the arrows. For this diagram, I estimated the lengths after listening to the conversations and analyzing the transcripts. Participants may have different opinions, and certainly, the relative power of any of the challenges will vary from individual to individual. Among challenges, single asterisks (*) mark the challenges that are likely to diminish naturally over time, such as fear and risk, or the intellectual challenge. As students gain mastery over new skills and make progress, the "unknown" becomes more visible, and practice with new skills leads to confidence. At the same time, however, the more intense and time-consuming aspects of the dissertation research absorb more and more of the student's time, impinging on family and job responsibilities, and leaving the student feeling more and more isolated. The challenges that may intensify are marked with double asterisks (**). It is more difficult to predict the behavior of other factors over time as individual circumstances will affect the dynamics.

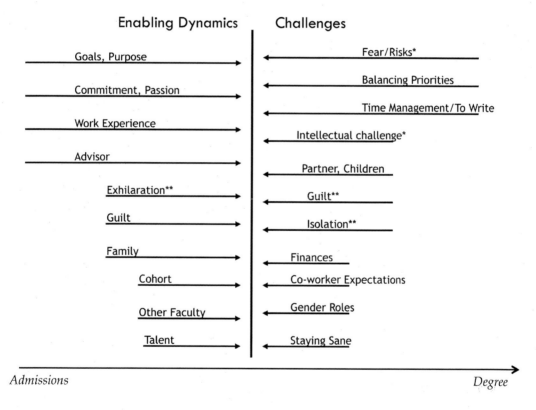

Figure 5.2 Challenges and Enabling Forces

The left side of the force-field diagram shows the Enabling Forces. Some have already been discussed, in particular, the passion and commitment associated with goals and purpose for pursuing the doctorate, and the wisdom and insights that accompany experience in the workplace. Notice that *guilt* is depicted by arrows on both sides the equation. As we learned, guilt can be paralyzing, leading someone to leave without completing the degree, or it can be a source of great motivation. The force-field diagram also identifies other factors, people primarily, whom participants identified as central to their sanity, progress, and success: teaching faculty, the student cohort, family, and the advisor.

The force-analysis contributed to the creation of figure 1.1 (see chapter 1, p. 14). In that dynamic figure the challenges are represented within the three loops "Progress," "Balance," and "Satisfaction." Student progress is at the center of the figure because our primary concern is to understand the elements that affect progress and lead to successful completion, from the "inside out." Each loop represents activity that generates strong emotions, and the direction of the arrows is important.

Some recent research suggests that departmental culture and program structure affect degree completion in important ways (Anderson, 1996; de Valero, 2001; Golde, 2005). From the discussion with these participants, it appeared that most of those effects were transmitted or filtered through interaction with the advisor, and so those loops appear as secondary dynamics in figure 1.1.

The significance of presenting the challenges in a dynamic mode is to appreciate that they feed one another. For example, if students are feeling that they can balance priorities and are getting some satisfaction from their work, those feelings will contribute energy to the effort required to get through the personal transformations, the writing, and bureaucratic hoops that must be jumped. However, if one of those loops, for example, balance, begins to generate a negative outcome, that negative outcome could shift the outcome of the entire "system," leading the student to have doubts about his/her ability to finish, reducing the motivation or energy available to continue.

In figure 1.1, many enabling factors are captured in the loops labeled "Peer Support," "Advising," and "Family." Few souls achieve goals that demand so much inner strength, like successful completion of a PhD program, alone. And that is where we turn our attention next. The next part is titled "The Supporting Cast," and in chapters 6 and 7 we will hear about and consider the roles these individuals played for the students.

NOTE

1.   The reference to Valdez refers to the Colombian coffee advertisement on TV, showing "Juan Valdez" and his (over-) loaded donkey bringing big bags of coffee beans down from the mountains.

Part III

The Supporting Cast

Between the 1960s and the 1990s, the expression of our sense of community evolved from that captured in Joan Baez's lyric "No man is an island," to "it takes a village." Whichever perspective you prefer, from participant comments we learn that the doctoral graduates who participated in this study relied heavily upon the support provided by family, friends, employers, their student cohort, faculty, their advisor, and others.

As early as 1969, the findings from his own dissertation research led Len Baird (editor of the *Journal of Higher Education* from 1994 to 2011) to identify the cohort as a key element in helping doctoral students resolve the role ambiguity and conflict inherent in the student context. Research conducted since then reveals more about the role peers and the cohort play in persistence and degree progress (Gardner, 2007; Golde, 2000) and in providing socio-emotional support (Gardner, 2010). Recently, authors have begun to address the socio-emotional support provided by spouses and children (Gardner, 2008; Yates, 2010). These and other authors have written about the advisor and advising in doctoral programs (Gardner, 2007; Golde, 2000; Millett and Nettles, 2009; Paré, 2010; Patton, 2009; Thomson and Walker, 2010; de Valero, 2001; Watts, 2010), including a book focused on advice for the advisor/mentor (Calabrese and Smith, 2010a).

So, we might ask, what will the reader find that is new and different? First, the examples drawn from our conversations reveal nuances that cannot be gleaned from surveys or journal articles where space is too limited to incorporate extensive commentary. Moreover, as these participants listened to each other during the focus group they elaborated and built upon each other's ideas. The longer we talked about the supporting cast, the more animated the conversation became as we clarified important points. A whiteboard and color markers captured the output on the spot. In this exciting process of "cocreation," the author/researcher and participants together generated insights about the relationships among the supporting cast that were not apparent from previous work.

Chapters 6 and 7 introduce the supporting cast and member roles. Chapter 8 transforms the insights into frameworks that can be used by students, faculty, advisors, and support staff to analyze the adequacy of support available to doctoral students in their own programs. But with the last comment we get ahead of ourselves.

Chapter Six

Insiders and Outsiders

I think my perspective changed throughout the journey because I was the one who started there and ended up divorced. . . . So I've been kind of reflecting on how did the support system change and how was that different. Certainly . . . the one constant is that I had kids to care for during that time. . . . It was obviously a pretty significant commitment to leave a full-time job and have, at that time, a husband who said, "Yes it's okay. You can go be a TA," even though I was primary financial bread winner at the time. Yet there wasn't the kind of day-to-day support outside of "Yes, you've got your freedom to go do this. I don't quite understand what you're doing, but go for it."

In many respects, the role of the cohort and the people at work and my advisor, . . . that support system didn't necessarily shift or change during that time. That kind of stayed constant. . . . Obviously, the impact of the divorce and taking a year and a half away to kind of get my own life back together before then being able to then clear the path to be able to continue to proceed [was really hard], but that kind of same support system was still there in similar forms. Obviously, my cohort accelerated ahead of me, so I had to look at cohort members from other years to be able to supply some of that.

In her poignant comments about her disrupted journey, Emily mentioned three of the groups in the supporting cast that were the focus of attention for the group: family, cohort, and advisor. Employers, faculty, and friends were the others. Very quickly the participants began to characterize the type of support each provided along two dimensions: working knowledge of the institution and the ability to influence the student's situation. Highly knowledgeable individuals are characterized as "insiders"; individuals with little or no knowledge are "outsiders." Influence really means the power to make a difference, and ranges from "low" to "high." Different types of power are included: structural, psychological, or emotional. Figure 6.1 illustrates.

Influence \ Knowledge	Outsiders	Insiders
High Power		
Low Power		

Figure 6.1 Characteristics of the Supporting Cast

The matrix presents discrete cells, yet each dimension really functions as continuum, and so the spaces were refined to include "boundary straddlers." A supporter could be characterized as more or less of an insider or outsider, and similarly, as having more or less power. It seems more accurate to represent the dimensions on a graph that depicts increasing levels of power and knowledge on two axes. Figure 6.2 shows the graph populated by the people in different support roles. We will consider each in turn, beginning with family. Along with family, we will discuss employers, cohort, faculty, and friends in this chapter. The role of the advisor will be addressed in chapter 7.

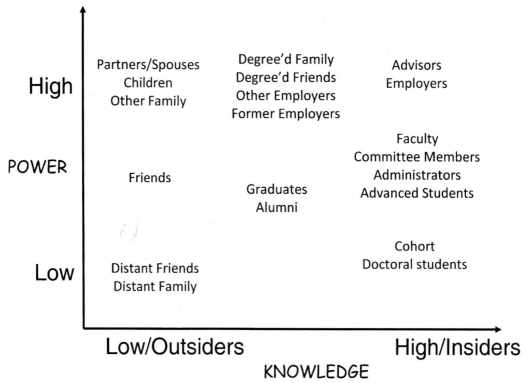

Figure 6.2 Supporting Roles, Power and Knowledge

FAMILY

Family support is among the most powerful for students. Outsiders, family members may have no connection to or any idea about the process of a doctoral program, yet can still be very supportive emotionally. Brad pointed out emphatically that his spouse made it all possible, in a way that created a rare and privileged situation.

> I was doubly fortunate to have a spouse who had a "grown up" job and to be child-free for the duration of my doctoral studies. As a result, I had the time to focus on my studies in a way that would have been impossible if I had had substantive work or parenting responsibilities. Looking back, I am grateful to have had the chance to take this time to develop myself as a scholar and professional. I also am keenly aware of how these relative advantages—in comparison to many in my cohort . . . were a privilege that shaped my experience. I enjoyed my doctoral studies immensely.

Ben said simply, referring first to the weekend of the conference and then to his doctoral program, "I'm indebted to my wife. She is mad that I'm taking a summer weekend, but she's going up to see our friends in Cleveland, and so they're going to go and have a good time this weekend with my kids. I really am thankful for her."

Listening to Ben, Stephanie remembered the conversation we presented earlier about how she felt being single. She felt that she had an easier time while Ben felt that he had the better deal because his wife did the grocery shopping and the laundry, and Stephanie had to fend for herself. Polly offered yet another perspective that showed clearly the importance of understanding the specifics of individual situations.

> I think there's a two-edge piece to that. There's—you never know because you don't walk in somebody else's shoes as to how their situation is different than yours. But I could never have had the freedom to not work and take an assistantship because my income was supporting family, so I had to work full-time the whole time through the program. Then yet figure out, even when my husband was helping with the other—the day-to-day type things, which was very helpful.

While some might have found the pressure of being the sole breadwinner overwhelming, because of the help her husband provided, Polly found it quite workable.

Yet, Kelly reminded us that there was a cost for partners. "All they know is their partner is in a bad place and they don't know how to help them." It was a cost she experienced several years later, when her partner went to school to become a nurse, a field Kelly knew nothing about. Experiencing it from the other side, Kelly ruefully remembered thinking, "As much as I know about how you negotiate higher education, there were times when I would just feel like, I got nothing for you. . . . That's when I got the sense of what it must have been like for her for five years, just having no frame of reference to help me through things."

In a similar vein, Ben had remarked earlier that spouses, too, needed a support network, and then went on to describe the strength of the emotions involved.

> But it really, I mean for those of us who have families who are part of the process, it is a family commitment, whatever that family makeup may be. It is absolutely a family commitment. My wife joked when I was done, because she had supported me through eight and a half years of graduate school—masters straight into the PhD while working full time all the time, and she's like, "If you divorce me, I will hunt you down and kill you." [Group laughter.] But lovingly in a funny way, but you know the fact is. . . . Because she supported me through that, and she said, "No double the amount of time it took for grad school, and that's how long I own you." You know in a joking way, but at the same time it is a huge sacrifice.

Emily jumped in at this point with an observation both about the partners and spouses generally, and also to illustrate a mechanism she used while writing to be thoughtful about time for her partner.

> I feel like knowing the spouses or partners of the people in my cohort, they became very much part of our community as well. . . . One of the things that was I think successful, . . . really became more a strategy of how to get writing done and thoughtfulness done. . . . We always used blocks of time to say, this is going to be the dissertation time. So there was a level of expectation on the part of the partner that said, "Okay, I know I can't have her during this time; but I know if she's going to be available the next—." So being able to have that schedule, I think, not only helped in being able to get work done, but also to say there's a dedicated time for that, and there's a dedicated time for family and people.

Family members sometimes surprise us with an extraordinary level of support, as did both Carole's mother-in-law, and mother, at different times.

> Of course, my spouse and six children lived through the transformation, and to their credit, loved me despite the firebrand approach during those five years. In the middle of the milieu, my mother-in-law moved in with us for four years. That was not planned. But she also, though, was a person who really stepped up to the plate and even though she was well, well up into years, she still is a little German woman that loved to cook. And it was like, "Yahoo! Okay, we're going to get to eat during these five years." So, you know, she did an awful lot of cooking and an awful lot of support so family, . . . was just really totally, incredibly, I think, supportive. They made enormous sacrifices. And when I went across the podium, it was not just me.

She went on to describe the way her mother rescued her in the final stages of her dissertation.

> I actually had a pretty major meltdown, I guess, as Davida called it, hitting the wall, when I had to do the final rewrite of my dissertation. I was just out of gas. I was out of anything left. I, there was just, I cannot take this thing apart again. I cannot rewrite this one more time. And so, I'm, starting to have this meltdown and it's like, I just can't do it. I cannot get past this. And my mother, who was—this was during the summer and she's off during the summer because she works an academic school year, volunteered to come from out of state to hold my hand. So, she comes in, bless her heart, she says, "We can do this. We can do this." So we're printing all these chapters, we had them all laid out. She says "We'll start with this. We'll start with that." So I have this personal editorial assistant—and then with literally her steadying hand, "You're going to get through this"—and I had a computer crash in the middle of all this. And anyway, it was all just such a nightmare, I'm never going to make it and she said, "Yes, we will." And I remember feeling so bad. I said, "You traveled all this way, this is so stupid, I'm a grown woman and I can't even write a paper." She says, "Now Carole, calm down." She said, "Most families don't have these resources; we're just very blessed. I have the time off because I'm not working right now. I can come over and help you."

In Kathy's case, "no one else in my world had a PhD . . . in my personal life. While they can be very emotionally supportive, and say 'You can do this, I believe in you.' They couldn't tell you about—they couldn't give you advice. They could just listen and let you get it out."

Some family members could be said to straddle the boundary between Insider and Outsider, because they themselves have graduate degrees, or are enrolled in college concurrently. With less knowledge of the specific institution, they are still able to provide perspective and informed emotional support for handling challenges. In Carole's case, it was her children who played that role. "Six of us were in college at the same time. So it was only my youngest, our youngest child and my husband who were not and so in a lot of ways it ended up being a shared experience, particularly with my older children because we were always commiserating on what was going on and in terms of, you know, encouraging each other et cetera."

In addition to his supervisor and the other PhD's in his professional life, Brian's partner played an extraordinary role, in part because he, too, was enrolled in school. The strength of Brian's emotion is apparent in the detail of his response.

> I do have a partner. He actually, for those of you that don't know, he went through the [this same] higher ed. program as well, as a master's student and he worked in college in university settings until I went back for my PhD. He actually chose to go back to school for his MBA during my second year of the doctoral program. And he was very familiar with what I was going through in terms of both the setting and the people and the process to a certain extent. But, he was amazing in terms of sharing that workload with me running our household.
>
> We do have three kids that are our dogs basically. Obviously, they don't require daycare and college and braces and whatnot, but it was challenging at times. You know, for two of the five years he was also in school and at times that was great because . . . I didn't feel like I was abandoning him because he was going through courses and so forth like I said, at the same time I was. But at the end of my program, my last year, post-defense, I had one more year after he finished and let me tell you, he really carried the burden for me. . . . Now that I look back on it, . . . at the very end I got my job at [new university] the last week of July '07 and then in August I had my defense of my dissertation and then did my post-defense cleanup. I graduated; we sold our house; we got a new house; we moved completely down to [southern city]. I left my old job and I started my new one, all by Labor Day weekend. So it was exceptionally chaotic during that month period and I remember that first weekend after Labor Day when I was here and Dan, my partner, is a consultant, and so he's on the road during the week and . . . I would say I got through it with your help and with Dan's help.

Davida plays this role for her brother during his PhD program.

> My brother, who is a PhD candidate at Northwestern, I think for a long time resisted that whole "you've got to go to college." But once he got there and found his footing, he, I think, realized that there's something there, and so I'd like to think that I had a little piece in encouraging him. Now, the funny thing, since we keep talking about hitting the wall, I think he has hit the wall and he's quite frustrated with the whole writing and the committee process. And as he's said, "I've rewritten this thing over and over and every time I go back, there's like one little piece that, you know, how did I miss it? And they drill me for it." And I tell him all the time, "It's a part of the process. You've just got to keep pushing through it."

The single students, those without partners, were faced with quite a challenge, as Seth pointed out. While they had the freedom and flexibility to use their time as they wished, the support was not there. "I think that the people that were partnered had a different kind of support system. I'd say stronger in many ways because they didn't have some of the financial worries, so to speak. They had somebody at home taking care of some of the things, and vice versa, I'm sure."

Other family members, with even less understanding, all but disappeared from sight. Interaction fades, a result of shifting priorities, as Davida explains.

> I wouldn't say family deserted me but I think some of my family members had a hard time understanding why I couldn't always come back home for a holiday or I didn't immediately return a phone call a day later because I didn't have time to return the call a day later. You know, it's like write or chat and at that point it was a little bit more important to write, so . . .

EMPLOYERS

Employers fell into two categories: those who headed offices within Ohio State and those who worked at other colleges or universities. Within those categories were supervisors with and without doctorates. Doctorate-trained supervisors who employed students at OSU were often the most influential. True Insiders, these folks are the most knowledgeable about institutional rules, procedures and flexibility, and their decisions about job responsibilities can make or break student success. Participants were exceptionally clear on this point.

The interchange among Kathy, Kelly, Polly, Brad, Ben, and me on this point accelerated as each finished the other's short sentences. The dialogue demonstrates an evolution in thinking as folks considered whether "bosses" were insiders or outsiders. Ultimately it led us to differentiate a category for bosses who worked in institutions of higher education, other than where students were enrolled. Kelly, Kathy, Ben and Stephanie worked for people at OSU during their studies. Polly and Brad worked at other institutions of higher education. The conversation began with Kathy answering the question, "Who else was important?"

Kathy: Employers

Kelly: Yes, I would say boss.

Emily: So what makes an employer an insider?

Brad: Being in higher education . . . and had already gotten the degree or a similar degree themselves. You know understanding this process.

Kathy: Yeah, mine was inside! . . . I was working in the College of Pharmacy in the Office of Student Affairs. My dissertation topic was studying the assessment technique for pharmacy accreditation, and so my immediate boss was supportive in offering me the access to the student population so that I could do my research and being supportive of that. Then the dean of the college being willing to use that data for our next accreditation, so in that case they were a part of the actual—

Emily: Actual study versus simply support you. Yeah.

Kathy: And they did both, but in this case it was actually a part of the research.

Author: For me, Brad, it is inside or outside the organization.

Brad: Discrete institutions.

Author: The discrete institution.

Ben: And it's those high insiders that can also make or break someone's ability to even complete the PhD. I mean . . . Stephanie and my experience with John [their boss, director of international education] was absolutely critical. I mean John's total support of us working on PhD and feeling like we were contributing to the department because of what we were learning, let us fly.

For Brian, continuing to work full time was the only sensible option from a financial point of view, in terms of both salary and the tuition credits that were covered through his employee benefits package. Thus, the attitude of his employer/supervisor was central to his ability to make progress.

> From a professional perspective, I truly could not have completed the program if it weren't for my supervisor—Dr. Linda [name]. She was amazingly supportive—allowing me to flex my hours around classes, and take personal leave around my candidacy exams and dissertation to write/ prepare. Perhaps because she, too, went through this process, she really knew what I was going through and kept me engaged and motivated.

Employers who were in higher education, but not at Ohio State straddled the Insider/Outsider boundary. Polly, who worked at a community college, mentioned earlier how she was able to confer with her dean to schedule work responsibilities and vacation time to allow time for writing. Brad had been concerned about taking on a new senior administrative job in another state, just as he was beginning the analysis of his dissertation data. "I mean for my example, I can say when I got to [new job] my vice chancellor, my boss, said to me, 'You're going to finish the degree and we're going to make that—we're going to get that done and you tell me what you need to make that happen.'"

THE COHORT

As we noted in the introduction to this part, previous research clearly recognizes the importance of fellow doctoral students. The two-and-a-half-day orientation workshop for this doctoral program which was initiated some twenty years earlier, along with the core courses taken by all the doctoral students, are designed to help the groups of doctoral students form an intellectual community. Less formal mechanisms, often organized by the students themselves, create more opportunities for cohort members to interact.

Insiders, members of the doctoral cohort play very specific roles according to our participants. "They're at the same place you're at and they get that struggle," according to Kathy. "They may be able to sort of step away from the struggle and look at it from a different perspective because they're right there in the middle of it with you. . . . And only they handled the empathy for the institutional thing," Polly offered. Recalling the incident of her towed car, Carole said, "Kelly came to my rescue because I was just beside myself. . . . 'Carole we can figure this out. There's got to be a way.'" And sure enough, Kelly researched the options for on-campus student parking and helped Carole get a permit. Because of her commute, however, Carole did not really identify with the cohort. "But," Brad felt, "they're low power."

Folks expressed varying sentiments about the power of the cohort, primarily because each incoming group of new students differed in size and in many other ways. Some years, because of budget and faculty circumstances the program admitted only two, three, or four students. More often cohorts were between five and eight new students and one year, nine were admitted. In addition to size, the students varied by age, gender, and professional backgrounds.

Most participants spoke of the cohort in terms of the students enrolled in the higher education program. All of the higher education students participated in an orientation program, a two-and-a-half-day event that, as Tina noted, could last well into the evenings, often referred to as "leadership lab." However, in the first year of the program, doctoral students in higher education and educational administration (focusing on K-12 administration) took three core courses together, one each quarter, fall, winter, and spring. So students would sometimes refer to the larger group as their cohort.

For Olivia, the cohort was influential. "I was part of a very strong cohort during the PhD program. I didn't realize in the beginning how meaningful, nor how much I valued, the opportunity to connect and dialogue about the PhD experience until those moments escaped me." Jaime felt the same way. "I really felt a strong connection to my cohort from the beginning, and we really bonded during breaks in 'Leadership Lab' and getting together periodically afterwards. They really helped me become comfortable and realize I wasn't in this alone."

Kathy and Kelly both talked about the close friendships they made during the program. Kathy said, "My strongest memories are of forming lasting friendships, balancing work, school and home and making ends meet financially. A classmate in my cohort and I quickly became friends because of the similarities of our situations and I think to some degree the similarities of our approach to work. We remain close to this day." Kelly added, "My best friend in my cohort—we met each other at the opening picnic and were pretty much inseparable for the next five years."

Laura was referring to the larger, combined cohort when she related her painful experience during the first quarter. Yet, in the midst of that experience, she formed her close friendship with Kathy.

> Many members of my cohort were secondary school administrators in their forties and fifties. I felt an absolute disregard and disrespect for my opinions and experience. I felt often that the more mature members of my cohort felt I was too young to be earning a doctorate. That bothered me. . . . I was one of the youngest in my cohort and generally felt that the more mature members did not respect my educational background and experiences in sports medicine. I was not seen as belonging since I wasn't an educator by training. . . . I tended to feel disrespected by them on most occasions. However, I did find one of my very best friends within my cohort. I feel as if she became my rock. We supported each other, vented to each other, and problem solved together. She was (and continues to be) a mentor, personally and professionally.

Polly also referred to the combined cohort as she chronicled how quickly it shrunk. A member of her cohort, who had been in the educational administration program, was hired as president of her community college a year prior to this conversation.

> I had a very small and kind of strange cohort, so I probably don't fit with the mix. . . . Ours was mixed [educational administration and higher education]. . . . There was only two that emerged out in higher ed. I think we were only—we started out with seven, two—we lost two after the first quarter, so that took us down to five. After the first year, two more didn't persist, so then we went our ways. Of course, one is now my new president. [Laughter.]

Stephanie's cohort was "incredibly supportive and helpful. . . . Two to three people during the dissertation process provided moral support, reading and commenting on chapters, always having someone to call to ask questions." Davida's doctoral cohort enveloped her in an entirely different experience than the isolation she felt as the only woman of color in her master's program, and contributed to the success of the entire group.

> I thoroughly enjoyed my cohort experience. We affectionately call ourselves the "Conspiracy Theory" because we believe that we came in as the most diverse and inclusive in recent history (there were three Caucasian women, six African American women, one Latino male, one Kenyan woman, and one Asian woman). Our objective, as we used to tell each other, was to prove the "naysayers" wrong, and to ensure that we all completed our programs. I believe that all have obtained their doctorates, with the exception of three; two are in the final stages. I enjoyed our classroom camaraderie and when we would get together for weekly lunches or Sunday evening

potlucks. My PhD cohort experience was dramatically different from my master's cohort experience, where I was the only woman of color and oftentimes experienced periods of cultural loneliness and isolation.

The six members of this tight-knit group presented an analysis of their experience at the Sixteenth Annual National Conference on Diversity, Race and Learning in 2010, titled "Believing in the Impossible." Many of their key points parallel the findings in this study. She went on to describe the way they interacted in more detail.

> And we all remain very close-knit to this day. I'm thinking about some of the women that come to mind. We've either been in their wedding or, most recently and unfortunately, one of our cohort members lost her sister suddenly, very suddenly and we have been trying to surround her as a sister-circle of support to let her know that we are here. One, we cook dinner for her for a whole week. I mean, those women again, I don't have many close friends, I could probably all count them on two hands but they certainly over the last couple of years have entered into my circle of friends and have a great deal of professional and personal respect for them.
>
> And the thing was, it wasn't always the classroom where we became tighter, it was outside the classroom. Those quick lunch dates or Sunday evening potlucks or going to the movies together that for me again, I can't speak for them, but I needed that sense of other women with similar life experiences, being able to surround myself with them and by them and that we could make it through all together. Now, we all ended up finishing on completely different schedules but I can say, . . . one of us or more than one would always show up at that particular student's graduation. If they had a graduation celebration, we were there. Again, other occasions where we had the opportunity to celebrate one another, somebody is there.

The participants extended the definition of cohort to include doctoral students who were admitted earlier, and also alumni of the program. For example, Brad, felt that "students who are farther along, who are not members of the cohort but who are second, could be closer to the high [power]. I mean could be low, but closer to the high. . . . Other well-advanced doctoral students that are—because, you know, they do provide advice and sometimes support." We recalled Davida's comment about her observations of the doctoral students in a class with combined enrollment she took as a master's student and how those students served as inspiration to her as she was applying to the program.

And then as a group we realized that alumni currently working at the institution also fit this category. Laura, a clinical associate professor in another program on campus, was our resident expert on mind-mapping software, and very good at experimental design. Kathy, director of assessment in her college at the university, and known nationally for her work, supervised several independent studies about outcomes assessment. Carole, who is a career management consultant, recently spent ninety minutes talking with a current doctoral student whose dissertation research involves career choice, directing her to resources in the literature and among the professional community outside of OSU.

> She's well into her program, and she called me. Ada had connected us, and we probably talked for an hour and a half with an incredible conversation. She left with just a whole different view, I think, of moving forward. I mean it was awesome for me on my side, because it was this very strong sense of giving back. She was obviously aware I was [in the program] a long time ago, but "I'm here to encourage you and here are the things that belong, here are the markers, etc." I really enjoyed the conversation. "Now," I said, "as you get further, let me know where you are." So now we are connected. I really enjoyed that conversation.

These busy graduates chose to take time from their jobs as administrators, consultant and faculty to respond to requests and become active in support mode. As the years went by, I often referred students to alumni who were in related fields, or who worked nearby. Carole was not the only one who found the interaction rewarding. Toward the end of the meeting as we approached noon on Sunday, Brad asked how "distant" alumni might be able to help, "Wouldn't it be interesting if it were some advisory—some advisory role, friendly advisory role where people's e-mails or phone numbers are given out. If students coming in had questions about the experience, they can give us a call." Laura continued, "So, it worked for us. That's one of the things we've already identified that we liked being able to talk to someone who is doing a similar type of research."

And Brad told her, "I went in and pulled out your dissertation and said, 'You know here are some ways of approaching this.' Again, there is a continuum there, and I will say I would welcome the opportunity to play a role like that because it reconnects me to the program at a time when my connection is becoming more and more tenuous." Following this interchange, we spent a few more minutes brainstorming about different ways to connect people with current students.

FACULTY

Faculty other than the advisor also provide essential support. As we built the chart of roles, most often participants acknowledged other faculty in the context of specific courses; Jaime referenced such a situation when she said, spontaneously, "thank heavens for Patti Lather," a nationally recognized expert in qualitative research who taught the course sequence that grounded her dissertation research. In reading the transcripts, I was surprised that only a few specific comments addressed faculty roles and some of those are indirect.

However, comments reported earlier like those alluding to feelings of "dependence," concern about "faculty egos," and "not being in charge of their own lives" convinced me the students were well aware of faculty influence. There are many situations where students need specific faculty support, such as committee membership, writing letters of nomination for scholarship or fellowship applications, or more extensive guidance with a research methodology. Participants may have been reluctant to say more, although Kelly was very explicit about one faculty member. He treated her in a manner she felt was so inappropriate that even though this person could have been a productive member of her committee, she did not pursue any further relationship.

> I remember sitting in my first committee meeting, preliminary committee meeting with all the whole group and one person had made some comment about a paper that I wrote for his class which he actually had given me an A on, but in the committee meeting, had referenced it and sort of tossed off-hand "Yeah, it really wasn't a very good paper." Now, ten years later, I remember that, right? Yeah. And he would have been very use[ful]—probably like one of the most appropriate people who should have been on my committee, but that was one of my moments in which I said, "Yeah, you know what, I'm too old for this." So I very humbly uninvited him. . . . He didn't care one way or the other, but at some point we start doing things.

Some faculty roles are so embedded in the process, for example, as committee members, that there was little need to make more explicit comments. Depending upon the student's dissertation research, committee members with specialized expertise were asked to become more active. For example, as a researcher, my strengths lie in the qualitative domain, so when I have students whose research is more effectively addressed through quantitative methods, committee members with that expertise are asked to play a more active role from the start.

Davida's dissertation focused on the lived experience of African American women who were university presidents. There was no ready-made methodology for the type of research she wanted to pursue, so we reached across the university to two experts in critical race theory and rhetoric. Both African American women were in high demand: one a professor in another department, and the other a senior administrator. Senior researchers in their fields and at the university, ultimately their commitment to join her dissertation committee and provide active guidance was critical to her/our success.

Most often the support offered by faculty was in a latent mode. Students "asked" faculty to serve on program and dissertation committees, or to provide independent study supervision so they could gain more expertise in certain topics. Chairs of key departmental committees, such as those that oversee the rules governing doctoral study also fit this category. Committees such as Graduate Studies are powerful because decisions taken about rules and exceptions can heavily impact student progress. With latent power comes the implication that there is a choice to be made about whether to use that power, and those personal choices often reflect departmental dynamics or politics that extend beyond the student.

Consider an untenured assistant professor teaching a course taken by the student, in rank for three years, and neither a member of the student's committee nor a department committee related to graduate study. This individual is likely quite knowledgeable about the institution, the department, and the program. However, if the student requested support for an action that required an exception be granted to a program or institutional rule, the only "power" available to this person would be conversation—with the student to help clarify thinking, or with colleagues to persuade them of the appropriateness of the student request. The inclination to act on the student's behalf would likely depend upon (a) any precedents, or reasonableness of the request, and (b) the person's need for senior faculty support in other contexts, i.e., dependence upon senior faculty for upcoming appointment reviews, or course or space assignments. While in principle all faculty have some power, each individual can choose whether to use that power to influence the student's situation.

FRIENDS OUTSIDE THE COHORT

The word friendship is practically a synonym for support, as we saw in the "Cohort" section. For the doctoral students, strong friendships outside of the program are sometimes sustained, sometimes weakened, and new friendships are often formed. Those with doctoral experience can become particularly important. The circle of people who provide key support might also include "a colleague or a friend," according to Polly. "If they have been through this same experience, they could actually come into the high realm. Yeah, because they know where the land mines are. They know where the good connections are. . . . When I did this problem, this is what I did, and it happens to be good advice."

Brian talked about the importance of folks who worked with him. "I was also surrounded by other PhDs in my professional life, which even through simple conversations about my research topic, methodology, etc., kept me focused and challenged me to think about my research from multiple angles." Working alongside him at OSU, these folks were Insiders.

PhD-trained friends working outside of higher education straddle the Insider/Outsider boundary. They are less knowledgeable than Insiders because they lack understanding of the personalities, pressures, or politics the student faces in this specific program, at this specific institution. However, their own doctoral training allows them to appreciate the experience of the student and they can represent a valuable resource.

And some friendships will not survive the sporadic communication and distance. Once part of a student's active network, these relationships did not survive the geographic and psychological distance from the doctoral student. Davida's rueful comment characterizes this group. "But I also lost a couple of people along the way, people that I thought were friends that, you know, again, I'm glad they—I learned that they weren't, or weren't in my corner and that's perfectly fine too."

REVIEWING THE ROLES

Figure 6.3 depicts the fully populated matrix, and offers category names for the different roles of the supporting cast. Participant comments helped with the identification of all but the Cheerleaders. Specific characteristics, such as having a graduate degree, or working and studying in the same institution, were used to situate different types of family members, employers and friends in categories described by the dimensions.

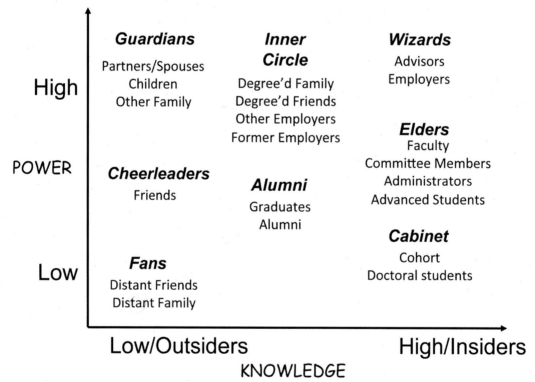

Figure 6.3 Wizards, Guardians, and Others

THE TRULY POWERFUL

To this group of Insiders and Outsiders we attribute the greatest ability to influence the success of the student in the doctoral program. Whether through structure, psychology or emotion, the attitudes and actions of these characters are supremely important. They appear in the top row of figure 6.3.

Wizards

Wizards, like Dumbledore (of Harry Potter fame), are very powerful individuals. They are Insiders, and the keepers of the keys to the kingdom. They point the way and open doors. They challenge students, encouraging them to engage their brains and develop their skills. The most powerful Wizard is the student's advisor, variously called advisor or program or dissertation chair. We will address this critical role in its full complexity in chapter 7. Along with the advisor, employers, or more specifically, supervisors are categorized as Wizards if students are employed in the same institution where they are enrolled for the doctoral program, Ohio State in this case, and if the supervisor has been through doctoral training.

Inner Circle

Straddling the insider/outsider boundary and still highly powerful are members of the Inner Circle. Employers, former employers, supervisors, family members, and friends who are themselves doctorate-trained or working on graduate degrees share a level of understanding that allows them to provide support at the Inner Circle level. Employers, family and friends who work in higher education also fit the bill.

Guardians

Guardians are soul-mates. They influence the student with same level of power as Wizards and the Inner Circle, but live outside the institution and higher education. They provide the psychological and emotional support so essential for stability. They know the student well and can be trusted to give straight feedback and to recognize signs of disintegration. The closest soul-mates are often family, partners, and spouses. Special friends belong in this category. For the single students, as Seth said, "There was no one to go home to and talk to outside of your personal supports." For these folks, friendship networks became even more important. With or without frames of reference, Guardians stick it out.

THE ROBUST RESOURCES

The middle row in figure 6.3 represents supporters who are somewhat less influential, have somewhat less power than the previous group but who, nonetheless, represent significant support for the student. They are named "robust resources" here because they tend to be more passive than active in their support. Students can mobilize them by asking for help, but their power is typically latent. The majority includes Insiders or straddles the Insider/Outsider boundary.

Elders

Typically, Elders are faculty, with substantial latent influence. They have less power than Wizards, but Wizards, especially the advisor, work closely with the Elders. They straddle the boundary between the Wizards and the Cabinet. Members of a student's program or dissertation committee are Elders. Advanced doctoral students in the program are also Elders.

Alumni

The alumni, doctoral graduates of the program, remain Insiders to some degree because they have been through the program. However, over time, they cease to be current in their information about the department, doctoral requirements, faculty, or institution. Yet, they have much to offer as resources for the student. Some few alumni, employed as faculty or administrators at the same institution, might be considered Elders.

Cabinet Members

Cabinet members are Insiders and trusted advisors who, in the manner of President Andrew Jackson's "kitchen cabinet" hold no official position. They know the system, however, and how to make it work and so serve as a primary sounding board. They bring empathy and experience to the table. Primarily comprised of cohort members, professional friends also play this role. Largely in an emotional and psychological support role, the Cabinet sits lower on the power axis than the Elders.

Cheerleaders

Cheerleaders are Outsiders who straddle the power boundary between Guardians and Fans. These are treasured friends or family members. Remaining aware and engaged, they make an effort to stay informed of progress, either directly or through contact with the Guardians. They regard the relationship as important, if temporarily less active, and can be counted on to celebrate milestones with the student.

Fans

Fans are background players. Outsiders, inhabiting a space that is at a distance both geographically and psychologically, typically they interact with the student only sporadically.

EVALUATING THE IMPACT OF CAST MEMBERS

The easiest way to gauge the impact of the supporting cast is to identify the factors from the force-field diagram (figure 5.2) that they affect. While the advisor will clearly have a substantial role, others will make noticeable differences. The most valuable impacts will be those that reduce the level of the challenges.

Guardians, in particular, can have a powerful effect in reducing the impact of challenges like *balancing priorities*, *time management*, *time to write*, and *guilt*. The Inner Circle can help the student address *fears/risks*, and the *intellectual challenge*. Elders, too, of course, can help with the *intellectual challenge*, as can Alumni and the Cabinet. Wizard/Employers are pretty much the only ones who can take an active role in ameliorating *coworker expectations*.

The Inner Circle, Cohort, and Alumni can contribute to the sense of *exhilaration* and stoke the fires of *commitment* and *passion*. Wizard/Employers can also facilitate the value of current *work experience*, by allowing access for research papers or simply offering time for reflective conversations. Only Guardians, of course, can address issues related to *family*, *partner*, and *children*.

So how should the student think about the supporting cast? Cast members are only valuable when they become active, and they become active when they are engaged. While time is the most precious asset for the doctoral student, it is worth using some of this precious time to build relationships with key players when the opportunities arise, particularly with Guardians, the Inner Circle, Wizards, Elders, and Cabinet members. Doctoral success is heavily dependent on assistance from the supporting cast.

Chapter Seven

Advisors and Mentors

> Ms. Gubar's students and younger female colleagues call her a warm and generous mentor—the kind of woman who will greet another with "Sweety!" and a kiss on the cheek. But she is also demanding. "She is like the perfect Jewish grandmother," says Jamie Horrocks, who was Ms. Gubar's research assistant the semester she became ill and is now an assistant professor at Brigham Young University. "She is nurturing, but she'll also kick your butt." (Wilson, 2012)

No, this is not a comment by one of the participants in this study. Rather it was taken from an article published recently in the *Chronicle of Higher Education* and refers to the advising style of Professor Susan Gubar, a well-known feminist scholar. The quote illustrates a key point: The biggest danger in categorizing the "advisor" as a Wizard is the potential for misunderstanding.

No more than Dumbledore used his powers to create a neat and smooth path for Harry, did the participants in our study expect the advisor would make their lives simple. They were clear that gaining the skills and expertise required great personal effort. While the words "no pain, no gain" were never used per se during the conference, their appreciation for the work required could easily be read between the lines of many, many comments.

Their comments about advising focused on concepts like respect, trust, feedback, accessibility, direction, and engagement. A good part of Saturday afternoon was spent clarifying the differences they perceived between mentoring and advising. As we entered the discussion, I raised a point that for me, represented the elephant in the room: how do we avoid centering the discussion on my advising, and keep the focus on their perceptions about the kinds of interaction and support that were meaningful?

The answer to the question is obvious, perhaps, but needs to be stated. The conversation was a mix of both. And so I face the same dilemma here: how to tell this part of their story without sounding self-serving? It was gratifying and often humbling to hear their words of appreciation. It was also sometimes startling and definitely eye-opening to listen to their examples and illustrations. Together we drew pictures (literally) of the advising terrain, and teased out the dimensions that differentiate advising from mentoring. Updated versions of the pictures we drew together are found in chapter 8. They show the dynamics of the advising relationship, illustrate the emotional swings of the student journey, and present a typology of advising modes. Perhaps more so than other chapters my voice will be part of the conversation here and in chapter 8.

How did participants understand the role of the advisor, and why is it so complicated? For Ben, the advising relationship and role were critical in providing support, structure and guidance. Kelly said simply, "the advisor is crucial." For Laura, the advisor

> knows the program inside out. Knows the facilitator, knows the roadblocks, knows the political landmines. They know everything you need to know. Nobody else can do that. The adviser is so different than the social support. . . . I think there's listening, there's emotional support, there's emotional challenge, there's shared reality and the adviser does all of that, but they provide a type of support that nobody else can provide because of their position in the system and their experience in the system. . . . You look for someone close to you who has had that same experience because you trust what they're saying. That's what the advisor does.

After listening to the Saturday afternoon conversation for a while, Kelly summed it up from her perspective. She remembered my telling her and Carole, that "they were taking me on" as much I was taking them on. They were my first two doctoral advisees and I was still finding my way through the advising protocols of the department and program.

> Well, exactly, and so the whole thing and kind of what I'm hearing everybody say is that the best advising relationship is partnership. . . . And that's what it was. You can give critical feedback to your partner. . . . A partner is a colleague. . . . And a partner is somebody you can be absolutely direct with, "Here's how the relationship is going to change. All right now that you've come—now that we're at this point." I mean I remember that conversation very, very clearly. But I also remember you saying, "You're going to be my first advisee. I'm not sure I know what we're doing. We'll figure it—we will figure it out."

Davida offered a similar opinion.

> I think for me personally . . . a good advisor is someone who is not necessarily desiring to be your friend but someone who can practice tough love. For example, giving those deadlines and sticking with them and upholding me to those. I think a good advisor is organized and can recount particular instances, strengths, and weaknesses. I think a good advisor is the person who tells you what you need to hear and not necessarily what you want to hear, who can help you be realistic about the possible outcome. And I think a good advisor keeps you either in their cell phone or a phone number handy at any time of the day or night, for emergencies and so forth. And really respects a lot.

Participant comments about the advising relationship could be clustered around five topics: (1) demonstrating respect for the student and valuing ideas; (2) trust; (3) providing challenge, feedback, direction, and conceptual support; (4) appreciating the difference between an advisor and mentor; and (5) investing in the relationship by sharing personal experience, while maintaining appropriate boundaries. The first three seemed to comprise the core of the advising relationship, while the fourth and fifth related to the heightened involvement of a mentor. Participants described their perspectives about these core elements with rich language and so we will explore the meaning of each in turn beginning with respect.

RESPECT

Why is respect so important? Basically, respect is a fundamental part of self-confidence, and self-confidence is necessary to take on and persevere through an endeavor as challenging and gut wrenching as doctoral study. Whether we rely on intuition to make that judgment, having watched friends and colleagues who gave up in the face of adversity because there was no one there to provide encouragement, or theory, such as Bandura's (1986) well-known work in self-efficacy, we know this to be true.

The goal of doctoral advising is to provide sufficient guidance and encouragement that the student engages fully with the intellectual and personal challenges, internalizes a set of new skills and writes a dissertation sufficiently robust to complete the degree and graduate. To a person, these mid-career graduates indicated that feeling the respect of their advisor was central to their ability to continue when they felt most daunted. Ben said it very clearly:

> It's that respect as an intellectual gets through those really difficult times where you just can't go any further and being able to really talk through it and have that feeling of being valued as an individual. . . . The advisor believes in that student, believes in that individual, and that individual has a sense that his or her advisor believes in them. That's really important to get through those hurdles.

Kathy added, "You always have confidence. When I didn't have confidence it didn't really matter because you had the confidence."

And what does respect look like? I asked this question directly. And Kathy's comment was, "not telling Kelly her idea was crazy," referring to the story Kelly had told about her temporary advisor.

> I knew I was interested in administration and policy, curriculum development but very much more in the administrative side. Okay, I like the politics. I like the negotiation. That's just kind of where my head is. I remember early on trying to have this conversation with my temporary adviser, and the person asked me, "Well, where do you kind of see yourself?" . . . because everybody in my cohort wanted to be in student affairs. I did not want to be in student affairs, so I was saying, "Well, you know I really like policy, and I'm thinking the right job will appear at the right time in a good place." The answer that I got back was, "Oh, you can never do that because you're not going to be faculty." That was a door slam, but I also tend to sort of go, "Well okay, that's one opinion." [Laughter.] So I didn't really like it.

Kelly had been admitted to the program on the basis of her experience, intellectual promise, and goals. About half the doctoral graduates of this program typically moved into faculty roles and half into administrative roles. The attitude expressed by this faculty member was inconsistent with the culture of the program and might have devastated a less resilient student. Kelly's sense of herself and prior administrative experience allowed her to maintain perspective in this situation.

In the context of remembering a lot of intense feedback and discussion, Brad said,

> I thought it was part of the contest for me, and a good one I think. But you know, I always felt that you would listen to my side. . . . I felt as though that willingness to listen leant significant credibility to the relationship and also it made me feel something closer as an equal, if you will. It wasn't going to be your way or the highway. . . . And there truly was dialogue. That's how colleagues treat one another, good colleagues or being colleagues, if you will.

In a similar vein, Emily related the importance of an enthusiastic response to her effort to construct a conceptual model for her dissertation. She returned some weeks after an initial conversation with something quite different from the version we had crafted together at the previous meeting. When she got positive feedback on it, she remember thinking,

That was really kind of an important moment, because it was a way for me to . . . to put it in my terms or my thoughts that wasn't anything like what . . .we had left with. A strong illustration of that way for you to not only take a back seat and listen, but demonstrate that level of engagement to say, "Yes, I think you have it, but what about this, and what about that? I think it makes more sense doing this, what do you think about that?" I mean that was huge.

In her reflection paper, Jaime had also pointed out the importance of the advisor listening to and learning with the student as well.

As an advisor, I took some risks in accepting students whose fields of expertise were outside my own knowledge base. Two dramatic examples are Kathy, whose background and focus were in pharmaceutical education, and Laura, with her focus on the new accreditation standards for athletic training programs. It seemed natural to me to work with them because my interests were in educational and organization innovation and these were excellent, cutting-edge examples in two professional fields. However, in the early stages of those relationships the "students" were far more expert than I was in several of the related content areas, and we discussed my need to catch up in order to provide appropriate guidance. The respect for her expertise was very important to Kathy.

I think another aspect we haven't touched on yet was you encouraged our expertise, our individual expertise. So in my case, it was this area of assessment of professional programs, and you said, "I don't know about this world. This is your world." And . . . you encouraged me to be the expert in that world. You encouraged me to be confident in my expertise in that world. There . . . are a lot of faculty members on this campus that there is no way they would ever admit there's something they don't know—let alone work with a student who wants to explore that area. There was a give and take, so the part that you brought that was your expertise helped encourage us to continue to develop our own. It gave us confidence in that.

The interaction with students with special expertise fit the category of partnership more naturally than with other students. However, as students work on their dissertation research, and certainly by the time they are analyzing data, they become "the" expert on their topic. Many advisors recognize this and faculty often encourage students preparing for the dissertation defense by telling them that, at least for a short while, they know more than anyone else in the world about their topic. For Ben, this translated into a very exciting moment of respect.

There was one point in the dissertation where I couldn't explain this phenomenon that I was trying to see. . . . So we started mapping it out, and I went home afterwards. I'm looking at this mess and trying to go, "Okay. How am I going to do this?" Well, it ended up being the central part of my findings, but it was really exciting because [during] that conversation, . . . there was a respect for me as an intellectual, as a researcher, as a professional. The coolest thing which I always describe to people is the shift in experience when you go in and you defend your dissertation. You walk in the room, and now you're the world's authority on this little piece of the puzzle.

Kathy really expressed the core element of respect with a pointed contrast. She felt it was critical that the advisor "learn who we are." In her experience, based in pharmaceutical research, "there are many people who would not take the time to do that." Rather, faculty seemed to feel that "you are the graduate student that was put on this earth to help me advance my research at this institution. You are merely a cog in a very big wheel—that I'm generating research and getting my NIH grants and all that. And they don't care that you're a person, and they don't care that they're expecting you to be there twenty-four hours a day, seven days a week."

In fairness, many faculty in the sciences with large NIH, or NSF or other grants, pay a great deal of attention to their students. However, Kathy makes two key points here. First, there are real risks for students who serve as research assistants on large grant projects, in the natural, physical or social sciences. Second, mid-career students bring expertise with them that enables them to define very interesting research agendas, and that is worthy of recognition.

TRUST

"Trust" is a big word. Merriam-Webster (n.d.) defines it as, "assured reliance on the character, ability, strength, or truth of someone or something." Ben underscored its importance when he said, "if there were not that trust and relationship, that intellectual challenge would push you right over the edge." Stephanie added even more emphasis by pointing out, that "you were the only person who understood where I started and where I needed to go. . . . My family didn't understand that, my friends, my cohort, no one else knew that, so that was part of why it was so vital to have that trust with you and why your opinion and what you said was so important to me." Her comment echoed Laura's comment about the advisor being the person who knew the program inside out. The third part of the Merriam-Webster definition included the word "dependence."

How do students come to trust an advisor? Kathy offered a baseline condition. "In my case, no one else in my world had a PhD . . . not in my personal life. . . . Here's the person who has walked in those shoes before, who has the credibility because they earned a PhD." So the advisor walks in the door, so to speak, with a baseline level of credibility. However, Carole was clear that it is also a process of continuing to build the credibility that leads to trust. In her words, "you would have to establish credibility with me for me really, my willingness to follow you." Using different words, many of the participants spoke about the need to establish a track record, a consistent track record comprised of the messages given to students, success of students in certain situations, and willingness to support students. Kelly was emphatic in talking about consistency and how that led to a track record.

> So I think the other thing to remember is that we talked to each other, you know, and that's kind of getting into the whole cohort thing. Students talk to each other, and one way in which you build trust is that if you have not—not you, the royal you, sorry—the message is always the same. Right? You know, you don't tell one person one set of things and tell a second person another set of things because people compare notes. All right? When I'm going around campus in time to help faculty understand what assessment means [in her current job], how you do that and the ways in which it will not come back to haunt them. It's very important that I give everybody that same message . . . because they're going to talk to each other.

The message under the microscope here was letting the student know they were ready for the candidacy, or general exam. According to Kelly, "Well, you told me explicitly, said, 'I won't let you fail.'" And when I jumped in to correct her language, indicating that I never promised she wouldn't fail, but rather wouldn't let her take them until she was ready, she said, "Right, 'I won't let you go until you're ready.' It's the assurance. It's that whole sense of 'I won't . . . let you go to generals [candidacy exam] unprepared.' And you tell enough people that it becomes sort of the message that develops the trust." Laura chimed in, "And the track record supports." Kelly continued, "And what that means is that when a student—when you tell a student I think you're ready for generals, they believe you." Olivia added another perspective about preparing for generals.

When someone said you said you wouldn't let us fail, you didn't say that, but what you did say was: "This is the environment we're going to go into, and this is how our relationship is going to be different. When you're sitting for the generals, this is how you and I have worked so far. Now this is how our relationship is going to change over the next six weeks while you're doing your generals." Or, "this is how our relationship is going to change when you're sitting for your dissertation defense." I knew how to—you prepared me to know how you needed to fulfill your role, and that helped me fulfill my role.

Laura provided an analogy to a person in physical therapy who had taken a bad fall. If the therapist says, "'In two weeks you're going to be able to have full flexion in your hip. Or you're going to be able to get yourself up from a chair,' the first time you hit a deadline, you gain more trust in the therapist. The more you hear these messages and the more they're confirmed and are true, the more people's trust goes up with advisors because basically what they say is intentional."

After she helped clarify the relationship between track record and trust, I asked "Why is this level of trust so important when you have your own ability to make judgments about so much?" These are, after all, accomplished, mid-career professionals. The answers from Brad, Ben, Kelly, and Emily were eye opening and reminded us of the fear and insecurity they felt early on in the program. Brad began, "I think we're all accomplished people. You know we all have intellectual, clearly intellectual abilities. . . . Even as accomplished as we are, you still question, can I do this?" Followed quickly by Ben, "Well, and we're apprentices in many ways. We are scholar apprentices and so we're looking to a master to guide us through that apprenticeship so that we too can become masters. It really is—I keep likening it to the monastic life, but in many ways it's similar in that respect." And then Kelly added,

> I mean that's the way the system is set up. There are different parts to graduate school, and we've kind of been talking about the intellectual parts. There's a whole other realm of things you've got to negotiate. Many are people's egos. There's a hierarchy; there are all [the] politics; and there are advisers who will just let their students walk into a hotbed of a committee that, you know, people are fighting with each other, and this person is caught in the middle. There is still a power differential and that's why—in some ways that's why I think that fear gets so big, because we know having worked, having come into this as mid-career, it's not—I mean most of us can recognize we're more in the middle of a political landmine that we can't fix. So you really have to have somebody that you trust to kind of help you negotiate your way through that. It's not—you might know what it can do, but you may not always be able to do it.

Emily extended the thought a bit further. "Who can I trust to provide me with information that will help without knowing their motivations? And I'm not in charge." And then Brad came back with another comment, accompanied by continuous muttered concurrence from Emily, Kathy, and Ben.

> In the sense . . . I always felt . . . that you had advocates with the other faculty members and with other folks on campus with whom I had to interact. So we had to direct some of this process or, you know, for example in preparing for the generals. I mean I have a recollection of us kind of talking about where we thought the committee members may be coming from, and how we would begin to anticipate their questions, and I don't want to be gaming it, because that's not exactly right, but kind of at that helpful guide but also knowing that you had our back, as it were . . . and that you felt that we were—when you moved us forward, when you felt that we were ready, and we could move through those things. . . . But I think the advocacy reason is important because it—you know we are interacting with other folks besides our adviser in a sense. Your relationship with those people, or your willingness to sort of to go to bat for us, I perceived was there as helpful at times.

Ben, then added, "and that built trust. I mean that really built that trust."

Brad led the group to a real "aha" moment by suggesting we think about this part of advising as taking the training wheels off a bicycle. The whole repartee is presented here because it shows the wonderful creativity of the dialogue, the true meaning of cocreation, and because it provided me, as an advisor, with insights as well. It also left us with the questions: How do advisors learn to recognize that moment when training wheels can come off? How do we recognize the moment when the student gains conceptual mastery? What clues can a student provide?

Brad: I mean it's just like taking the training wheels off the bike as it were, you know.

Ada: Say a little more.

Brad: You know take the—when my son was learning to ride a bike there was a day where we just decided, okay, this is the day that these wheels are coming off.

Ada: Right I understand that part.

Brad: And for the parent or to do that is to affirm something to the child that you're ready for this.

Ada: You have to have a sense—

Ben: Even though they may not feel ready.

Brad: Even all that.

Ada: You have a sense that the kid has some balance; that she's not going to kill herself.

Brad: Well that, but I think—hopefully, if we're doing our jobs—this is—let me play this a little bit. If we're doing our jobs as parents, we're setting our kids up to be successful. I think, so the analogy here is that your training wheels are off, and you could trust in her to kind of wobble for a while and sort of play it out rather than saying, no and kind of—

Ada: To pick up the word balance, and just staying narrowly with the training wheels thing, I think it's a nice analogy. You're willing to take the training wheels off when you think the kid has enough balance; that they're not going to fall over the minute you let go.

Brad: Right.

Ada: And that they can kind of get themselves down far enough that if they start to fall, they're going to put their foot down and kind of hang on and get themselves up and get going.

Brad: There's a leap of faith on both sides.

Laura: Right.

Ben: That's the one day I say, "You're going to learn how to ride your bike."

Ada: That's a very specific moment for me, and I'm picking up on it I think because one of my current students just got there with her second chapter. . . . And I sent her an e-mail last week. . . . All I said was in the subject line, I said, "Breakthrough." Because her first version had been very simple, and the second version, while it still needs a great deal of work, got the full complexity of the topic and was starting to get the depth and the nuance and all the pieces, and I could see the pieces of the picture puzzle were there. The puzzle wasn't yet totally—every piece didn't quite go in its little nook. But she got all the pieces. She got the picture.

These former students and the one I was working with at the time (who graduated in March, 2012) learned to ride the bicycle. They persevered through their fears, kept practicing and were rewarded with a new skill. What about those who did not? Stephanie reflected on the experience of a classmate, one of my former advisees, who left the program after course work, having been unable to develop a dissertation proposal over a two-year period. Curiously enough, the issues seemed to be a combination of lack of trust, and a new issue that Stephanie observed: attitude on the part of the advisee.

> Yeah. I just wanted to add something because [we mentioned] a few advisees that were lost along the road, and all of us sitting in the room or watching the room are successful advisees and finished, we defended and we have our PhDs with [this] adviser. One of the people who did not continue with [her], and didn't know if they ever succeeded in the PhD contacted me after I left for Luxemburg and said, "How did you work with [her]? I'm having difficulties. She keeps telling me to rewrite things or look at something a different way, and I'm having problems with the letting go, and I think the way it's written is fine."
>
> So my advice, of course, was "Well, you have to be open minded and have to trust what she's saying, because she's been there, she's done that and she's graduated other people. So if you want to graduate, my advice is then listen to her and try and listen." But what the story tells me is that it's not 100 percent [the advisor], it's also us and our, again, whether it's maturity or investment or whatever we decide, it's also our attitude and our willingness to accept the feedback and to accept the help. Whether that is the trust . . . or whether it's something else. There's obviously people couldn't do that with [this advisor] as well. So that's something to answer.

Stephanie not only points out that a productive advising relationship needs both people to make the effort, but also that some students and some advisors are not suited to work together. Whether it's a matter of personality or cognitive or coaching style, sometimes it is more productive to look for a different advisor and make the switch. Olivia, Kelly, Polly, and Tina demonstrated that in reverse. They made the switch from other faculty advisors to me.

My style of advising involves a lot of direct feedback, and while we will explore feedback per se in part IV, participant responses to a direct question from me relates to the matter of trust, track record, and this two-way relationship. I asked, "I wonder whether the equanimity or degree to which you could accept feedback is a product of a word we don't like to use very often: maturity. Is that part of the difference with mid-career folks?"

Ben, Brad, Kathy, and Laura kicked this question around. All four gave one word answers immediately: "Trust." "It's trust, not maturity." "That is the key." Kathy ventured, "It may be because maybe the maturity piece comes in being able to have a more mature relationship with your advisor. I mean, I don't know." After a few moments of quiet, she then said, "Yeah, it's more about trust. It's about the fact that you could give direct feedback to me, because you were almost as invested in what I was doing as I was." Laura and Ben picked up right away, "That's the word. That's the word. Invested, yeah." Laura continued, "I think it is a lot with feeling like the person delivering the feedback is invested in seeing you succeed, and you can handle that feedback because you know they're telling you that because they think you have the potential to be better."

Kathy came back to the question of maturity versus trust a few minutes later, offering an example from personal experience that suggests maturity may be quite central to the ability of this group of individuals to hear and use feedback productively.

> I'd like to echo or add onto that, and I'd say that while I agree 100 percent that trust and having someone who is invested in your project is critical to being able to accept that feedback, I think for me personally it *was* a maturity thing, too, because I can think back to a time when I was a professional in the pharmaceutical industry. My boss was a medical writer, and I thought I was a pretty darn good writer. I had a master's degree at this point. I had survived writing a master's thesis, and everything I would give to this woman would come back marked up with red ink. I vividly remember a conversation with her, and her telling me "When I am correcting what you've written, this is in no way me correcting you as a person."
>
> I had to learn that lesson, and I think having learned it and then going into anything that I did in the future, I was so much better off. But there was a time when red ink on paper was a criticism of Kathy, and I did learn that lesson, and I think that was a maturity thing for me. So I do think there is a role, at least for some people, for maturity and not discounting the trust or the investment question.

Stephanie's reaction to some pretty "in-your-face feedback," as we termed it, highlighted a perspective that seems a combination of trust and maturity. Not once in the several years that I worked with her did she get upset. Time and again, she would say, "This is great. This is great. This is great." Knowing that each individual possess a different tolerance for criticism, I asked her to talk about that.

> For me there are two reasons to say I was able to take feedback. One was that I was being offered the feedback. I knew a lot of people who didn't hear any feedback and then when they got ready to finish writing, they were told the wrong track. So I appreciated the fact that I got feedback in time to change it. So that was one big piece. . . . The second piece was after generals, I think, is when I started looking at the PhD program as a whole bunch of hoops that I just needed to jump through. Chapter one was a hoop, chapter two was a hoop, chapter three was a hoop, four, and five. If you told to me write six, seven, and eight, I would jump through those hoops, too. Every time I got feedback and knew I had something else to do, I was ready to jump if you told me, and that was partly my optimism, feeling that I was really going to finish, and it was partly my relationship with you that I trusted. If you told me it needed to be changed, it needed to be changed, and I could fight it, and I could cry and get upset, or I could get on with it and move forward.

FEEDBACK, CHALLENGE, SUPPORT

Advising involves a mix of interactions with students. Foremost among them are providing guidance, support, a roadmap to the program, and challenging them to be more analytic, to write more clearly, and giving feedback. Participants commented on all these interactions, and indicated those that contributed to their feelings of trust.

Perhaps the biggest challenge for an advisor is to sense the moments when students can be pushed to "do more," when the ideas are very close to being embedded in a new conceptual map. Laura called this "the appropriate question at the right time." There is a time when you can "give us a challenge and . . . pose a question to get us to reflect and think about the next step. I do think that that was part of the fear/exhilaration cycle . . . that when we were getting very, very scared and retreating and thinking maybe I can't do this, there was an appropriate challenge presented that made us refocus and realize that there was [a way forward]."

Lest the reader think the conversations are all sweetness and roses, Laura went on to say, "I think I cried once in her office when she told me I had to do qualitative research." She barely finished the words, when Polly added, "That one made me cry, too." It was certainly not my goal to induce tears; however, if and when the research methodology needed expansion into an area that was not part of the student's repertoire, not in their comfort zone, in my view it is up to the advisor to assure that consistency and rigor are maintained.

Laura was skilled in quantitative methodology, and so moving into qualitative research was a stretch for her, particularly as she considered the data analysis. Even worse, because she/we determined that it would be inappropriate for her to do the interviewing because she was the instructor in her experimental design, she had to cajole Kathy, also an accomplished quantitative researcher, into serving as the interviewer.

Carole nearly gave everyone the hiccups as she talked about her reactions.

> I never felt, like, personally attacked, but yet I certainly many, many times, as I think I shared with you . . . yeah, I have that, you know, almost ninety-mile trip home. It's like after one of our [advising] sessions, invariably I'd get back in my vehicle and then I would just bawl all the way home. It was like, "Oh, oh, my goodness." It's like I just got all pulled apart again and "Oh, my goodness." And it's "Oh, oh, oh" and then I'd get myself back together by the time I'd get home and I can't let anybody know. It's like, "Oh, I went down to my advisor today, bawl, bawl, bawl." And, but yet, it was always couched with you really focused on my success, my completion of the program and it was always done, it was like—I don't know, it was a combination of tear you down but build you up. I don't know if that's a good way to explain it because, you know, it was, it was tough at times. The conversations were tough messages. And I'd have to come back and go back and go at it again.

Quite often participants remarked about conversations where we identified options for improving material. Laura characterized "a type of support that is more of a challenge in that 'you can take this avenue, you can take this avenue, or you can take this avenue.'" Polly provided an example related to her dissertation, when the first draft presentation of her findings resulted in a mammoth chapter.

> I mean a big "in-my-face" for me that I went back home and said, "I don't know if I can continue doing this." In writing [the] dissertation, . . . I put together this mammoth chapter. I think it was chapter five—mammoth chapter. And I was—said, "Okay, I finally got it now." I got all these pieces all laid out, blah, blah, blah, and came in, and we talked about the chapter after you had spent some time reading it, and you said, "You know, I think you have to have two chapters. It's not just chapter five, you've got to have a chapter four and chapter five written. And we got to think about a different framework for how to put these pieces together."
>
> Was kind of like, "Oh my God." . . . It was just, "Oh my God. I cannot do this." But the more we worked through this, the more you kind of added in some ideas for how this massive change could be looked at in a different way. You didn't just send me away to say, "Go figure it out." You sent me away with something in my hand that I could make sense out of, and I could go back and reframe that data in a meaningful way and actually separate the chapters so they were—and they were a much better product in the end. But I never would have thought it would be a better product when you first told me that information. It was kind of like, "I cannot do this again."

Jaime offered a similar story. Confronted with feedback that began, "We need to change this," she got through the fear because alternative approaches were suggested.

I mean I'd freak out, and then you'd say, "Okay. Okay." Then you lay out something for me; I get, like, that it's my writing, you know, away from here, but you'd lay out exactly what things I could go back and look at. You'd offer the steps and answer the questions I had about how to move forward or what wasn't working and that just really helped me focus . . . and so it wasn't as much. I could have been a lot, lot worse.

Polly's image for this type of feedback was "poking a hole in the bottom of the glass, so the water started leaking out." The key for her, which she called "pouring some water in the top half of the glass so it evened back out again," was the conversation that followed, directing her attention to other dissertations that could be read, or an article, or a technique (like a matrix), that might give her a tool for reframing the analysis. Polly never experienced the feedback as prescriptive. Never "'You have to do it this way.' It was always, 'This isn't working for me because I'm not seeing these connections. You might want to try to think about it this way.' Or providing a grid," suggesting how her concepts might line up. "Then I'd go away and think about it and come back. . . . The writing and the thinking was mine. The 'how you frame it to make it a little bit better sense out of it than you did the first time' was the assistance."

Emily reinforced this notion. "But it was the role of the adviser that didn't prescribe that for us but allowed us the choice to do it but gave us examples of how others were successful. I think that's a really important distinction that in some perhaps less successful cases, it was the adviser's way or the highway. In your case, it was, 'Let me tell you how these four people have done it, but ultimately you have to find what fits for you.'"

My experiences with previous advisees became part of the conversation when I hoped they might help the student figure out some variation that would work for them. More advanced students and former advisees who lived locally (and some who did not) were always at risk for being contacted by a current student at my suggestion.

Sometimes the advisor simply provides the perspective, as Kathy described it, of "someone who was going alongside us in the journey who could then take a step back that was much more removed from it, and say, 'Here's where the issue is.' Once we had someone to find that issue for us, then the solution became so much more clear. Once we had a definition of the issue, then we could fix it, but sometimes you just couldn't define the issue because you [we] were too close to it." This is the same invaluable role we can play for any of us working on a project or manuscript, by bringing fresh eyes to the project.

Brian made a similar comment about feedback on his writing, remembering ruefully,

> Writing the longest first draft of chapter 2 known to mankind only to have it edited down by about half at the follow-up meeting with my advisor. . . . Having an advisor who thought about things very differently than I did was very helpful. I remember some of our review sessions where I'd hand in a chapter. . . . I thought I wrote about it in the most salient and transparent and clear way and you'd be like, "I don't get this. Why is this important?" and it would cause me to take a step back and say, "Okay, maybe there is a better way to say this." I've never had my writing so scrutinized in my entire life.

Couched in a compliment, Davida included a hint about the directness of the feedback, as well. "I have always admired her attention to/for detail, ability to proof and 'flip' a piece of writing, and very 'blunt' perspectives when I would stray from the writing path."

Apparently, not all feedback is created equal. In addition to offering alternatives and illustrations, Laura was emphatic that "there's an art to good feedback." Words like, "this needs to be more clear," or "you need to add more sentences about this" seemed to be more easily heard than "I don't understand this." Focused and precise feedback did not create anxiety for either Laura or Kathy, because they "knew exactly what they had to do to improve."

As Olivia remarked somewhat earlier, being told about the type of interaction to expect made it easier for the student to keep perspective. Seth had graduated only two months prior to the two days of discussion that August, and recalled a conversation from his very first year. According to Seth, I said something like, "This is what to expect as you go through the writing process, and this is how I'll probably give feedback." He went on,

> So I always kept that in perspective. I like direct feedback, so when I got it, and sometimes it was very direct, but I walked out of there, went home and started writing. I didn't really think about it because that's the expectation from day one that I always expected. It wasn't a surprise to me, so I think that expectations and being clear from the beginning were really good; not just about the dissertation but the entire PhD program. I feel like I was very prepared to know what to expect, . . . and I went home and kept on working because that's just what I did. So I didn't walk out of there getting upset. Things like timelines, I think we all share that in common and life circumstances, but other than that I don't think I ever felt frustrated walking out of there saying, "What do I do next now?" I felt like I always had a good direction.

Providing overall structure was also important for Ben.

> I think a necessary criterion for an adviser to help somebody to get through the process is what Olivia was just saying, and that is providing the structure. Because one of the things that I heard in our periodic get-togethers as a cohort was that Christine and I were at a real advantage over our peers in that we had a structure and a map. And I had colleagues who finished without having some times—well, I mean not despite their adviser, but they didn't have the sense of having a roadmap and a clear map. I think it was Brad maybe an hour ago who was talking about this idea of a map, and I keep visualizing that. I had a sense throughout the whole process of what the map was.

The map was actually a diagram that depicted a staircase with "bubble people" expressing confusion at the bottom, juggling in the middle, and celebration at the top (see figure 7.1). The commentary along the steps explained the sequence of the program. It was a simple diagram that I created to use at orientation with the incoming doctoral students early in my tenure as faculty. New students were first presented with a blank version, no annotation, just steps and bubble people, and then were given the annotated version. In addition to our detailed curriculum materials, it offered a step-by-step guide for progression through the program. Later it helped me track student progress.

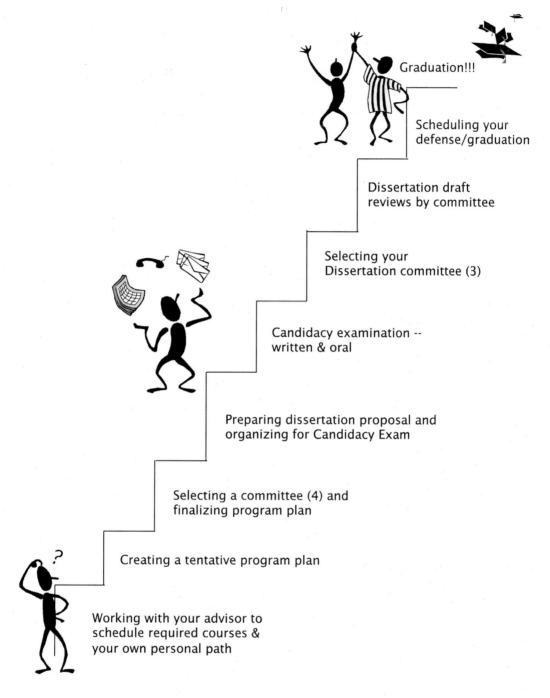

Graduation!!!

Scheduling your
defense/graduation

Dissertation draft
reviews by committee

Selecting your
Dissertation committee (3)

Candidacy examination --
written & oral

Preparing dissertation proposal and
organizing for Candidacy Exam

Selecting a committee (4) and
finalizing program plan

Creating a tentative program plan

Working with your advisor to
schedule required courses &
your own personal path

Figure 7.1 The PhD Schematic

Brad felt the diagram served as the basis for conversation where we "individualized the map in a way that helped us see what lay ahead." Ben went on about the role the map played. "There wasn't a sense of uncertainty other than our own natural uncertainty, insecurity, all those other things we identified, but that's a critical criterion for helping someone through the process. Because without that map, oh, my gosh, there's so many pieces to the puzzle. How do you get it all put together?"

This doctoral program differs from some others because students are required to write a decent draft of the dissertation proposal prior to the candidacy (or general) exam. Students working with me knew it is as the "85 percent" draft. Faculty felt this helped the students in several ways. First, students were better prepared for some candidacy questions, particularly those related to methodology and the core of their dissertation research. Second, writing the candidacy exam always produced insights that would improve the dissertation, and could be incorporated directly into the draft proposal. Third, students benefited from being closer to faculty while they were struggling with the elements of the proposal, for example, defining research questions, methodology, and writing clearly. They avoided some of the sense of isolation that often undermines proposal writing. Finally, once the exam was completed, the student could revise the proposal, submit the protocol for human subjects review, and begin their data collection, the core of their research. The timing helped them keep momentum.

Sometimes students got frustrated with the timing, as they watched their peers move into generals. Other times, as they heard peers struggle with dissertation proposals, the advantages became clearer. As Ben said, writing the proposal "was kicking my butt at the time, but I'm so thankful and I remember getting that affirmation, 'Okay, good.' I'm getting the support that I need."

ADVISORS VS. MENTORS

Participants insisted that there were very real differences between advisors and mentors. One of the key differences according to Kathy, involved "acknowledgment of you as a person with a real life, not just as a student here at Ohio State. . . . What are you struggling with at work? What are you struggling with at home? And maybe some of your less successful advisers . . . are all about just this one part of your life rather than being considered as a total person." Laura exclaimed, "I have a boss that doesn't even know if I have kids or not." She felt strongly about the distinction and offered a lot of insights. First, "what gets you completion is the mentor." And then she continued,

> I think a critical challenge is part of quality mentorship. I think that is a very critical component to success. It's not so much just the support. All of us need a shoulder to lean on. All of us need to talk to someone about the guilt we're feeling, but it was almost like being shown the path to success, while allowing us to pick which path we'll take. In my mind an advisor is just someone who gives you advice about classes and advice about a dissertation. [A mentor does] way more than that. It wasn't just advice about school and classes and homework it was advice about careers. It was advice about, "don't take this job Brad."

Ben remembered feeling that while he was challenged intellectually, because he was asked "are you okay right now?" in the middle of a conversation where his draft had been turned inside out, he could accept the intellectual challenge. "I'm appreciated emotionally and we've got a relationship here and we're going to work together. . . . That trust was critical because I had to take chapter five, and make five, six, and seven."

Another dimension involved accessibility. Emily, Laura, and Kathy spoke to this point several times, in different contexts. Emily worked full-time and found herself derailed for a year due to her divorce and family responsibilities. Access to her advisor throughout the year allowed her to continue to make progress when her time and emotional energy permitted.

Well, I think one of the other pieces that was important as mid-career folks is your availability to do it at the timeline when we had the time. To me, that was key; that is, some advisers . . . they're not accessible certain quarters. They will not give feedback during the summer, and as working people, it was really important that when we had the time and ideas started to flow, we carved out that space. You, as much as you could—I mean you still gave your own parameters, but for the most part it was you were available when our ideas started to go. So it was the ability to mold with that timeline because otherwise, we had to—when that was happening, and we had to put ideas on the shelf for a quarter, that could have just stopped us in our tracks.

For Laura, the immediacy of access was important. She valued being able to talk even if it meant her traveling to off-site locations, where conversations were fit in between other activities. Kathy underscored that by commenting on two aspects of advising she sought to emulate.

One is that student's projects come first, and so when I get something from a student that goes to the top of my priority list. Even if it's the most unreasonable time for me to get it, it goes to the top of the priority list because that's their project and their timeline. I try to honor that, and being available to them for advice, and making time in my schedule to meet with them and counsel them, so those are the two things. I'd say time for their papers and time for them.

Kelly framed accessibility in emotional terms. "I looked to my advisor for the answers and for what it was worth and what it was going to be, and all the other support was kind of the current—the here and the breakdowns, the cries. You were a different source of support for me. I wouldn't call it support. It's mentorship. I think that's different."

Olivia and Laura both appreciated having examples of other students who had been successful, when confronted with similar challenges. Laura called it "shared reality in psychology. That's a very settling thing for people to know that they're not weird." Brad called it "modeling possible applicants for success." And Olivia, underscored it.

Especially when you're in a process where you don't connect with a lot of people who are on the same roadmap with you. I think it's critical, the shared stories. I feel like we're really like, I didn't know Kathy, but I felt like I resonated a lot with Kathy's experience, and it was nice to have that perspective because you don't get it other places on your own. You don't find that without you making some connections.

Laura had already mentioned "feeling like the person delivering the feedback is invested in seeing you succeed." This theme came up in an unexpected way when Laura mentioned that it had been very important to her to celebrate completion at various times in her program. She mentioned being taken out to eat. Others, like Ben, Emily and Polly, remember the sense of enthusiasm. "Reaction was enthusiasm first, not 'you didn't go with what was suggested earlier.' I still have those kinds of e-mails that were sent that the 'theme was not, you're not quite there, but keep going.' It was, 'You have made the next step,' and that was so confidence building." According to Ben, "Each of us has received that e-mail from you. Each of us." Kelly said, "We can't see it until you tell us we've just had a breakthrough."

Ben explained more about the sense of support that helped overcome uncertainty and vulnerability.

I think it's . . . that idea of you developing a sense of competence. "Okay, I can do this, and I'm going to do this. I'm going to get it done," but when we were most vulnerable, had we not gotten support . . . I think that could have deflated that movement forward. Because I know for me there were a couple of moments where I was definitely driven, but if I were really having some struggling there, had I not gotten that support when I needed it right then to get over that hurdle, that could have been really devastating.

His comment echoed comments from Kelly and Laura's use of the word *partnership* to define good advising. And Polly, who was already a department chair at a local community college, took the notion of support further. "I think the hurdle is an important thing because I think we all have whatever hurdles they were; whether they were personal hurdles or hurdles in the dissertation concepts or wherever they were, and so there had to be something that happened to help get over those. . . . In some respects it was a lot of how [the advisor] handled—helped us handle the hurdle."

Ben summed up this part of the discussion for us.

> The thing that keeps resonating with me and hearing that we're talking about is the mentor has a respect for our intellectual capacity and our creativity as individuals, and we have that trust and that relationship, and so, Kathy, that's what you were talking about. That's what—you know in terms you get that affirming e-mail and each of us received that. You get that affirming comment on that chapter that you've been beating your head against the wall on for so long, finally it's there.

Who knew a simple e-mail, with "Breakthrough" as the subject line, could be so empowering?

INVESTING

Investment in the relationship seemed to characterize the difference between an advisor and a mentor. Participants defined investment in several ways. One example was not giving up when the student seemed to be having more than the usual difficulty with a concept. As Emily said about the interaction that finally led to her conceptual framework, "I can remember the many strategies used to help me try to get a conceptual framework. I think you used every trick in the bag." Kathy added, "You know a good adviser isn't just punching a nine-to-five time clock and isn't a checklist of things that people need to get done. They really do spend some time getting invested in what those things are."

Investing can also mean sharing personal experience, to help a student make sense of particular situations. For an independent study one quarter, Laura needed access to documents from three other universities. She set out to make contact, and received

> a very nasty e-mail from one of them, that said, If I was doing an independent study, I needed to have a syllabus, and I needed to give it to him, "and it needed to have at least twenty-five resources on it." I was so angry, because I thought who are you? My adviser comes from Harvard. [Laughter.]
>
> I went in and talked to you, and we had this huge philosophical discussion about you being in the Institute of Science [International Institute for Applied Systems Analysis, Austria] as the only woman and the interaction the first day you showed up: One of the guys folded his coat and asked you to get him a cup of coffee. So that is not an adviser. That is something way more to me.

Another example involved inviting students to experience part of the advisor's life that might be outside of the university. The simplest case is to visit the advisor's home and to interact with other faculty and students in a personal and informal setting. Once each year, my husband and I hosted a potluck get-together for the doctoral students at our home, usually late on a Sunday afternoon. All current students were invited, as were faculty. Each was asked to bring an inexpensive appetizer-type dish for six to eight people, such as salad, cookies, dips, cakes, homemade bread, or even a basket of Kentucky Fried chicken wings. Over a fifteen-year period, these grew from a few students to gatherings of forty or fifty students and spouses (or significant others), and faculty with spouses and partners. Halfway through the gathering, I would give a small speech playfully recognizing the progress of all students, not only those graduating or completing general exams, but even the first-year students for simply having survived. There was a lot of clapping and whistling!

Participants also seemed to appreciate the chance to see their advisor in the context of activities that were special or unusual. In this case, their advisor owned a horse, was training as a dressage rider, and competed in local shows from time to time. Most folks do not have the opportunity to be "up close and personal" with a horse, and so when students were not enrolled in courses with me, they were invited to visit the barn. Laura, who had herself owned a horse and competed as a high school student, actually assisted with several competitions. She recalled, "I brushed Starlight [the horse]. That doesn't involve school. . . . I was at the barn. I think maybe that's what is unique about it." One by one, Emily, then Olivia and Tina brought this up. Olivia said, "and I brushed a horse. I forget which one, but I've been to the barn, too." [Laughter.] Sharing a part of my life that was very important to me outside of school, and that put me in the position of being the learner (training to ride), was very meaningful for them. Emily recalls my using analogies to riding lessons in classes, and had the sense that my experience with feedback from a trainer affected my ability to give feedback.

For the advisor, it raises a fundamental question of how to set and avoid crossing boundaries. My rule was: No one visited the barn when they were enrolled in one of my courses. And, it was crucial for me that students never feel that someone was taking advantage of them. I worried terribly about that when Laura assisted with the dressage show and reiterated that during the conversation. She reminded me, "You told that to me every time I came to a show." Olivia recalled a conversation about boundaries that happened when we were discussing her dissertation research. The more deeply an advisor engages in the creative process with the student, the greater the risk that the result resembles the advisor's conceptual work, rather than the student's. Olivia said, "You were explicit about that. You would say, 'I want to be careful not to turn this in the direction that I would make it go.'"

A MATTER OF CREDIBILITY

What was the source of their willingness to accept feedback and to act on recommendations? Why "do what their advisor said?" Carole's thoughtful reflection touched many of the elements that illustrate the complexity of relationship. She began talking in terms like Davida's, and expanded her thoughts in response to a question.

> But there's this incredible personal element and it's really the relationship and I do think it is built on mutual respect. And so, kind of that whole coach/cheerleader/drill sergeant all wrapped up in one and I think there also has to be respect. I think for me, I would not have moved probably with success—been able to create a successful relationship with an advisor that I did not have incredible respect for. And that was a real important element for me because, not only do you need to be real, but you've got to establish credibility with me and when you do, you know, I'll walk through fire for you, so . . . it's a combination. I think it's hard to kind of put words to but that's, that's kind of my first, my best attempt.

As she continued, Carole articulated more clearly the importance for her to feel that the advisor was credible. If she was going to follow directions from this person, she wanted some sense that the advisor knew her stuff. When asked to be more specific about how the advisor could do that and whether a curriculum vitae and list of publications was sufficient, she described credibility as more of a process of interaction.

> Hmm. Well, I don't know that published . . . you know, certainly professional accomplishments and being professionally accomplished would be part of that. I don't know. I don't think you can fake it. You knew what you were talking about. You really knew what you were talking about and I don't think—I don't know, it's like if it had been fake, I think I would have seen through it. Bringing your work experience, your professional experience, your personal experience all to the table and a willingness to lay it out there and always, always an idea person, and I'm bringing information and you're reacting to it and "have you thought of this and have you thought of that? Well, what about this?" And so, it's like I'm bringing all this stuff and it's like, okay, well, what do we do with all this? And so it's like reining me in and, you know, kind of sending me off. And . . . I'd bring it all back and then you'd push back again. And so it's really, it's a willingness to push back and creating a safe space to do that, honoring who I am.

With these words she seemed to have captured the group's sentiments about the difference between advisors and mentors.

Chapter Eight

Images That Illuminate

VISUALIZING THE JOURNEY

It has taken many pages and thousands of words to capture the sense of the journey lived by the participants during their doctoral programs. In the spirit of a "picture is worth a thousand words," figure 8.1 illustrates the journey visually. The illustration depicts several key aspects of the journey.

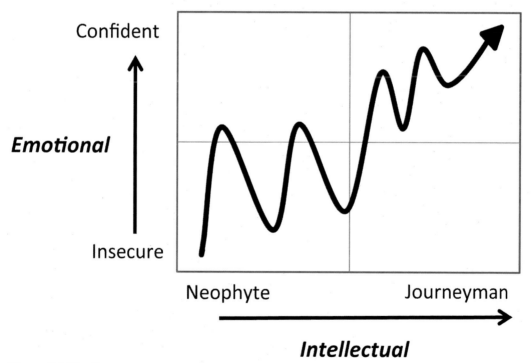

Figure 8.1 The Journey

The two axes represent two paths that the students are traveling simultaneously as they seek to become confident scholars: an emotional path from insecurity to confidence, and an intellectual path from neophyte to journeyman. "Journeyman" is an old term that seems apt in the context of higher education where faculty are sometimes described as guilds working with students who are their apprentices. The term journeyman connotes the achievement of the set of skills necessary to function as an independent craftsman, or in our case, scholar. Here its use is gender neutral.

The figure indicates the bumpy ride student experience, as they first gain skill in one area only to face a new conceptual or intellectual challenge that undermines their self-confidence, until enough practice produces skill in that area. Each new research paper, each course in methodology and content offers new knowledge and challenges them to develop new analytic tools and lenses.

The first year was particularly challenging for a combination of reasons. Brian recalled, "The first year was really rough, as I chose to do my residency the first year. . . . Weekends were devoid of anything fun for a good chunk of my program, and were spent catching up on reading, writing and occasionally sleep." For Laura it was the "first ten weeks. It was the first quarter where I felt bipolar, where I was, 'could I do this?' . . . Whatever challenges came . . . after the first quarter, they just didn't seem as large of obstacles."

Brad articulated his feelings of loss. "I mean having made that shift and being in transition that first quarter that you were really mourning what you had given up . . . but then that transition was tapering and now you were this side of that, you were a doctoral student and not what had happened prior." And moments later, Seth echoed his comment, "The first two weeks when classes began and I realized that I was just another student, and felt a sense of loss." Laura quickly chimed in that she only made progress when "I quit fighting the identity and who I was previous, is not who I am now. If I'm going to be successful in this, I got to change who I am and to change my identity. I'm not an athletic trainer anymore. I'm a student." Ben reminded Laura that she and Kathy had "the added challenge of having to learn the jargon and theories that kind of undergirded all this stuff." So the big dip that year resulted from time pressure, the challenge of the new student role, and a sense of loss during a transition that left folks in a no man's land.

The second year was hardly mentioned in the conversation. During that period folks settled into their course work and began to try out topics for dissertations. Choosing a dissertation topic was often time consuming. A few people like Stephanie, zeroed in very early. "I drove my advisor, my professors, and my cohort crazy by being too clear on my goals/focus/topics. I remember being told I had to pick a topic other than one with an international focus for a paper, and I refused. . . . I absolutely knew what I wanted to study." During the second and third years, people began identifying their community and faculty whose interests related to their dissertation topics, and who might serve as committee members. By the middle of the second year and certainly by the third, members of a cohort were no longer in synch with course work or timelines for generals. Job and/or family responsibilities impinged on time frames, and often meant friends saw each other less often.

The biggest "dip" in the middle of the graph represents the period of time, often in the third year, sometimes the fourth, when students are writing the dissertation proposal and preparing for the candidacy or general exam, as it is often termed. Preparing for and taking the generals was "brutal" according to Ben. Every student was pushed to the wall. Yet, while the requirement to write draft proposals prior to generals added to the pressure, it really served its purpose for Ben.

> You know I think about it, I wrote my first three chapters just before my son was born and did my generals when he was three months old. Had I not had those three chapters written, because I was so exhausted after the generals . . . I think I took about a month and just [collapsed]—but it was an exciting experience to do the general. I mean actually I think that was the single hardest element of

the program. The dissertation, I loved it. It was a hell of a lot of work, but it was—I really enjoyed that. But the generals were brutal, but had I not had those three chapters when I came out of that month, I was like, "I can't do it," but I kind of picked up the three chapters and I went [sound effect breath] okay.

He, like many others, saw the generals as a rite of passage. Brian had thought the rest of the program would be easier to manage after his residency, but found in his third year, "when it came time for 'independent work—writing the proposal, prepare for candidacy exams, the entire dissertation process—this was the hardest time to manage."

The dip in the upper-right quadrant has already been graphically described by both Davida and Carole as that point toward the completion of their dissertations when they hit the wall, or just ran out of gas, but they dug deep and found the energy to finish. For Tina, that period stretched across three years. She remembers, "the intensity of the three consecutive summers when I prepared for the general exam, conducted research, analyzed data, and wrote the last three dissertation chapters—an intensity that I often describe as an 'ascetic' experience, that I now associate with scholarship. Sometimes I yearn for that intensity again."

The figure also indicates the intense interaction between the emotional and intellectual domains. As people gain confidence in their ability to accomplish tasks, they are more willing to take on more complex problems, and the cycle feeds on itself. Unfortunately, if they lose confidence, they are likely to shy away from new challenges and that, too, feeds on itself, and can lead to serious delays as students regress to more incremental progress, or even stall out. A key task for an advisor, according to the participants, is to recognize those moments when a student is about to fall off a cliff and offer encouragement and practical guidance to help get them back on track intellectually. When the student can see a path forward through the bush, as Polly, Jaime, and others indicated, they can generate their own energy and clear the trail. But at those moments, they need help framing analytic or conceptual options in order to regain momentum.

ADVISING DYNAMICS IN ACTION

Carole's comments about advisor credibility, presented at the end of the last chapter, directed our attention not only to the complexity of the advising role, but also to its dynamic nature. Two individuals, even those agreeing to work together, do not immediately form a trusting partnership. It takes time and much interaction to develop credibility and to become trustworthy. Figure 8.2 shows the dynamics of the advisor-student relationship. Using the clusters that we identified at the beginning of the last chapter, the diagram shows the interaction among the clusters, centering the advising relationship on three key elements: Respect, Trust, and the quality of Feedback, Challenge, and Support provided by the advisor. The continuous lines represent the core advising relationship, and the dashed lines indicate the additional dynamics that shift the relationship into mentor mode.

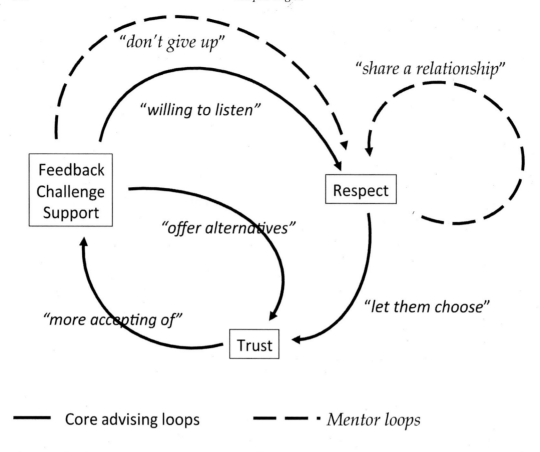

Figure 8.2 Advisor and Mentor Dynamics

The figure is drawn in the style of a systems dynamics model, which means very simply that it depicts feedback loops. So each arrow represents a statement of consequences. The way an advisor provides feedback, challenge or support affects the degree to which the student feels respected. The level of respect the student feels affects his/her trust in the advisor, which in turn affects the student's engagement in the relationship. The feedback loops "accelerate" the quality of interaction and result in either positive consequences, as shown in the diagram, or negative consequences.

As drawn here, illustrating positive dynamics the figure can be read in this way: If (or when) the adviser provides feedback, or challenges the student in a way that is helpful and shows a willingness to listen, the advisor demonstrates respect for the student. When the student feels respected and is given choices about how to proceed, trust grows, and the student becomes more accepting of feedback from the advisor and more engaged. Thus, the interaction feeds on itself. When an advisor offers constructive alternatives to illustrate the meaning of feedback, or new concepts, the student understands the feedback even better and that interaction enhances the process of building trust. It is this type of interaction that Carole's comments described in different words.

We could describe negative consequences of the same feedback loops in this way: If the advisor insists, or appears to insist, that the student follow his/her directions in an inflexible manner, appearing to show disrespect for the student's intellect or opinions, the student loses trust. If these demanding and inflexible interactions are repeated, the student becomes less and less willing to meet with, or listen to, the advisor. The feedback loops would result in a deteriorating relationship. As an example, after having a disagreement that reflected a serious difference of opinion about where he should focus his time and energy while preparing his dissertation proposal, another of my advisees changed to a faculty colleague. The argument had disrupted the trust cycle shown in figure 8.2 and sent our dynamic in a negative direction. Fortunately, we both realized that we were having difficulty before the relationship completely deteriorated, and we organized his shift to another advisor. In an impromptu hallway meeting a year later, we were able to share his excitement the afternoon he defended his dissertation in the summer of 2010.

The diagram helps illuminate the dynamics of the core relationship and draws attention to the key role of respect in the relationship, where several dynamics converge, making it a powerful accelerator. Two loops in the diagram incorporate the key elements that differentiate the mentor relationship with the captions "don't give up" and "share a relationship." Emily's comment about realizing that her advisor had tried "every trick in the bag" during conversations about her conceptual framework, and the different opportunities for students to engage with the advisor outside of the doctoral program provide examples of these dynamics. In the diagram, these two loops contribute to the dynamics in the same direction as the core relationship, enhancing and strengthening the impact on the student's sense of being respected, and moving the relationship into a partnership mode.

THE ADVISING MAP

The scope of the advising role is potentially huge. More than a dozen areas could be extracted from the participant conversations related to content knowledge, the process of moving through the program, and dissertation and professional growth. Table 8.1 lists those that emerged from these discussions. Imagine showing this list to a randomly chosen group of faculty. How do you think they would respond? Some might respond that the list seemed incomplete. A second and more likely response could sound something like, "I never signed up for all this." Hired, rewarded and valued for content expertise, research, and teaching skills, many are unprepared for, and others do not seek, the complexity of the advising role. They perform the role very differently.

Table 8.1 Scope of Advising

• Content knowledge	• Choosing a committee
• Inquiry skills	• Negotiating the committee
• Issue comprehension	• Negotiating the system
• Roadmap	• Connecting professionally
• Dissertation topic	• Gaining visibility
• Writing coach	• Professional coach
• Research rigor	• Survival coach

Another way of describing the scope of advising is shown in figure 8.3. The ovals in the diagram represent the domains of a student's life, all of which are affected by the doctoral journey. This particular diagram was created on a white board during the Saturday afternoon discussion as participants sought to identify differences between advisors and mentors. They concluded that the mentor operates in the center of the diagram, where all five domains intersect, marked with the asterisk.

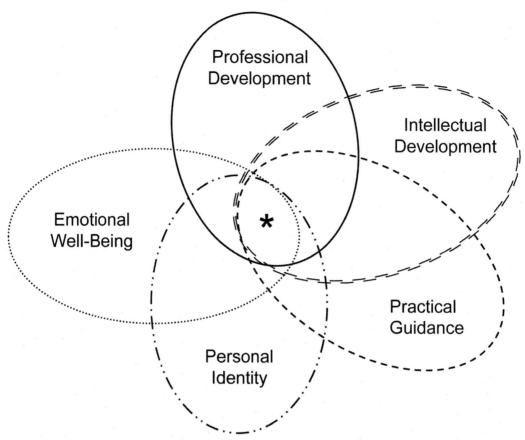

Figure 8.3 Student Domains

After examining their comments in more detail, as we did in the previous chapter, I believe the diagram can be used to characterize the input not only of mentors and advisors but of other members of the supporting cast as well. Different domains demand attention at particular times in a student's life. Brad's, Laura's, and Seth's comments clearly demonstrated the challenge to professional identity they experienced during the first year. Certainly, effective advisors and mentors, are likely to be involved more fully in the domains labeled "intellectual development," "practical guidance," and "professional development" than the small area of intersection at the center suggests. A willingness to venture into the intersection, particularly related to "emotional well-being" and "personal identity" may distinguish mentors from advisors.

Many folks are involved with emotional well-being, for example, all the Wizards, the Inner Circle, and Guardians. In a similar manner, Elders and members of the Cabinet engage with intellectual development, and Alumni and the Cabinet offer practical guidance, along with advisors and mentors. If we consider the items in table 8.1 and the domains that participants identified together, then it is easy to see that we need more precise language or terminology to describe a range or family of advising types to accommodate the preferences, styles and talents of faculty involved in advising doctoral students.

Figure 8.4 borrows from the original Blake and Mouton "managerial grid," and presents a typology of advising modes. The managerial grid described effective management in terms of either a "people" orientation or a "task" or "production" orientation. The people orientation is the "degree to which a leader considers the needs of team members, their interest, and areas of personal development when deciding how best to accomplish a task." The production orientation is "the degree to which a leader emphasizes concrete objectives, organizational efficiency, and high productivity when deciding how best to accomplish a task (Blake and Mouton, 1968; Mindtools, 2011)."

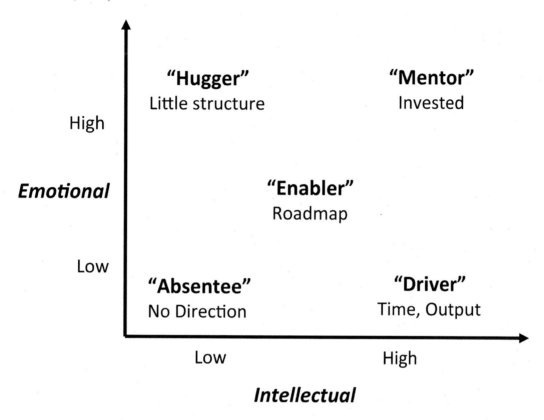

Figure 8.4 Advisor Grid: Intensity, Style, Skill, and Preference

This grid describes advising modes in terms of the intensity of emotional or intellectual involvement. Only one of the positions on the grid, the "Absentee" in the lower-left quadrant, represents an unworkable situation. Regrettably, like the participants, we have all observed faculty colleagues who are so laid back or have so little interest in their doctoral students that they are completely unaware of the intellectual isolation or the emotional distress caused by their lack of direction. How many of you, faculty readers, have rescued students who come to you for advice because their advisor was inaccessible? The four other modes are all workable, although two of them are skewed toward either productivity or emotional well-being.

The "Hugger" is an empathetic individual who will take as much time as needed to talk with student about the life challenges the program represents, but provides little guidance regarding the research process (choosing a topic, crafting researchable questions, choosing an appropriate methodology, or the structure of the program), when and how to choose a committee, preparing for the candidacy exam, and following departmental or university procedures in a timely manner. Ironically, the lack of intellectual and procedural guidance can cause even more emotional distress thereby undermining student confidence and progress. Olivia pointed out that these folks care about the person, but were not able to get people to complete. Like I can think of a number of faculty members who care about people individually, but they don't create the same structure for the opportunity. . . . I know other faculty members who I think cared deeply about people and do not have the same track record. . . . You meet with them. They ask about your family and about your kids and whatever, but then they just kind of, once you're back out the door, you're still left in more of a mode of isolation to do the work.

The "Driver" is a professor with an eye on the research ball. With or without a grant, very likely the student is working closely with this individual on a research project where the goal is output—research results, conference presentations, publications, grant applications. "The Research" and results are top priority; student concerns come second. As Kathy said, "You are merely a cog in a very big wheel. . . ." These faculty will always seek to advise students whose research interests coincide directly with their own. The faculty member may fail to attend to student questions about various aspects of the research they do not understand well, and ignore the personal costs that accompany an all-out focus on the work. Student concerns about making progress on dissertation research, time away from family, or taking care of their own physical and mental health are simply not part of the relationship. The Driver's inattention can add to the student's sense of isolation, or feelings of guilt, and overall lack of balance in his/her life. The risks are that the student might come to resent the intensity of the research experience and over time feel the demands of program to be so insurmountable that they are not worth the effort, and leave.

Effective advisors, as described through participant conversations, display the characteristics similar to effective managers in the early Blake and Mouton managerial grid. Effective advisors are those who can handle both domains equally well, and appear in the center and upper-right quadrants of figure 8.4. According to Kelly, advisors can range from mechanistic, those who just tell you the steps, to being in the middle, "if they're kind of okay," but when they reach the high end of both, "they have to be an advisor/mentor."

The "Enabler" fits in the middle ground, recognizing that the student needs guidance intellectually and will be facing emotional challenges. The inference to be drawn from the grid is that Enablers share an awareness of both and a willingness to attend to both. It would be inappropriate to infer from the grid that the emotional stability of the student is the advisor's responsibility. Rather, the Enablers treat the student with courtesy and respect in the process of providing programmatic and intellectual challenge and guidance. And, if the advisor senses that the student is in some distress, he or she will be willing and able to listen and to connect the student to other resources on campus—be they counseling resources or writing workshops.

Consistent with the distinction made by participants, the graph illustrates the difference between an Enabler and a Mentor as a matter of intensity: the degree to which the advisor is invested in the success of the student. We could define a Mentor as an Enabler on steroids. Manifested by going the extra mile to help a student develop a conference or grant proposal, or to submit a scholarship recommendation, perhaps on short notice, the Mentor is focused as much on the student's success as a student and as a young professional. The Mentor accepts the student "with baggage" one might say, taking the time to consider the context in which the doctorate is being pursued, and the student's personal aspirations and career goals. A focus on the student's success characterizes the Mentor. The risk to Mentors is that time spent on advising might be at the cost of time spent on their own research.

The title of the figure is central to this part of the conversation. Like everyone else, faculty come to their roles with different temperaments, orientations, skills, and preferences. Some are extroverts and others are introverts. Some love the interaction with their students and their lives; others prefer a more task-oriented relationship—whether as simply a matter of preference or because of the pressures they feel to obtain grants and show research productivity. Some truly love research. Talented researchers and, perhaps, kind individuals, they are at their best in an analytic mode. Many are simply unaware of the complexity of the mid-career doctoral challenge and might engage with students differently if this information were available. Others are comfortable working with students in more holistic ways and enjoy the process of assisting a young scholar to find a personal research focus and career path, different from their own.

Carole defined a good advisor, as a

> cheerleader, a drill sergeant. I think they need to set expectations; I think they need to process. I think they need to be intentional about moving you through that process as opposed to, whatever. In other words, more—maybe it's because my personality, I like structure and I really respond to somebody that has a system and structure and accountability and I think that's really that intentional piece.

"We're talking about a skill set," according to Kelly. "I mean I think those are incredible traits that an advisor/mentor needs to have, but not everybody in academe who finds themselves thrust into the role of the advisor has the slightest idea of how to do that." In the worst case, "We're talking about an inability to relate to people. We're kind of characterizing as 'you're either this wonder mentor, or you're absolutely not.' I think there really are a lot of people sort of in between."

The Advisor Grid is an attempt to provide language for characterizing styles of advising. How might it be used? Faculty could use it to think about where they might fit on the diagram, and whether they wanted to consider taking the time or gaining the skills to move into the Enabler-Mentor trajectory. For example, some Huggers may default to that role or that quadrant of the grid because of uncertainty about a student's willingness or ability to accept more direct feedback about ideas or writing. Participants in this project indicated that almost all were capable of accepting critical feedback. Setting up the expectation ahead of time, and using language with a bit of care made it easier to hear and integrate criticism. Everyone who spoke up indicated the feedback was certainly trying at times, but was worth the effort.

If modifying their styles were not appealing, then advisors could make a point of connecting students with other folks to complete the advising support. The set of advising tasks remains the same, no matter the style or preference of the faculty advisor with whom they work most closely. For a program or department, that translates into the notion that "it takes a village" to support a successful mid-career student.

Who constitutes the village? Folks who can assist with intellectual guidance and career connections; who can serve as role models, sponsors, and institutional advocates; and some who can provide support as the student makes a substantial personal and professional transformation. They may be other program or departmental faculty, as Golde and his colleagues suggests with their model of team advising (Golde et al., 2009), faculty elsewhere in the university, members of the student cohort, administrators carrying responsibilities in areas related to student interests, student affairs professionals, or members of a local professional community. It is unrealistic to expect a single individual to play all these roles; it is equally unrealistic to expect student to succeed without these resources.

Students could use the grid in a similar manner, to assess the types of support they might want from an academic advisor. Those with strong family, friendship, or professional networks might work very well with faculty who fit somewhere in the Driver arena. Others might feel the need to connect in different ways.

Research and participant experience indicates that the choice of advisor is central to doctoral success. However, individual doctoral students display the same range of characteristics as do faculty, for example, introvert or extrovert, task or people oriented, and not all faculty share the skill sets of Enablers or Mentors. So once enrolled in doctoral study, or perhaps even at an interview with faculty, students need to consider carefully the mode of advising that would serve them best. For example, a student with strong people orientation might work well with an advisor with a strong content or procedural orientation, such as a Driver or Enabler, bearing in mind that the kind of support a Hugger might provide could be sought informally. Alternatively, this same person might work well with a Hugger, but make sure to find those who can provide the full range of intellectual guidance and procedural information that will be essential to making timely progress. Faculty teaching pertinent courses or on a graduate studies committee can play this role, as can student affairs professionals in the department.

As Jaime said so clearly, "The mentors I've had, professional experiences of my assistantships, and collegial relationships I formed all contributed to my professional and personal identity coming out of the program on the other side." Taking the initiative to get to know other departmental faculty and students in the department and to reach out to administrators and faculty in the university community whose responsibilities seem consistent with individual life experience or career goals will be fundamental to success as a doctoral student and emerging professional. The key message for current or aspiring doctoral students is to be prepared to take the initiative to seek out these resources, and to put together an effective support team.

Part IV

The Never-Ending Journey

"Finishing the Journey" was the title of this part in the draft manuscript for the book. After writing chapter 8, I realized that would have been a serious misnomer. As you will see in the following chapters, completing the doctorate was the first step toward the "next phase" in the lives of the participants. Their perspectives about the transformations are presented in chapter 9.

The process of learning and developing is, of course, not unique to doctoral students, and that is the subject of chapter 10. There we will explore the connections between the mid-career doctoral experience and human development theories related to life transitions and culture shock. While this book is structured differently from research articles and for a much wider audience than doctoral students and faculty, it is research based and more insights can be extracted from the experiences of these individuals by comparing and relating them to a few well-known models and theory.

In the last chapter I will offer my own reflections about mid-career students, advising, and my role as a faculty advisor.

Chapter Nine

Transformations

Once I completed this doctorate—I don't say this out loud very often—but I honestly feel I never had to explain anything to anybody again or prove myself. Explain in the sense of proving myself. I have met that particular challenge which to me was the highest academic challenge I could meet. So I have never retired, but I resigned from higher ed. . . . But it's easy for me to say I'm having the time of my life because I don't have to prove anything to anybody anymore. The doctorate is, well, besides all that I learned, it opens doors sometimes to do other things.

—Tina

My identity changed as a result of the program and what I was learning. I came into the doctoral program an athletic trainer, and I left an educator. I still feel this way; I feel as if I am a substantial voice in terms of educational preparation, curricular design, and clinical preparation for athletic trainers as opposed to being strictly a clinician.

—Laura

For me, it totally, completely altered how I viewed the world, and unlike any other educational experience I've been through.

—Carole

Personal growth, professional development, and new intellectual perspectives resulted from their doctoral studies according to Tina, Laura, Carole, and the others. The experience was life altering for all of them. Six found themselves in exciting new situations that could not have been anticipated. Nine now hold positions of substantially greater responsibility and influence within their original fields. Each quest was profound; many were similar, and some are still in process. In fact, we might say that all are still in process because every single participant gained new ways of observing, questioning, and understanding the world. This skill or perspective of "deconstruction" always leads to new questions and ideas. So, in the truest sense of the phrase, the participants learned how to learn deeply.

The transformation was a process that began as early as the first quarter of the program for some, like Laura, who said earlier, "I quit fighting the identity and who I was previous. If I'm going to be successful in this, I've got to change who I am and change my identity." Seth, Kelly, and Brad, as you recall, described the painful transition to the student role. While each person traveled a different path because of family and job circumstances, there were many commonalities and similarities. At the most basic level, everyone experienced intellectual changes. For most, these translated into changes that helped them improve as professionals. And for many, the impacts altered fundamental beliefs and identity. In the Sunday morning conversation, folks also identified "reentry" as an explicit period with issues that arose when they had their degrees in hand and no longer had to make time for course work, dissertation research and writing. So we will explore the nature of the changes, finishing with reentry.

VARIATIONS ON THE THEME

Intellectual Socialization

Intellectual changes ranged from learning new skills, such as Jaime's delight at discovering qualitative inquiry, to exploring new philosophical lenses, like deconstruction. Brian described his new way of approaching issues, always asking "why we do things." Other people, he feels,

> they jump to conclusions—even some of my colleagues, in terms of how they respond to situations or . . . student crises or policy decisions. I think the process of going through a dissertation and a doctoral program in general, has really caused me to sort of stop and take a minute to absorb all sorts of facts. I'm usually the one who asks tougher questions, I would say, in our staff meetings, more critical about what we're doing and why we're doing it as opposed to a lot of my colleagues who, I think, sometimes just look for what this is or what's most practical and go with that.

Kathy called the process

> intellectual socialization . . . learning how to think critically and to evaluate things to really become an intellectual. . . . There are times when I can tell, working with people, those who have had the opportunity to engage in this intellectual endeavor and those who haven't. . . . And whether they've actually earned the doctorate or not, it's the fact that they've engaged in that environment and the kinds of ideas, and what they can bring to the table is very different . . . when they have had the opportunities that we had to engage in this—I guess I'd call it intellectual lifestyle.

Socialization is often used to connote socialization to a professional work environment. More than half the participants used the term to mean socialization to the intellectual milieu of higher education. As mid-career professionals, they did not have to "grapple with" socialization to work environments, to use Kathy's words. As Ben said, "The mid-career folks have developed this sense of professional identity." Polly, Ben, and Olivia talked about getting "back into the intellectual community and ways of thinking and ways of interacting," "figuring out some of the norms of that intellectual side of socialization," and "learning the jargon and the mores of the institution" that were fundamental to professional progress in an academic setting.

Learning how to think for themselves, deciding whether or not to agree with the professor, and then backing up their thoughts with evidence required a whole different mind-set, according to Davida. It was about synthesizing material, not just reading it. Carole echoed Davida, saying, "When I got into this level of courses, I quickly figured out that I was going to have to approach this totally differently than I had ever approach any course work, and that included my master's program."

Styles of Perception and Judgment

Carole and Brian then explained in some detail how the demands for analysis, and interpretation not only broadened and improved their analytic abilities but also altered their profiles on the well-known Myers and Briggs Type Indicator (MBTI) personality inventory (Myers and Briggs Foundation, n.d.). Carole extended her strong concrete, realistic modality into a more interpretive, connective mode, and Brian increased his comfort with decisiveness. For those who use MBTI regularly, understanding "type" becomes a useful language, and also part of identity; that is, it provides a shorthand description of preferences in the way people use perceptions and judgment. Their changing scores (behavior), prompted both Carole and Brian to revise self-images and identity.

Career Trajectories

Most folks entertaining the idea of a doctoral program anticipate a result that would enhance and accelerate their career trajectory. Among this group, nine remained in their original fields: Emily, Brad, Brian, Kathy, Laura, Polly, Stephanie, Jaime, and Davida. For those like Laura, the results were realized, and satisfying.

> The most exciting change is the opportunity to improve yourself. I was a good teacher/educator prior to entering the doctoral program, but the theories and tools that I learned and acquired while in the program made me an excellent teacher/educator. There is not one day that goes by in my current career as the director of clinical education and associate professor that I do not use something that I learned in my doctoral program.

For those remaining in the same career but seeking new jobs, satisfaction was hardly immediate. At the time of these conversations (summer 2010) Davida was frustrated professionally, as her expectations had not been met.

> I'm at a point where I don't think I have felt the effects of the PhD yet, in terms of my occupational trajectory. . . . On a day-to-day basis, it is quite frustrating because my thought was, I would get the PhD, perhaps find a position that would allow me to teach and do administrative work at the same time. It would put me sort of on the fast track towards the vice presidency and that hasn't happened. . . . When I was doing all the job searching last year, I mean, I really, oftentimes, every time I got a rejection letter, it's like, "Hmmm, I've done everything I was asked to do and it's not falling into place," and I know the economy has a lot to do with it. It's just not five people competing for one associate or assistant vice presidency of student affairs, it's like hundreds.

Both she and Seth (who changed careers) entered the job market just as the recession hit.

The stock market collapse decimated the retirement savings of many faculty and administrators in higher education. So, instead of finding a wide array of job offerings resulting from the retirement of Baby Boomers, Davida and Seth found themselves in a very competitive market where experienced professionals were applying along with recent graduates for the few positions that were advertised. Only in 2012, did the job market begin to open up again. And, Davida now directs a center in her field.

Six members of the group found themselves in new situations: Ben, Kelly, Carole, Tina, Olivia, and Seth. Ben's career took "a different course from what I had expected. I became very passionate about international education, as I told you all, about Japan, and was foreign student adviser and saw an opportunity at Columbus State and shifted to working in community colleges, and now it's become my passion, my love. Career technical education, in particular, is a real area of interest, so we'll see where it takes [me]." He expressed excitement about the change, and has since moved into STEM-related educational projects. [1]

Kelly expressed a similar level of excitement when she described her job as a senior administrator in a large land-grant university. Her first appointment involved a three-year contract focused on handling the types of program assessment prompted by changes in accreditation.

It was probably about a year and a half later that my three-year contract turned into sort of an ongoing contract, but I'm responsible for accreditation at institutional levels, so I kind of worked for all that stuff, the regional accreditations. . . . I work with departments and programs that are programmatically accredited, so like we don't have a pharmacy school, which if we did, I'd be working with them. Assessment is all about that, and the accrediting agencies only want those who bear that interest. Then we started program review a couple years ago. It just made so much sense to pull all of those things together because all three of those things really sort of force areas to ask a set of questions about what it is that they do. How long do they do it? Why do they do it? What would happen if you just stopped doing it tomorrow? You know, what's the impact in having it?

So that's really—that's my title. I also kind of think I'm the director of all things that need to be done. . . . Yeah. But you know it's okay. It keeps life very interesting, and I love my job. I absolute love it. I firmly believe I could not do it and would not have it if I didn't have this doctorate.

Careers and Professional Identity

For several participants, career change deeply affected self-image and identity. Carole ended up on an entirely different career path, and the repercussions of the change were earthshaking for her.

I, in fact, made a de facto career change and wasn't planning on doing it. So, . . . for me there was a huge loss and I had to go through kind of a whole grief process of really losing my dream of what and why I was even at [this university] because I'd brought that dream with me and I was going to continue to grow in that particular field. And that didn't happen. So, of course, I had no idea that ultimately I would find a new identity and if you had told me that I would at the time, I would have laughed because I would never have conceptualized myself as having a different identity. And the fact that I was going through that whole process and then creating a new one was unexpected.

I had a very preconceived idea of what higher ed. would look like for me and it's ended up evolving into something very, very, very different. . . . It was a torturous journey it seemed at times. And it would have just been so much easier if I had known, like, "Oh, by the way, you're going to spend your whole next decade as a consultant." I didn't ever even conceptualize myself as a consultant. That had just never entered my psyche, because there was just one way and that was inside the institution, and being an integral part of a higher ed. student services team.

There was some discussion about the reasons professional change extended into deeper personal changes. Was it the result of the length of time the student spent in the program? Or was it a matter of age? For those like Tina, Emily, Ben, Stephanie, and Davida, who spent more than the average five years, there was more opportunity to digest intellectual and professional insights and to generate personal change.

Tina spent the longest time in the program and among the participants was also the oldest when she enrolled. Because she held a full-time faculty position at a local college, the number of courses she could take in a quarter was limited, and serious writing was accomplished in three successive summers when she was not teaching. Hers was a radical career shift. She first commented on her situation in her reflection paper. When I invited everyone to participate in this project, the project title was "Beginning Again in the Middle." In her reflection, Tina wrote: "The title of this project for my experience might better be expressed as 'Beginning Again Near the End; And Now I Can't See the End.'"

After obtaining her degree, Tina left her institution and started a consultancy and program for "third age" people at the local community college. She now heads a center offering outreach programs for the community, space for group retreats, and an art gallery. She still maintains the consultancy working with older adult programming. She voiced her thoughts about the process in these terms:

When I started the program, my [early] objectives were career based, to become a dean of adult programs, but because I was at it for so long and because things just changed, I changed, I guess. It became more of a personal journey. . . . By the time I finished it was a very personal—well, outcome. . . . So I speak about it differently maybe. I'm attributing it to age and stage. Maybe that's not the factor.

Well, the fact that it resulted in such a radical change in my life. The fact that, to this day, I have not had an income comparable to the one I left in 2002 in order to pursue the path where my heart was taking me. I mean I've been fine with that, but just the whole total change of how I wanted to proceed with the doctorate, and the people I've wanted to somehow impact or help them achieve their goals and thereby impact them.

Brad, younger than Tina by two decades, and whose doctorate enabled him to take a senior administrative role in his field, disagreed that it was a matter of age, saying that he, too, felt personal changes.

Well, it seems as though we were something close to consensus yesterday that there was a career decision to start, but I wonder—I mean certainly this on my part was personal as well. . . . One of the themes by which you would achieve success in this, perhaps, is by internalizing it and saying, "This is what happened, and this is my product." I'm not sure about the age—you know, I think we all had to take it on in our own away.

When I followed up by asking whether age was the key factor, both Jaime and Seth, who are about five years younger than Brad, said, "I don't know about that." And Polly, who was closer in age to Tina when she enrolled, had advanced along her same career trajectory.

I was forty-two when I started the program in 1995, so you know I'm around the same age group that you're talking about, but I didn't do a career half-change; I enhanced my career up the ladder upon completion. Although, of course, I had to internalize the programs and had a lot of struggles and hanging on to it and moving forward, but it just came out different. I don't know if age is a determinant in terms of your outcome of totally switching focus of career. I think that that's probably something within where you were traveling anyhow.

Personal Change

People spoke of a variety of personal changes, from new perspectives to entirely new family situations to reframing personal identity. Emily certainly exemplified one of the most difficult changes. "I think my perspective changed throughout the journey because I was the one who started there and ended up divorced." Laura felt much more "in the here and now."

I will have to say that in terms of life journey, like when you think about some of the outcomes of this, I think I'm much more in the moment now, having spent so much time not in the moment. Now that I have an opportunity, I'm much more in the moment. . . . I feel like I'm much more in the moment, because this opportunity to not be in the moment gave me more appreciation for that now.

Much later, nine years after finishing the program, Laura, too, was divorced, and attributes some of the cause to dynamics that were a by-product of her doctoral experience. Would she have changed her experience?

At the end outcome we have to weigh it. What things wouldn't we change, and I can certainly look at it and say there's far more things that I did in the program that I would not change if I could go back and do it differently. There are one to two things I would approach differently. I think that's the positive outcome, and despite all the struggles and all the things we encountered, when you look back and reflect, there's very little you would change. We talk about this so frequently. That on a given day the stuff that we use, the theories, we use it every day with students. This has been probably the thing that I utilized; this has been a very valuable degree. Not just on the piece of paper but what I learned. The knowledge has been very, very valuable.

Ben had raised the question of personal identity when the group first constructed the Venn diagram (figure 8.3), calling it the "internal makeup of the individual." At the time he raised it, I shied away from incorporating it into the diagram because to me it seemed a domain that could not, and perhaps should not, be the responsibility of an advisor or mentor. However, the group insisted on including it because it represented a domain impacted by doctoral study.

Among the group, Carole is probably the poster child for radical personal change, prompted by exposure to new ideas and analytic frameworks. Far more than her MBTI type was altered.

> I am so profoundly a different person because of the experience. . . . I felt very grounded when I started the program and I had a very naive assumption that . . . I really wasn't going to be particularly impacted by the experience. . . . What I underestimated was that I was actually personally going to be impacted. . . . I really had to totally unpack my entire belief system. And then I'm going to repack it back together and was there any, anything of the original parts of me even there? . . . moving forward . . . I started to see a broadening between me and my social group, the people that I had known and interacted with for decades. And I could see that I was the one doing all the shifting in this process and everybody else was staying sort of in the same place.

We asked her to "give an example of something she might have thought before, and something she thinks afterwards." Carole chose to tell us about the way her views of women and work changed.

> Probably this area that immediately came to mind was probably how I viewed women and work. And I came in probably angry at some level and that, actually, that is a lot of energy that got me through five years because I had—I was working in a private system, in a nonprofit and it was a very heavy patriarchal system and I'd been pushing against this glass ceiling for many, many, many years, and so I had all of this—whatever—about that and I became convinced that if I were going to have a seat at the table I had to have some big guns, and to do that, I need to get more credential. If my voice was ever going to be heard, I needed to do something to bring some credibility to my voice and so as I'm starting to move through this process and, of course, I'm still within that same system, I am starting to become much more of an active voice.
>
> And, but yet it was still angry. That's the part, when I look back, I'm kind of chagrined about. It's like, "Oh my, I should have been a little less." So, but then coming through the whole process, then—a lot of my research was around women and work and there's still—even when I go back and I read my dissertation I'm like, "Oh my goodness, I was still angry. Whoa." I mean, I could just see all this in my writing like I had this point to prove.
>
> And what I'm finding ten years later is that actually a lot of the issues are much more universal. They're not just—I was seeing it through such a huge gender lens and it was myopic and that coming out on the other side of it now, I don't know, yeah, I think that I, that it opened up a whole new vista and I'm a lot more broader. I'm so much more inclusive; I'm so much more willing to embrace another viewpoint than I was then. Does that make sense? So women and work, it, that, I would say that I definitely shifted my view. I'm not—the angry voice is gone. It is replaced now by a much more inclusive voice, understanding it is complex for all of us.

The Period of Adjustment

Carole's time frame for fully digesting and integrating her "new self," constructed piece by piece from the perspectives gained during the program, was about fifteen years, that is, five years in the doctoral program, and the ten years since. What about those who graduated more recently? Brian, who graduated three years prior to the conversation, felt that "in some ways, I'm still figuring out how it changed me." During the job search, he discovered that his PhD made him appear overqualified for some positions that appeared to be a logical next step. "Fortunately for me, I found an institution where, you know, they kind of took a different approach and they valued the fact . . . wanted to hire a staff of people who have the motivation and drive to pursue something like that."

Davida, an even more recent graduate, shared her feeling.

> Okay. I mean, I would echo some of the same sentiments. I think I'm almost soon to be two years out from the program and so I think for me, I am, like I said earlier, still trying to find my way. So I would say I'm probably still a work in progress and evolving. I often catch myself when people say, Dr. [last name], I pause for a minute and look around and think, "Who are they talking to?" And then I think, "Oh it's me, right." And so, you know, that whole notion of credibility and credentials and that automatic assumption that I am somebody, so respect me. I'm not there yet . . . and I'm not sure when it will happen and when I'm completely at ease with what I have accomplished. . . . I'm not sure, when that will come.

Remembering the dramatic analogy she used when talking about completing her dissertation, I asked: "Davida, that's a particularly interesting comment to me because a few minutes ago you were talking about slaying the beast and that you were going to finish the dissertation. So did that not, in fact, give you a sense of confidence in your ability to do something incredibly complicated?"

> Yeah. Yeah, I killed the beast by—but that doubt monster, I don't think ever goes away. And I mean, I see that sometimes in my own professional decisions, you know, it's almost like I still have this sense that I've got to prove myself and show that I belong here and what I'm adding is of some value and that I'm not just talking off the surface of my brain. That, you know, if I'm going to come, I'm going to come correct. I'm going to come with the research. I'm going to come with the evidence. I'm going to come with showing you this is how someone else has done it. And that people understand that I had something here, you know, I had something to bring to the table.
>
> I don't think that monster will ever go away. But again, that's why I say I think I'm still a work in progress, still ever evolving.

While many recent graduates tell of situations where they fail to respond to their name preceded by the "Dr.," Davida's example brings to mind the "Imposter Syndrome." First researched by Clance and Imes (1978), it refers to the lack of confidence that can affect performance. They uncovered these feelings in research on high-achieving women. Summarized in a nutshell, very capable and competent women in senior positions still worry that someone might discover that they are actually incompetent imposters. Curiously, Carole voiced much the same sentiment a while later in the conversation,

> I was just going to say that. I was going to say . . . I just kept thinking over and over and over, "Oh, here's the imposter syndrome and here's what I experience all the time and it's the oddest sensation." Actually by the time, you know, I finished my PhD, I put more pressure on myself. When I walk into a room and now it's Dr. [Carole] walking into the room or it's Carole [name], PhD, and I've got to start presenting. I put, I quadrupled the pressure on myself because I had completed it. And yet, I had this sense for a long, long time—in fact, you put me in the right situation I still, it's

like, "Oh my goodness, if you really knew and if I talk for one more minute, I will have told you everything I know on this topic and no, I don't know it all." And so, professionally I've actually found that I, I really tangled, and it's interesting because I talk about the imposter syndrome in my research and yet, I can't get away from it. It's like this little thing. It's in the back of my head and it's like it, it's like everywhere I go, it's like every time I get up I've got to prove again that, yes, I—it's, you know, I have legitimacy, I have, you know, to be up here and to be talking and using my voice and giving my voice and, you know, I don't know if that is a giant that I will ever, you know, totally slay.

But, and of course, in the literature they talk about—and I'd be really interested to see Brian's perspective, they actually use that solely in terms of women. So I don't know if that's true for other individuals with that dealing with and describing it as this sense of being an imposter and you're going to find out that I don't know nearly as much as you think that I know. But I start[ed] using this mantra, "Fake it 'til you make it." And, I've done so much consulting inside of organizations and it's like, I'm just making this stuff up. I'm like, "You have no idea that I have no idea what the hell I'm talking about but I'm going to go for it." . . . If you're that confident, well they're going to believe that you know what you're talking about, and when you really don't.

Seth's comment in chapter 4, about attending an academic conference (ASHE), and feeling like an academic fraud suggests the imposter syndrome may apply to neophytes of both genders! Brian, too, felt pressure to live up to standards that seemed undeserved.

I, too, have felt times where, because I have "comma PhD" after my name, there's a higher expectation in terms of what I contribute to conversations or what I bring to the table. . . . I think a lot of the times my colleagues and peers—how do I say this? Let me give you an example maybe. The dean of the undergraduate students, he's an associate provost, he is a faculty member but is an administrator now and he will not give any credence to anybody that comes into his office unless they have "comma PhD" after their name. And so a lot of the times when there are initiatives in student affairs that they want to see go through, they tag me along because for some reason they think, as I'm part of that PhD club, if you will, that their cause will be advanced . . . probably the biggest . . . example I could use of times where I felt like, "Wow, this PhD really is preceding me and setting a higher bar than I feel like I deserve."

So we are left with an open question about the characteristics or circumstances that result in these feelings. Considering the comments at the beginning of the chapter, we might conclude that age or experience makes a difference. However, neither Tina, Polly, nor Kelly mentioned these feelings. On the other hand, Carole was among the oldest of the students and Brian and Davida were in the middle of the age range. Whatever the source—age, gender, discontinuity in personal identity, expectations of others—their feelings were distinct, and had provoked reflection long before this conversation.

REENTRY

In the months leading to graduation those who enrolled in full time doctoral study are in the middle of an intense emotional roller coaster as they send out application letters, request references, respond to telephone interviews, and interact with potential employers on-site about jobs. Those who continued working during the program are considering how best to use their new skills and new credential. Carole described her process.

Upon completion of my program, I evaluated my options, and initially wanted to pursue opportunities in higher education, all of which were out of state. However, with family considerations and my spouse's business, I came to the conclusion relocation was not an option. At this critical juncture, I hired the services of a career coach to facilitate a career change to private business and industry. Little did I realize, the company whose services I engaged was delivering career management services in a retail setting that were closely aligned with my research area. When we discovered the synergy, I accepted the offer to join their team and left higher education. As I developed my consulting practice and moved into a train-the-trainer position, I began to connect the dots in significant ways and develop my unique philosophy and approach to career decision making, career development, career transition, and talent management based on a plethora of influences— my training, my research, and my personal experience. Today as a career management consultant, my personal journey and transformation is a significant strength and element I bring to my role as a career coach and talent management consultant.

With all of this activity alongside the final stages of dissertation writing, the intensity of the doctoral experience reaches a real crescendo during the last four months. Finally the dissertation is defended, revised, and submitted, graduation comes and goes, and it is time to rejoin the "rest of the world." More than half the participants referred to a period of time following completion of the program as "reentry," and the picture they painted vibrated with a sense of unease that Brad and Ben called "the new normal." "Yeah, my wife and I have been married for almost thirteen and a half years. Eight and half of those I was in grad school. So, you know," said Ben.

The "new normal" signals the personal changes that have occurred for the students, now graduated, their partners and/or children. As we have already seen, the participants were different when they finished from when they began. While they were students, mentally and physically, absent—in class, writing papers, meeting with research groups, advisors and working on dissertation, partners were not only taking care of living arrangements and children, but they, too, were growing and changing as a natural part of adulthood. Some were intentional about figuring out how to best use the available time to find new interests, or new ways of earning money. And, of course, children who might be part of the family were also growing and developing. Laura offered this unhappy comment.

> Now that I have finished my doctoral program, it has been a continual struggle to get my husband to create time for us. He adapted to my schedule during the doctoral program by doing home improvement projects for us and others. This was a great way to give me uninterrupted time while I was a student, but now I struggle to get him to say "no" to friends' requests for him to come over and do home improvement. I am having difficulty getting our family to slow down and readjust to a less chaotic schedule.

Olivia picked up her point immediately. "And how do you go back—to, like, I feel like I'm two years out, and I still don't know how to go like back to normal. When I was reading yours [reflection paper], I was like God dammit, how many years ahead of me is she, and her life is not back to normal yet! [Laughter.] I was mad when I read that."

Laura continued, "So I can't get him to readjust. I'm slowing down. I can't get him to slow down with me. So I never felt that that would affect him as—you know we're in it. I felt, yeah I'll be the one. . . . It will be hard for me to slow down and take some time. It's affected him equally."

You may recall Brad pointing out his "negotiation" with his wife. Once she completed her master's program, it was the green light for Brad to start his doctoral program. They made an agreement to swap incomes. Now, he says, "We've reverted to slightly more typical roles, but there is still this sense in our household that you took those five years out, and so you owe me X number of years of this. I mean that's okay, that's how we approached the problem."

The reentry discussion took place on Sunday morning. Saturday evening, the group had dinner together, and there was lots of time for one-on-one conversations that were not recorded. Laura related her conversation with Olivia.

> Olivia and I talked about this last night, too, and it's a part we haven't talked about. What makes this different is this comes to an end, and then you have to reintegrate with each other in a normal schedule. I wrote about it in my reflection paper, and Olivia was telling me how depressed she was that ten years later, we are still struggling with "quit taking overtime. Quit taking the job that takes you two states away. We don't need that now. I have an income." I think that's something that's different too. There comes a point where this ends, and you have to reintegrate back to a point where that is not all consuming in your life.

Kathy, too, was clear about the challenge, "Yeah, I had more trouble with reentry than I did with the period of the dissertation." When asked whether she meant reentry into the job, or to the relationship, she clarified.

> Reentry into life after dissertation. Because I had met my husband two weeks before I started in pharmacy, and then we got married two weeks before I started in here. So he had only ever known me as a student, and this other part of my life. He had a very, very—we met when we were both older and established, and he has a very satisfying hobby or second career, if you will. He flourished in that because he had all this extra time. Then when I came back and said, "Okay it's time for us," and he was really hitting that point where he was becoming very successful in this second career that he had.
>
> So we had a little bit of readjustment to, "What do you mean you have six games this weekend to officiate? I have time to spend with you." That was difficult for me, but we have finally figured that out, and I have now a second sort of hobby thing that I do, too and we share in that. I go to games, and he comes to concerts, and we figured it out. But that was harder for me.

Carole had always been concerned about the impact of her studies on her relationship with her husband. Sunday morning, she added, "I think to your point that reintegration is like 'Okay I'm done now. And now what? What does that mean for us moving forward? How do we integrate this new me, because I am very different than when we started this journey?' there was a sense of how do you bring all that together."

In the midst of this animated and heartfelt expression of frustration, Kathy realized that someone had said, "It's like being incarcerated." The cross-talk for the next ten minutes was so animated, we never did figure out who said it first. Laura then followed, "And you're released back into the population." [Group Laughter.] To which Brad adds, "Orange jumpsuits on." And after more cross-talk, Laura finishes, "And they wonder which percentage of us wants to go right back into incarceration the minute we're in the real world!"

Coming back to Laura's point about slowing down, Emily added, "I put myself having another different kind of sense of guilt. Before it was guilt for not writing, and then it was guilt for I should be . . . doing something. I said, 'You don't have to be doing something.'" In the cross-talk that followed, someone said, "I thought that kind of guilt would go away and it should have been freeing but I was so used to feeling guilty." Followed by, "Absolutely, yeah."

"Yeah," Kathy echoed, like an "amen." Carole remembered that "it took me about three years to recover and to really start to feel like I had, I don't know, like I was getting back to some sense of normal and not this inner urge that I should be doing something, I ought to be writing tonight, type of thing."

While incarceration was one analogy, Davida offered a second that sounded more like recovery from addiction or dependence.

On the time afterwards, that you feel overwhelmed, glad you're done and then I think there's a process of withdrawal, like you've been doing this for many, many years and then all of a sudden, your life switches. And then for me, at least, I began to process what the previous seven years of my life had been like and then trying to think about what the next seven years will be.

The participants described the doctoral experience as a process with an entry point, a honeymoon period, followed by lots of hard work leading to completion, and then withdrawal and need to process. As he listened, having completed his research about faculty retirement only a few months earlier, Seth found a parallel to models of transition that incorporate stages of departure, redefinition, and reengagement. Like retiring faculty, upon graduation the students "departed" the role of doctoral student, then went through a period of redefining themselves as they anticipated moving back into full-time work and lives, and reengaging into relationships and rhythms. We will come back to these points in chapter 10.

SUCCESS FACTORS

As the time to close the discussion approached, it seemed appropriate to ask the participants their advice for those considering enrollment in a doctoral program. Could they identify the factors that either helped them be successful, or that they felt would be critical for success? I was bringing the conversation back around to the question faculty are so often asked in application interviews: What makes a successful doctoral student? Their answers covered a range of topics.

Both Carole and Ben highlighted three points: (1) identifying a doctoral program that has a schedule, (2) faculty who are sufficiently flexible to accommodate a student working full-time, and (3) finding ways to relate the doctoral coursework and research to the work setting. Ben began, weaving several points together.

The key is to always relate what you are learning to your work and vice versa. They feed each other and excite in both contexts. One of the most critical things is to identify a doctoral program that will work with you working full-time. I was fortunate to work at [this university] while pursuing my doctoral coursework. It never would have worked at [the community college where I work now], in that people are not allowed to take classes when they are scheduled to work. I was fortunate to begin my position at [the community college] my last quarter of course work.

And Carole continued with emphasis on the third point, "One of the biggest benefits of working full-time was the synergy between my work with students and my own awakening and discovery process and experience." Olivia's comment about being very intentional about making those connections was reported earlier. And the coursework and research for Polly served as the training for her new administrative position, dean of a division.

Once I was settled and working toward my research area, what I was reading and studying correlated with the new administrative job role I was growing into at work. Because there was no orientation of any kind for my job, the pieces I was lacking were knowledge about leadership, organizational change, higher education legal issues, decision making, etcetera. . . . I needed to know how to be an academic leader and this marriage of study and work was making that happen for me.

The work setting can represent an advantage rather than a disadvantage. It presents a laboratory where either through observation or hands-on trying out a new way of advising or presenting or analyzing a political situation, the working student can test out the value of theories and models and more fully internalize those critical thinking skills. In those settings, the student learns about the power of these tools, and selects those that seem most effective and useful.

Brad focused on the need for planning. "Given what you know now, and obviously things change, people have accidents, and we can't control all of that stuff, but you need to be thoughtful on the front end about how this is going to work and what you're going to give up. That's part of this process—and understand that you will be giving up." Planning, looking ahead a year or more, to schedule the large blocks of time that would be essential for focusing on writing the dissertation proposal, the candidacy exam, and later, the analytic chapters of the dissertation was one of the most important of the success factors.

Kathy reiterated the importance of the choice she made "to go to a 50 percent position. I don't think I'd be sitting here today because I don't think for me, I would have been able to finish without having taken my work requirements to a more manageable level so I had the intellectual time to write." Polly, who had to negotiate writing time with her dean, followed up. "Earlier knowledge, that is important, because had I known earlier in the process that I was actually going to take the time, I needed to take the time to do this, I would have applied for a sabbatical. But not figuring that out until closer to the time frame, I was past the sabbatical application date so couldn't do that. So I had to figure out another way to garner time." Her comment reminded everyone about the enormous challenge finding time to write presented.

Every one of the participants rearranged work schedules to free up blocks of time. For Kathy it meant reducing her work appointment from full, to half-time. Stephanie and Polly negotiated with supervisors to use vacation time for an initial large block of one or two weeks, followed by three or four long, four-day weekends. Tina used summers. Olivia got up at 4:30 in the morning, a lot. Ben worked at night after the children were in bed. Seth, Kelly, Jaime, and Davida held assistantships. Carole, Brian, Emily, and Laura muscled the time somehow out of their work schedules. Faced with a daunting writing schedule Brian learned "that you have to be independent, and find a way to create structure" for managing time. "Self-discipline" was another word that surfaced. Davida extended both thoughts.

> I would agree. I think along with that self-discipline that you have to be able to persevere. You have to have something that motivates you and keeps you focused. You have to have structure. This process will drive you crazy, if you can't set deadlines and meet them. You have to negotiate the "time" you spend, researching, crafting and writing. You have to have some type of control over the process or it will get out of hand. And, you have to be willing to ask for help. . . . If you're not open to letting somebody else with, again, that credibility and sense of respect to look at your work and review it and offer constructive criticism, then you aren't going to be successful. . . . If you're not into that whole team setting, a committee of folk who are part of the community of scholars trying to guide you, then, no, you're not going to be successful after the core requirement."

Ben's comments took the point about "asking for help" one step further. Prompted by a comment Tina had made earlier, he focused on attitude and a willingness to learn.

> You talked about an openness that has to be inherent in the individual, and I wanted to make sure that we captured that because there has to be a sense for the individual that they have not yet arrived. There's not this—you know, they can't be coming in and just using this as something for utilitarian. "I'm going to get this because I need it, and then that's it." There has to be a sense that, "I want to learn. I want to become a student. I want to become that neophyte," if you will. Kelly talked about it kind of—she put it [as] the guru, but that idea that you have to be open to learning again and no longer being the authority, or no longer knowing it all.

Tina talked about Zen mind, beginner's mind. Now that I've accomplished this PhD, I feel like a student again in a different capacity now—like a lifelong student. There's more openness to learning. There's more openness to constantly expand it, and if you don't have that to start with, you're not going to succeed, and you're going to run into those walls that when you're given feedback, you're not going to know how to take it. But if you're open, and you have the trust and relationship with the giver of that feedback, then it can help you to overcome those hurdles in really positive ways and be able to realize your intellectual and professional potential. So I just wanted to bring that back, because I thought that was important.

Sometimes attitude translated into patience, as people remember classes that were, frankly, "boring," and situations where they learned to just "let it go" and not waste energy. In her own advising, when students ask her "what characteristics does a person need to be successful?" Kathy's insistence on perseverance was echoed immediately by others. "It's how bad you wanted it and how much you were willing to work for it that really made the difference; not how smart you are. I mean certainly there has to be some baseline level, obviously, but that's what the admissions process is for." Davida called this being "focused, really dedicated and committed." At another moment, she had said, "And so, it really is a test of endurance." Brian felt, "You need to be fully invested into it and realize the ramifications of what that decision will have on you professional and personally. I think that that passion needs to be there."

Carole used more colorful words that are worth repeating.

Well, I often tell people that you need to have a burning in your belly and you need, it can't—and it's the only way that you can quench the fire, because this is going to be a really, really, really tough experience. A very demanding experience and if there's any other way that you can have that fulfilled in your life, I recommend doing it. But, if you come to the conclusion that the only way to quench that fire is to put your feet to the test and move into a doctoral program, it will be a life-changing event. But you've got to really, really want it really, really down deep in who and what you are. I mean, I absolutely could not explain to anyone rationally why I was on the top of my game professionally, at a job that I loved, why I would subject myself to this experience. And I just kept saying, there's a bigger world out there and I, I've got to go there. . . . While there were external factors influencing me, it was the internal push that was the most compelling.

Several participants agreed emphatically with Carole's forceful statement about the choice of dissertation topic having a great bearing on a student's ability to stay focused and maintain momentum.

When it comes to research, pick a topic that you really, really, really like because you're going to be really, really, really sick and tired of it when you're done. But, you know, you have to pick something that . . . you feel strongly about because it's going to take a lot of energy to keep plodding and plodding and plodding through in ad nauseam. If I didn't feel strongly about my topic it would have been a lot tougher, I think, to stay the course.

Brian jumped in to agree immediately. "I personally chose something that I was very interested in, more just in terms of something that I found to be challenging as opposed to something that directly related to my professional goals or interests."

Why did Carole use such stark language about the topic and the research process? Dissertation research is no different than designing and implementing any complex project. Think about making a good-sized vegetable garden. If you don't love the idea of harvesting and eating your own vegetables, then the process of getting good soil, tilling it, choosing and planting the seedlings, weeding, watering, fertilizing, protecting the plants against pests, whether insects or chasing rabbits, day in and day out for several months, just won't be worth the effort. In fact, if you don't find that you love getting your hands dirty or listening to the birds, or watching the seedlings grow into larger plants, or just being outdoors, the whole process will get pretty tiresome. So it is with research.

Many steps are involved in conducting good research, beginning with learning how to do it. Research questions need to be crafted carefully, current literature searched for pertinent articles and books, those compared and analyzed for gaps and a methodology designed consistent with research goals and epistemology. If the research involves people, every university requires the submission of protocols for "human subjects review" of some type, which begins with certification as a principal investigator and then for each project, completing forms, submitting protocols and meeting university deadlines. Developing survey instruments is a multistep process, and human subjects reviews might be required at each step, such as exploratory interviews, the pilot survey, an expert review, as well as the final survey. Scheduling time and places for interviews or focus groups for qualitative research can be tedious and frustrating. There is humdrum and humbug, in every complex project, and success depends upon maintaining the motivation to keep going through less-than-creative tasks and procedures. Like the vegetable garden, payoff comes at harvest time, but motivation is sustained by enjoying the process itself. The end-of-project excitement comes from analyzing the data, learning the results, generating the insights, extending an existing theory, or coming up with an original model.

The list of success factors included choosing a program to accommodate the working student, being self-disciplined to create your own structure and deadlines, the passion and internal motivation to support perseverance, the willingness to learn and be open to feedback, finding a dissertation topic of great personal interest, and the foresight to plan for the intense periods of writing and research. The composite emerged as people reflected on fifteen highly individual experiences with doctoral study.

Common across these different experiences, was the great strength of each and every participant. At the outset of the conversation on Saturday morning, I asked each of the thirteen participants then present to introduce himself or herself by explaining when they graduated, their current professional position, and by sharing their reactions to the reflection papers which had been distributed to everyone earlier. Their comments about the reflection papers capture their appreciation of circumstances and qualities of their peers.

I think what struck me in reading the reflections was the adversity faced. I was just really awestruck at what some of you went through.

—Kathy

What struck me was the incredible strength that people have.

—Kelly

What struck me about the reflection papers—I just thought it was an incredible group of people that had so much courage who decided to wander off into something that was an unknown and really make themselves vulnerable.

—Carole

What struck me about the reflection papers, I think, yes the commonality of experience, yet the diversity. I think that one thing that I picked up from all of your stories was how this program broadened your horizons and gives you a different sense of appreciation.

—Olivia

It's just a tremendous growth experience personally for anybody doing it, and there's a lot of decisions to be made on what you're going to change or what you're going to hang onto and what you can do during that period of time. I just think that reading the reflection papers echoed that. Some of the stories in there were just tremendous.

—Polly

What struck me in the reflection papers was how so many comments that were made were the same, and so many comments were different. So we clearly all had some same comments, and I think that was the support and energy we had in being around our cohort and advisor, but also so many people had really very different experiences in this as well.

—Stephanie

When I opened up the other reflection papers and started reading, I thought, "Oh my goodness," you know. "This is really quite different" . . . so it was interesting to see—to realize how privileged I was, as it were to have the experience I had and not have those other life responsibilities that many of you all did, and so how that did flavor my experience and flavor yours as well.

—Brad

In looking at the reflection papers and the different stories that were completely different than mine, just looking at the database of what people put as their priorities. They were pretty much different than mine, so I thought that was really interesting.

—Seth

Some of the reflection papers I could have written myself. I mean some of them I was reading and thought I could have written a lot of what people said.

—Jaime

By the time we left at midday on Sunday, the group had achieved a sense of closure—the satisfaction of a job well done, recognized by others who had been there, too.

NOTE

1. STEM stands for Science, Technology, Engineering, and Math, and refers to a portfolio of educational programs designed to bring more students, and particularly girls and women, into these fields.

Chapter Ten

Broadening Perspectives

My reason for embarking on this research project was straightforward. I wanted to understand the mid-career doctoral experience from the inside—to learn how it differed from the experience of other doctoral students. I wanted to understand the phenomenon from the perspective of the students themselves.

Simply telling and organizing the stories achieves several of the purposes of the study. The first is to document the scope of the doctoral experience so that former or current doctoral students can compare it to their own and either take comfort in the recognition of similarities or examine the differences. Another is to present rich descriptions of a complex journey so that folks considering doctoral education can be better prepared for both the intellectual and emotional challenges. A third is to illuminate the black box for faculty and advisors so they have a better appreciation of the differences between mid-career students and younger students. There are significant differences between these folks and younger students moving straight through from masters to doctoral enrollment.

It is important to acknowledge, however, that the participants in this project represent a very specific population: students in higher education and student affairs, working with a single advisor in a single research institution. Neither the "sample" nor the research methodology typically support generalization per se (see the appendix for further discussion), nor is that the purpose of qualitative research on this scale. The questions we are left with are: How common is the experience of these graduates? Are their experiences unique to this field (education)? Or this university? Or this advisor? Without interviewing dozens or even hundreds more students and graduates at many institutions, we cannot answer these questions directly. Yet, for the reader, these are very important questions.

There are two strategies that we can use to test the possibility of extending this research to a broader population. The first is to compare the results of this study with the results of other studies about doctoral education. The second is to compare the results of this study with theories and models that have been validated with larger and more varied populations. If we find similarities, the simple mathematical principle of transitivity may allow us to extend the applicability of the results. We may be able to assume their experience to be more generally representative of the population of mid-career doctoral students in other fields and other institutions than might have been assumed from the sample size and methodology alone.

WHAT DID WE KNOW FROM PREVIOUS RESEARCH?

In preparation for the meetings, my research assistant Alycia and I reviewed a lot of the literature about doctoral students, and their success. However, I decided that presenting that information early in the conversation could skew the discussion toward "someone else's list of important topics" and chose to facilitate the conversation as it evolved through the late morning and early afternoon.

The conversation with participants in August began at 9:00AM on Saturday with an hour for introductions and another hour devoted to setting the agenda for the rest of the day and Sunday morning. I provided a thematic analysis of their reflection papers as input to the agenda-setting. Of the thirty-one topics culled from their papers, fourteen were mentioned by at least three people (20 percent of the group). Listed here from most to least frequently mentioned, the topics were:

1. knowing how to set priorities
2. finding time to write
3. fear
4. role of the cohort
5. having life experience to relate to theory
6. changes in your identity
7. finding time to study
8. family obligations
9. clarity of goals
10. becoming a "neophyte"
11. loss of income
12. impact of the dissertation
13. why and how we returned to grad school
14. life after PhD

As the agenda-setting conversation proceeded, the group chose a handful of topics for discussion from those fourteen, and added the role of the advisor, and the difference between advisor and mentor to that list. At that point, we took a break, and then launched into the discussion.

In early afternoon, I asked the participants if they would like to hear about some of the other research, and we presented the following list to them. The list was not intended as an exhaustive literature review, but rather to highlight results from some of the better-known authors. The author references are added here for completeness, but were not part of the original list we gave participants on Saturday. The italics added here indicate coincidence with participant experience. Previous research indicated the following:

1. Half or more of those who begin PhD programs, do not finish (Ehrenberg and Kuh, 2009; Lovitts, 2001; Nettles and Millett, 2006).
2. Much (if not most) of the research for the past fifteen years has focused on the reasons for this huge level of attrition (Ehrenberg, Zukerman, Groen, and Brucker, 2009; Ehrenberg and Kuh, 2009).
3. There is wide variation in completion rates by discipline (Gravois, 2007; Lovitts, 2001; Millett and Nettles, 2006; Nettles and Millett, 2006).
4. Departmental culture has an impact on student success (Anderson, 1996; de Valero, 2001; Gardner, 2008; Golde, 2005; Protivnak and Foss, 2009).
5. Institutional culture has an impact on student success (Tinto, 1993).

6. Students do better in collaborative departments (Anderson, 1996).

7. *Students need interaction with a faculty mentor, who might be someone other than the advisor (Patton, 2009).*

8. *Mentors in general (peers, faculty, professionals, people outside of the university) are important (Gardner, 2007, 2008, 2010; Golde, 2005; Nettles and Millett, 2006).*

9. *Many PhD students express ambiguity and confusion regarding the policies and practices of the department, institution, and discipline; this ambiguity and confusion leads to stress, frustration, lower satisfaction ratings, and lower persistence rates (Gardner, 2010; Golde, 2005).*

10. *The advisor is key in adding clarity to the process (de Valero, 2001; Gardner, 2010).*

11. *The advisor is also key for providing socio-emotional support, especially during the dissertation process (Golde and Dore, 2001; Paré, 2010; Tinto, 1993).*

12. Teaching assistantship (TA) and graduate research assistantship (GRA) positions help integrate students into the profession/department (Baird, 1972).

13. Students with GRA, TA, and fellowship appointments are much more likely to persist than students who are self-supported or are being supported by their families; this may be due to greater access to socialization experiences, peer and faculty mentors, opportunities for collaborative work, and/or financial support and tuition waivers (Ehrenberg and Mavros, 1995; Nettles and Millett, 2006).

14. The greater the level of integration, the more full the socialization (Gardner, 2008; Golde, 2000).

15. *There is a need for assistance and guidance regarding the writing of the dissertation (Golde and Dore, 2001).*

16. There is a need to help students figure out how to publish (Millett and Nettles, 2006; Nerad, 2004).

17. *There are more older students in education [and one other field] and they do just as well or better than younger students (Millett and Nettles, 2009; Nettles and Millett, 2006).*

18. Fewer than half the students are intending to go into faculty positions in many fields, such as education and engineering (Nerad, 2009).

19. *Many students cite the importance of peers for both socio-emotional and academic/intellectual support (Baird, 1969; Gardner, 2007, 2010).*

20. *In addition to faculty and peer support, outside sources of support (e.g., family, spouse, mentors) also seem to play a key role in encouraging students to persist (Gardner, 2007; Millett and Nettles, 2006).*

21. *Students who do not "fit the mold" of the traditional graduate student (e.g., older students, minorities, women, students with children, etc.) face a unique set of challenges and are more likely to leave their program of study before completing their degree than students who do "fit the mold" (Gardner, 2008).*

22. *Students with children take longer to finish than students without children (Ehrenberg and Mavros, 1995).*

23. Minorities and women face a unique set of challenges that may make them more "at risk" for attrition (Gardner, 2008; Johnson-Bailey, Valentine, Cervero, and Bowles, 2009; Nettles, 1990).

24. Most students cite a number of factors when discussing their decision to leave a PhD program; there seems to be no single overwhelming factor that leads to attrition; each individual has a unique set of factors and challenges that play a role in their decision to either leave or complete a program (Golde, 2000, 2005).

25. *Many PhD students express feeling lonely and isolated, and cite this as a major challenge to completing their degree (Gardner, 2008; Golde, 2005; Herman, 2010; Morrison-Saunders, Moore, Newsome, and Newsome, 2005; Tinto, 1993).*

The twelve italicized items relate to aspects of the doctoral experience that were identified by the participants in this study. Four items address the advisor or mentor relationships (7, 8, 10, and 11). Two point out the importance of peer and family support (20, 21). Three address sources of stress (9, 21, 22). Two others highlight the need for guidance with the dissertation (15) and the sense of isolation and loneliness (25). Notice that only three items on this list (17, 21, and 22) address the circumstances that describe mid-career students.

Very few of the more than eighty research-based articles and book chapters we read addressed mid-career students specifically. Gardner's 2007 and 2008 articles address issues of older students seeking to balance doctoral work with family responsibilities, mentioning feelings of guilt. Like this project, that research was interview based. Golde (2000) highlights the impact of unanticipated breaks in the program, caused by events such as an advisor leaving, and indicating that those breaks may lead to attrition. Five of the participants in this study—Olivia, Jaime, Brian, Tina, and Polly—overcame advisor departure, and sought out a different advisor. What was the source of their resilience? Evans (2010), Walker and Thompson (2010), Watts (2010), and Yates (2010) explore emotions and changes in identity experienced by part-time students, including those with family obligations. However, the realization that only a handful of researchers focused on the circumstances of mid-career students strengthened our collective resolve to focus on those differences.

How would I describe those differences now—after listening to the fifteen hours of conversation, and spending months reading and analyzing the transcripts? The essence of their experience is emotional intensity associated with a journey, a passage through complex personal and intellectual transformations.

MID-CAREER PARADOXES

Much of the emotional intensity associated with the mid-career experience as depicted by our participants seems to stem from contradictions inherent in the journey. The stories that emerged through the August weekend and later video conference present the mid-career doctoral journey as turbulent and full of apparent contradictions that challenge us to look deeper in order to fully understand these experiences. Situations that contain such contradictory or incompatible elements that are nevertheless found to be true are often called paradoxes (Demb and Neubauer, 1992, 5). Here are six of the paradoxes that seem most apparent to me.

Paradox 1: Experienced, Yet Intimidated

mid-career students come into the doctoral program with years of employment experience. In this group at the time of enrollment, previous work experience ranged from three to about sixteen years, when the students first enrolled. Polly, Kelly, and Carole held substantial administrative positions. Tina had been a professor for sixteen years. As a result, they, and perhaps the program faculty, held some expectation that these new doctoral students would "know what to do," or could take care of themselves in large measure. In fact, the role and setting were new to them. They knew neither the norms, rules, nor procedures in this new milieu and so found themselves ill at ease, and even intimidated. They were in serious need of substantial guidance.

Paradox 2: Savvy, Yet Vulnerable

mid-career students bring organizational savvy to their doctoral work. They grasp organizational structures and politics, which might make it easier to acclimate to the new setting. And, in some ways, it did for this group: they were aware of the power relationships among the faculty, knew how to scope them out, and were prepared to figure out the rules. However, that same knowledge also led to a greater appreciation of their very real dependence on their advisor and the faculty, their lack of status and position as the "low person on the totem pole." They felt undervalued, insulted when classes were boring, and vulnerable. Supervisors determined workload and time available for classes and writing; the department and its committees set rules regarding course sequences and hours; "graduate school" rules governed the definition of progress; and faculty were in charge of grades, framing candidacy exam questions, and approving dissertation proposals and research results.

Paradox 3: Neophytes, with Sophisticated Insights

mid-career students, like most new doctoral students, are typically research "neophytes" who need to learn how to frame questions and conduct research. Writing analytic papers may be new for them, likewise becoming comfortable critiquing published studies. They may fail to speak up in class and or be reluctant to criticize readings about theory and research in the first year of course work. Faculty might wonder about their capacity for critical thinking or analysis. However, their experience on the ground gives them insights about important problems that can generate potent and insightful research questions. Conducting research to address these questions in some cases requires truly sophisticated methods beyond the basic skills typical course work provides, and challenges faculty to help these students craft appropriate research designs.

Davida combined approaches from rhetoric, performance, and critical race theory in order to frame her research about African American women college presidents. She spent an entire year exploring these methodologies. Kathy developed a survey instrument to assess curricular outcomes and deployed it to both faculty and students in her college so that perspectives about learning outcomes could be compared. Olivia developed an original survey instrument about faculty engagement that generated the first database focused solely on those activities. Brian and Jaime focused on special subsets of the student population at opposite ends of the spectrum, students supported because of their academic record, and students on scholarship because of economic disadvantage. Kelly, Ben, and Brad followed different groups of students through year-long experiences that substantially extended their dissertation research timetables, as they interviewed students multiple times at different stages of their programs.

Paradox 4: Supported by Networks, Beset by Guilt and Pressure

mid-career students are often well embedded in work situations and may enjoy the comfort of family life. Those who remain employed benefit from the continuity of employment, income, and status associated with their positions. Evidence of professional value was clear to Tina, Emily, Polly, Kathy, Olivia, Carole, and Brian. Those with families benefitted from the emotional and practical support family members provided. Ben, Brad, Brian, Carole, Tina, Polly, Kathy, and Kelly were all assisted by committed partners. However, both job and family situations were the source of much guilt, pressure to make progress quickly, and envious attitudes from family and coworkers who felt the students might be granted unfair privileges. Davida, Stephanie, and Polly recounted the ever-present distress that resulted from constantly balancing competing priorities.

Paradox 5: Committed, Purposeful, and Fragile

mid-career students embark on this new venture with enthusiasm. Their commitment is substantial whether enumerated in terms of time (three, five, or more years of their lives), money (paying tuition and fees or giving up a full-time job for an assistantship with a modest stipend), loss of control (the daily, weekly, and monthly rhythms of life are now determined by others) and isolation (missing family, family occasions, and friends' weddings). Despite the depth of their commitment, most participants in this group lacked clarity about the end result, or end point of this effort, beyond obtaining the degree itself. This uncertainty created an unease that undermined faith about eventual success when progress felt unexpectedly difficult, or was stymied. The risk of failure appeared enormous when the potential gains became undecipherable. More than a few entertained the idea of walking away at some point during the program.

Paradox 6: Prepared, and Profoundly Surprised

The mid-career students in this study embarked on this journey seeking a career outcome from the doctorate. They expected to learn new ways of thinking, new research skills, new content related to their interest areas. They expected the work of writing and analysis to be challenging and time-consuming. Few in this group, however, anticipated the depth of personal transformation that resulted from these intellectual challenges. They were prepared for long hours and hard work. They were unprepared to deconstruct their belief systems and reassemble fundamentally new perspectives about the meaning of knowledge, identity, class, gender, power, and other concepts that formed the basis of their understanding of themselves and the world around them. Intellectual challenge morphed into highly emotional and unanticipated personal transformations.

TRANSFORMATIONS ILLUMINATED

Participants revealed the depth and shape of their transformations through the many stories they told. In chapter 8, we illustrated their experience as a journey along two dimensions: emotional and intellectual (see figure 8.1) because their comments had left no doubt about transformation and growth in both emotional and intellectual terms. A few previous researchers (Gardner, 2010; Millett and Nettles, 2009; Thomson and Kamler, 2010) do present the doctoral experience as a set of stages. The stages they articulate are helpful. The first two relate primarily to the mastery of the intellectual challenges, while Thomson and Kamler address identity issues. Thompson and Walker (2010a) describe their approach to identity development:

> We have suggested that we understand doctoral education as a process of identity formation. This involves crossing a kind of borderland, transforming an identity as an experienced, highly skilled professional to one of researcher. We have certainly heard our own full-time doctoral students remark, in particular, on not underestimating the difficulties of suddenly no longer being a valued and respected professional, in becoming "just a student." What one might have been very good at and very secure about in one's own practice is suddenly of rather less significance. For part-time

students the disruptions may work differently, in that students remain grounded in the workplace but are required to scrutinize it in new and often discomforting ways. Yet these disruptions, while difficult, are also productive of the new critically reflexive identity (2010a, 19).

As I listened to the participants in this study, it was clear that challenges to personal identity and belief systems were so intertwined with intellectual growth that they could not be separated. mid-career individuals are much further along in the life process of developing a personal and professional identity than younger students, and have based more of their life choices on their belief systems. Thus, challenges to identity are profound and destabilizing.

In the following two sections, I will connect these transformational journeys to well-known theories of human development and behavior dealing with transitions and culture shock. The theories focus on the dynamics of particular life changes and helped me understand the experiences revealed by the participants. The strength of the parallels suggests to me a core of universality about the stories that have been told here.

Job and Life Transitions

Career advancement was the primary motivator for embarking on doctoral education for these participants. Some sought to turbo-boost along an existing trajectory, while others were in more of an exploratory mind-set, wondering about new pathways that might be appealing.

Fourteen of the fifteen were in the prime period of productivity: Emily, Olivia, Brad, Brian, Ben, Jaime, Stephanie, Seth, Kelly, Kathy, Polly, Carole, Davida, and Laura. Tina seemed to be in the midst of a more reflective period that may have signaled her transition into a generative phase. Prompted by her research on third-age learners, after a period of study that had extended to eight years because of her college teaching responsibilities, she could begin to identify with those older learners, as she was only a decade younger herself. All were eager for a change of some sort; they were in a period of transition. No matter their ages, they were restless.

As was mentioned in chapter 2, both Sheehy and Levinson's research attests to the commonality of these life transitions and the developmental issues and questions that prompt people to feel restless and seek changes. Levinson's estimate of the time required for a transition was from four to five years, "not less than three and rarely more than six" (1978, 19). So what happens during this time? To better understand, we might use theory specifically developed to illuminate the nature of major professional transitions.

Bridges's (1991) model helps conceptualize more specifically the emotional and psychological aspects that might occur by proposing a three-stage process: Ending or Letting Go, a Neutral Zone, and Revitalization. His research focused on transitions within an organizational context, highlighting transitions as both processes and major events for individuals (Bridges, 2004). Central to his model are the processes of dealing with loss, moving through confusion, and finding new direction. Fishman (2010) recently used the model effectively in an academic context to analyze faculty retirement. The parallels to participant descriptions of their journeys through the doctoral program are extraordinary.

The first phase, *Ending*, involves letting go of something such as a role or status and creating a necessary ending. The individual is challenged with the decision to let go. Recall Laura's rueful comment about letting go of her role as athletic trainer for the women's basketball team at her previous institution. Both Emily and Kelly initially expressed regret about no longer being asked to participate in departmental decisions where they worked as graduate assistants. The university offices where they worked treated them as graduate students.

Coming to terms with letting go leads into the *Neutral* phase during which an individual realizes previous habits and behaviors are no longer as useful or needed and new skills begin to emerge. Often, individuals in this phase expect to move directly to the next phase, in a straightforward manner. However, this rarely happens. Rather, while in the Neutral phase individuals face anxiety, ambiguity, mixed levels of motivation, and may feel confused about what is happening to them. Carole offered the most dramatic description of this process as she spoke about the deconstruction of her personal belief system.

Bridges also referred to this phase as an "emotional wilderness" (1991, 5). Frankly, "wilderness" seems a much better descriptor than "neutral." Whether Bridges intended it or not, it brings to mind the biblical story of the forty years Moses spent wandering in the wilderness before arriving at the Promised Land. It has been said that the purpose of so many years of wandering was to allow the generation that had known slavery to die so that only the generation born in the freedom of the wilderness would enter the Promised Land. The challenges presented by wandering in the desert were expected to engender new ways of thinking.

The intensity of the candidacy exam can leave students mentally exhausted and result in a period of wandering that can last anywhere from several weeks to several months. In our doctoral program, the participants (like current students) were required to have submitted a substantial draft of the dissertation proposal prior to taking the candidacy exam. Often students feel a bit lost while writing the proposal. By having a draft due prior to the exam, if they do get lost, their guides are relatively close at hand. In other words, we might describe the purpose behind this requirement as helping students reduce the time spent wandering the wilderness after the candidacy exam. With a draft in hand, the next step is to make specific revisions requested by faculty—often growing out of the exam, and then move directly into data collection.

As confusion diminishes and the path forward begins to emerge, people enter the third phase, *Revitalization*. During this phase, individuals move forward to new endeavors, invigorated and excited by a new sense of purpose. In drawing the parallel to the doctoral journey, it seems that for some individuals this phase could begin during the early stages of dissertation research, while for others, it may occur closer to completion, during the job search. Kathy, Ben, Polly, Davida, Jaime, and Brad developed new approaches to dissertation questions that were at the heart of their (then) professional identities. All but Ben remain professionally immersed in the same content area. Ben's dissertation focused on the racial identity development of students in a study-abroad program, and although he is no longer involved with study abroad, his current work does involve student identity development. Kelly, Carole, Seth, and Tina represent four individuals at different ages and stages of career who demonstrate the excitement and satisfaction of finding new paths.

What do these models reveal about the mid-career doctoral experience? First, the energy that prompts enrollment in a doctoral program probably results from the combination of a desire for career enhancement and a sense of restlessness or dissatisfaction with the individual's personal productivity. It is possible that while both are necessary, neither alone will suffice to propel the student through the most difficult periods of doctoral study. Second, there may be distinct stages to the emotional roller coaster experienced by mid-career students. Those who actually depart current employment in order to pursue their studies will go through a period of grief, as they mourn the loss of status, perquisites, engagement, and financial stability. Those who remain employed also face a shift in status, including the loss of control of their personal time and energy. In order to become a successful student, both the full-time student and the part-time, employed student will have to admit the insufficiency of their own skills and knowledge. Accomplished professionals, they are de facto admitting weakness. Moving into a new environment they no longer know "how the world works."

Third, they may find, as Kelly did, that the new status is liberating. However, like Moses in the wilderness, they will be surprised by the length of the journey and the complications they encounter. While individual courses may seem manageable, internalizing new perspectives and integrating new skills will require openness to change, fortitude, and perseverance. They may wonder whether the outcome is worth the effort when the goal recedes before them in a virtual sandstorm of framing and reframing dissertation questions and methodology. Confusion will be rampant, and while necessary for learning, it is destabilizing.

Fourth, while the student and advisor may be able to anticipate these first three take-aways, the moment when the student passes through the gate into that period of revitalization and excitement will be less predictable. For some, it will come when dissertation questions are clarified and the path forward finally seems free of debris. For others, it may come during data collection, through the interaction with interview or focus group participants, or during data analysis, when interview or survey results begin to show patterns. If the dissertation research fails to generate excitement, then the dissertation process will feel like a lot of shoveling. For those who struggle through the dissertation, we hope that the job search will mark the entry into the revitalization phase.

Culture Shock

A major change in job, profession, or milieu presents the professional with the challenges that result in circumstances that seem similar to the stages outlined in models of culture shock, the second type of theory that appears useful in understanding the mid-career experience. One of the leading researchers in this area suggests that "by metaphor, culture shock may relate to life crises in a variety of areas other than the experience of travel to another country. A person experiencing any radical change in his or her life may experience a process of adaptation or accommodation that parallels the condition described by culture shock." (Pederson, 1995, 11). Theories about culture shock tend to be stage based and address the developmental path an individual follows while gaining the skills to move from dependence to independence.

Paul Pederson's seminal work *Five Stages of Culture Shock* (1995), serves as the source for the model used here. Drawing on previous work, he describes five stages of culture shock:

> The first stage of initial contact, or the "honeymoon stage," is where the newly arrived individual experiences the curiosity and excitement of a tourist, but where the person's basic identity is rooted in the back-home setting.
>
> The second stage involves "disintegration" of the old familiar cues, and the individual is overwhelmed by the new culture's requirements. The individual typically experiences self-blame and a sense of personal inadequacy for any difficulties encountered.
>
> The third stage involves a "reintegration" of new cues and an increased ability to function in the new culture. The emotions associated with this stage are typically anger and resentment toward the new culture as having caused difficulties and being less adequate than the old familiar ways. Because of this out-directed anger, persons in this stage of culture shock are difficult to help.
>
> The fourth stage continues the process of reintegration toward gradual "autonomy" and increased ability to see the bad and good elements in both the old and the new cultures. A balanced perspective emerges that helps the person interpret both the previous home and the new host cultures.

The fifth stage is described as reciprocal "interdependence," where the person has ideally achieved biculturality or has become fluently comfortable in both the old and new cultures. There is some controversy about whether this stage is an unreachable ideal or whether persons can actually achieve this stage of multiculturalism (1995, 3).

The way individuals experience each stage is affected by many factors such as age, experience, gender, and previous "travel," or in this case, job or professional relocations. Yet, like grief, the stages remain somewhat predictable and are easily recognized in the stories of our participants.

Laura and Carole probably offer the most dramatic examples of a quick passage through the honeymoon stage into disintegration. Laura described a very, very difficult first quarter, where she had to leave behind her identity as an athletic trainer and come to grips with her lack of familiarity with the language and knowledge base many of her peers brought to classroom conversations. Carole spent much painful time in the disintegration and reintegration stages. While she achieved an extraordinary level of autonomy, eventually running her own career counseling consultancy, she speaks about a process of reintegration that lasted almost ten years. Tina followed a similarly disorienting path that eventually led her to a whole new career.

When he began the program, Seth had anticipated a dissertation focused on campus ecology, followed by a job search leading to career advancement in administration. Intrigued by an exciting topic discovered during his second quarter of course work, and encouraged by his success as a teacher in his graduate assistantship, he proceeded cautiously, but steadily into the stage of disintegration. He willingly tried on new content areas and new roles. The degree to which he achieved autonomy became clear postgraduation, as he persevered in his search for faculty positions through a dreadful job market, ultimately landing a successful teaching position.

For those participants who were in turbo-boost career mode, the first two stages were less disruptive, as they recognized the value of the new language and culture. Their hard work involved mastering those new skills as they sought to internalize conceptual frameworks and theoretical perspectives. Through no fault of her own, Polly wandered in a state of disintegration for more than a year, because she lacked the faculty guidance that would have placed her earlier with the appropriate content and cohort. Once properly located in the higher education program, her reintegration proceeded more smoothly as she energetically sought to gain the competencies for her new administrative role. Despite some struggles with her data analysis, she progressed toward autonomy with alacrity.

Brad, Ben, Stephanie, Brian, and Kathy moved more directly through the first three stages than the others. All five set out self-consciously to progress along on established career trajectories. Later, as we learned, Ben shifted gears, moving from a research university setting to a community college, and then from international student advising into directing projects to assist students in the science, technology, engineering, and math fields.

Jaime and Kelly experienced the disintegration stage, bit by bit. Both questioned their status, and both spent considerable time and effort identifying and framing their dissertation research questions. For each that was the defining challenge because it required reframing skills and purpose. Jaime was working with a population and topic that were completely new to her, and to which she was firmly committed. Kelly's commitment to her dissertation research translated into an unusually long research timetable, as she pursued a topic that required participant interviews over the course of a full year.

Emily found herself stuck in a disintegration phase that only partially related to her doctoral program, which raises a key question for us. Do we use this culture shock lens to examine only the doctoral work, or should we consider that mid-career doctoral students may be traveling parallel tracks, experiencing the stages of transition and culture shock in their personal lives as well as the doctoral program?

Certainly, Emily fits that case. Her divorce could be described as a tectonic disintegration, a volcanic eruption, in that it derailed her doctoral program completely for almost two years. In parallel with her dissertation research, this talented administrator, an action- and decision-oriented individual, struggled with learning an entirely new language of conceptualization and theory, and spent more than a year moving through disintegration to reintegration. The nuanced analysis of her dissertation data demonstrated that she did, indeed, achieve substantial intellectual autonomy and was able to use her rich administrative background to develop a new conceptual framework.

Olivia's path resembles the bouncing path of a stone skipped on water, as she touched down briefly in the earlier phases and then bounced into autonomy. She had entered the doctoral program pretty directly after her master's work, and that allowed her to acclimate more quickly to the student role. Her dissertation research represented a daring foray into brand-new research territory. Never before had anyone created a database solely devoted to research on her topic. Previous research on the topic had utilized databases derived from existing national surveys that included, at most, half a dozen questions directed to the faculty behaviors we sought to illuminate. She found the situation wonderfully challenging and displayed an unusual degree of confidence (autonomy) as she developed the conceptual framework, definitions, pilot survey, and final survey for her research. Like Emily, however, in the personal context, she voiced concern about the length of time it was taking for reintegration.

Davida's effort to find and eventually, develop, an appropriate theoretical framing for her dissertation research required that she spend a great deal of time moving between the stages of disintegration and reintegration. It is testimony to her powerful sense of purpose that she was able to sustain the search through several disappointing initiatives long enough to identify the frameworks that she eventually wove into a rich new approach to her subject matter. The time she spent in reintegration resulted in new perspectives that gave her the foundation for an unusual level of autonomy, and an ability to function comfortably with both old and new frameworks (cultures). She, along with Tina, and perhaps Carole, may have achieved the biculturality that some said was out of reach.

As I consider participant experience through the lens of culture shock, there seems to be a lot of evidence that students are traveling two parallel tracks: intellectual or professional growth, and personal development. Olivia and Emily's experience surely provide evidence consistent with this perspective. Kathy's comments about the adjustment she was making to the rhythm of her husband's work and hobbies provides more, as do comments offered in the discussion of "reentry," or reintegration with partner relationships by Laura, Ben, and Brad. Polly was certainly navigating two tracks during her son's recovery from his accident, as was Carole, whose personal growth changed her role in her community. Jaime, Seth, and Stephanie, our single participants, made it clear that a parallel track was very much on their minds. Seth's wonderful comment about the implications of graduate student status for his dating prospects made us chuckle but reflects an important aspect of life for the mid-career student in his or her thirties.

I am now convinced that mid-career students are actually progressing along two parallel paths that intertwine much like the long, twisting, ladder-like strands of a DNA molecule. Each strand impacts the other through a variety of connecting moments and events like missed soccer games, lost evenings, accidents, illness, and long-distance commutes. It may well be that the illustration presented in figure 8.1 should show two lines, superimposed on one another!

APPLYING CULTURE SHOCK TO DOCTORAL STUDY

In his book Pedersen makes specific recommendations for helping those dealing with culture shock. The recommendations seem to echo much that we heard in the earlier conversations in chapters 6, 7, and 8 about the support, supporting cast, advisors, and mentors.

> While we may not be able to explain culture shock adequately, there are generally accepted approaches to dealing with this phenomenon that apply to a wide variety of crises situations . . .
>
> First, . . . *any important life transition is like to result in stress and discomfort as a usual and normal consequence.* The pain of culture shock may be seen . . . as a normal response to change.
>
> Second, the maintenance of personal integrity and self-esteem should become the primary goal of someone experiencing culture shock. Visitors often experience a loss of status in the new culture, where language, customs and procedures are strange and unfamiliar. *These visitors will need reassurance and support to maintain a healthy self-image and to restore their sense of self-efficacy.*
>
> Third, time must be allowed for the adjustment to take place without pressure or urgency. Persons adjust at their own rate dependent on the situation. *Ultimate reconciliation of the new with the old may require a longer period of time than is convenient but which is nonetheless necessary.*
>
> Fourth, recognizing the patterns of adjustment will help the visitor develop new skill and insights. *By charting the process of changes leading up to culture shock and predicting future stages in a logical sequence, the process may become more concrete and less ambiguous.* . . .
>
> Fifth, labeling the symptoms of culture shock will help the visitor interpret emotional responses to stress in adjustment. *Knowing that others have experienced culture shock and have survived or have even grown stronger from the experience can be comforting.*
>
> Sixth, *being well adjusted at home does not ensure an easy adjustment in the foreign culture. In some cases, visitors may find themselves more homesick if they were much better off back home.* . . .
>
> Seventh, although culture shock cannot be prevented it is possible to prepare persons for transition to new cultures and thereby ease the adjustment process. *Preparation might include language study, learning about the host culture, simulating situations to be encountered and spending time with nationals from the host culture before traveling there.*
>
> In all instances, the development of a support system is essential to help the visitor reconstruct an important identity or role in the new culture. *The visitor learns important lessons from culture shock that can perhaps not be learned in any other way.* To that extent culture shock actually contributes to the formation of a stronger bicultural or multicultural identity. (Pedersen, 1995, 9–10)

This culture shock model pertains to long-term sojourners, folks who will spend substantial time in the new culture and who, therefore, need to become fluent in the language, culture, and norms of the new setting. More than tourists who might easily make short-term adaptations, the sojourner has embarked on a journey of personal growth and development that requires deeper adjustments resulting from true appreciation of the logic of others.

Doctoral study produces similar results. Course work and subsequent research endeavors at the doctoral level challenge assumptions and demand deep reflection of the student for the express purpose of developing new and more complex ways of understanding the world or worlds in which we live. Excellent students, successful students who willingly open themselves to learning will come away profoundly changed.

"TRUTH" BY COMPARISON

While it can be fun to explore theory and research, the point of this discussion has been to answer the questions we posed at the beginning of the chapter: How common is the experience of these graduates? Are their experiences unique to this field (education)? In other words, can doctoral students or aspiring doctoral students in other fields, at other universities use this book as any sort of a guide? What can faculty and advisors in the sciences or humanities learn from this project?

In my years as a researcher, I have learned that truth is fundamentally a relative term. In other words, reality is in the eye of the beholder. Each person constructs a view of reality that guides behavior, consciously or unconsciously. Moreover, the logics people use to construct reality differ from individual to individual, and the belief systems that underlie these logics vary from industry to industry, region to region, culture to culture, and certainly, from country to country. So, we must always be skeptical about transferring knowledge from one setting to another.

Yet, if we accept the proposition that truth is a personal construction, we are presented with the ultimate conundrum: How do we learn from others? On what should we base our actions? How do we discern the patterns that might be moved successfully from one setting to another, that are transferable? Quantitative researchers have devised many sophisticated methods for enabling generalizations. Qualitative researchers typically depend on rich, thick descriptions of specific settings, leaving the reader to determine whether there be a sufficient environmental or contextual match to support transferability (Creswell, 2007).

Through my work in international settings and in different industries, I have come to believe there is another litmus test that can reveal approximations of truth from qualitative research about human behavior: When I come across similar results, substantial parallels in the findings from research that has been conducted in settings that diverge dramatically in structure and logic, I believe that those results reveal some sort of universal truth.

Let me offer an example. In the late 1980s, Professor Richard (Dick) Chait and his associates conducted research about the boards of directors of independent colleges in the United States. During that same period, Dr. Fred Neubauer and I, then based in Switzerland, separately conducted research about the boards of directors of multinational corporations in eight different European and South American countries. I had not met Dick Chait, and neither of us was aware of the other's research project. His book was published just as my coauthor and I sent our manuscript to our publisher (Chait, Holland, and Taylor, 1991). A friend who knew of our project sent me a copy. The parallels in our findings about the behavior of the boards and their effectiveness were uncanny.

That same friend soon introduced us and after Dick read our book he invited me to give a seminar on our research to his project team (Demb and Neubauer, 1992). We were both surprised and fascinated by the similarity in our findings and recommendations about the effectiveness of boards of directors. In fact, the only point on which there was any significant difference related to the ownership structure of the organizations, which my coauthor and I had addressed in the corporate context but that had not been part of their college study. These two sets of findings, resulting from independent projects conducted in wildly different contexts, represented learning that could be transferred.

Like the two research projects on boards, there appear to be clear parallels between the stages of culture shock and the stages of transition in the Bridges model. Both focus on transition as a process and incorporate the notions of disintegration and reintegration. The disintegration process that Pedersen discusses seems to resemble a combination of the letting go and wilderness stages in Bridges's model, and Pedersen's stages of reintegration and autonomy seem very similar to Bridges's revitalization stage. Thus, the two sets of theories seem to reveal a stage-based process of transition that may be universal. To the degree that participant experience aligns with these theories, their experiences may also be more universal and apply to a broader population of doctoral students than the structure of the project might initially appear to support. If A (participant experience) = B (transition and culture shock models), and B (models) = C (broader population), then the relationship between A and C is certainly worth careful consideration.

Chapter Eleven

Reflections

Did you ever stop to wonder about the courage it took for Christopher Columbus and his men to board their three little ships and set sail across an unknown ocean? As the crow flies, his route from Spain to Haiti was about 4,100 miles. The largest of his ships, the *Santa Maria*, was 75 feet long and 25 feet wide. There were forty men aboard. To put the size in perspective consider: A football field is 160 feet from *sideline to sideline*; the length of the *Santa Maria* was half that distance. A typical Coast Guard patrol boat, the ones we commonly see in pictures, is about 110 feet long. And the famous World War II destroyer escorts, the "Tin Can Navy" that served so well in the Pacific, were 300 feet long, the full *length* of a football field (Hornfischer, 2005).

What about the courage it took for John Glenn to get into that little capsule that was slung into orbit around the earth in 1962? "When John Glenn launched on the United States' first orbital spaceflight 50 years ago today (Feb. 20), NASA scientists weren't sure where he'd come down—or if he'd even survive the trip" (Wall, 2012). Or when the crew of the Apollo 11 set off to the moon in 1969? Earlier models of the Atlas rocket that carried them had been blowing up on the launch pad for months.

These are some of the images that come to mind when I reflect on the experiences of the participants in this project. Yes, they had more resources than Columbus and his crew, and a better map. No, they weren't going off to war. And we fully anticipated they would remain on Earth throughout their journey. But neither did they board a Royal Caribbean cruise boat, or a quick commuter flight from Boston to Washington, D.C.

In October 2011, I presented some findings from this project about the role of advisors at the Annual Conference of the National Association of Academic Advising (NACADA). In order to create an appropriate mind-set, when I began I asked the audience to respond to a few descriptors, one by one: "Raise your hands if you were married or partnered, working full-time, had children, were single parents, or all three, that is, married/partnered working full-time with children." There were very few in the audience who did not raise their hands. Everyone led a busy life. I ask you now, the reader, to do the same. When would you have raised your hand?

Then I asked the audience to imagine for the next two years, that they also

- would attend class for two–three hours, on campus, two–three days each week
- would have 100–175 pages of reading each week

- would meet with a class project group for one hour each week during the quarter or semester, beginning the second week of classes, for two of their courses
- were expected to "post" comments to a website about class readings
- would take a midterm within five weeks, or submit a major reflection paper, for three of their courses
- would turn in a major research paper or take a final exam, within eight to ten weeks, for three of their courses.

By this time, many in the audience were shaking their heads, or muttering quietly. Then I reminded them that those expectations pertained only to the first two years of a doctoral program. After those two or two and half years, they would then be required to:

- define an original research project
- write a formal research proposal, articulating research questions, presenting a literature review, defining the epistemology and methodology for the research, and outlining the research design
- take (and pass) the candidacy exam, to demonstrate their mastery of the major theories and research related to their segment of the field
- conduct the research
- analyze the research results and write up the findings
- in a two-hour panel session (the defense), respond to faculty questions about the research

The goal of my opening comments was to make the parameters of doctoral education "real" for the audience (Demb, 2011). That has been my goal with this book.

By now, you might surmise that my first reflection will echo the words I used in the preface. mid-career students are brave, strong, and committed people. Anyone working with good doctoral students is aware that they keep long hours and work hard. After listening to these former advisees with whom I had already spent countless hours over many years, I realized that, metaphorically speaking, faculty see only the tip of the iceberg that represents the totality of their lives. I believe it was Bette Davis who once said, "Old age is not for the faint of heart." Well, neither is doctoral study. Yet, these folks were willing, even eager to sign on for the duration, without a full understanding of all that would be asked of them.

With this in mind, let me offer more reflections for those considering doctoral study and for faculty advisors. My reflections here stem from the conversations chronicled in earlier chapters and also my observations as an advisor. At the time of the project conference in August 2010, I had graduated sixteen doctoral students, all of whom agreed to participate. One dropped out before the conference because of some major life changes. Since then, four more of my advisees have finished, and three others are in dissertation. So my observational sample is twenty-three students.

REFLECTIONS FOR ASPIRING STUDENTS, AND STUDENTS

The decision to enroll in a doctoral program will change your life. After reading this book carefully, give it to whoever will accompany you on this journey. The decision to enroll in doctoral study will affect the whole family. Talk about the implications at some length. Think about it.

Define your goals. Know your reasons for pursuing a doctorate. Where do you believe it will lead? Go interview folks in those roles, or look them up on the Internet. In a dissertation defense on June 6, 2012, one of my colleagues said, "Fewer than 3 percent of Americans have doctorates." To me, that means there are a lot of exciting and capable people enjoying their lives and being productive, without doctorates.

Choosing an environment where you will live and learn for the next five years is important. Visit different institutions, and if you have a partner, go together. You will both live there. Speak to faculty and students about as many aspects of the program as possible. Ask about advising and opportunities to work with faculty one-on-one. Get a feel for the institutional environment and the locale. If you like sports, does it have sports facilities or teams? If you like the arts or music, is there adequate cultural richness? If you have children, talk with students who have children. Visit schools, and day care. Look at housing options. Ask about medical insurance and facilities.

My observation is that students who succeed make the doctoral work a top priority. They put in real "sweat equity." They have the support of family and others and they are willing to rearrange their lives to make time available for the work.

Successful folks are willing to take intellectual risks. They ask questions. They choose topics for course papers that are somewhat unfamiliar and stretch their thinking. Like speaking a new language before becoming fluent, the willingness to use a new skill demonstrates commitment and motivation. It builds relationships and can lead to focused and more helpful feedback as you seek to perfect the skill. Successful students are open to new ideas, and seek critical feedback. However, in the process if they feel uncertain, they get help. They talk with faculty and with other students.

The cohort is terribly and wonderfully important. Almost to a person, each participant in this project spoke about the support and encouragement they gained from members of the cohort. They spoke of meeting with more advanced students and graduates of the program, in order to take advantage of that experience. Social interaction with members of the cohort helps build the community that serves as the support network. That network can also be very important for partners and even children.

Employers play a key role in enabling a student's success in the program. Stephanie and Ben were clear, as was Brian, about the support they received. Polly also was well supported, but felt she could have made better arrangements for her writing, had she realized how much time would be needed. She would have worked out a sabbatical leave. Talk with your employer from the beginning. Be realistic about managing time and responsibilities, and discuss options for the period when you are writing your dissertation proposal and preparing for generals. Blocks of time away from job responsibilities will be essential. With enough lead time, that can probably be arranged as a special leave or vacation time.

The quality of a student's writing is central to progress and success. If you are a good writer, you are fortunate. If your skills could be improved, get help. Good books that address organization, style, and specifics such as how to write a literature review are available (Galvan, 2006). Every good university has some sort of writing center, and tutors are usually available. Focus on building this key life skill.

REFLECTIONS BY, AND FOR FACULTY

What have I learned from this project as an advisor? Over time, I had already accumulated a number of "rules" for myself. This project underscored the importance of some and added more to the list. Here are ten of my personal rules.

Rule #1. Students need and deserve respect. A mid-career student who commits to doctoral study is worthy of respect. Use their time wisely. Teach well. Listen. Do your best to answer their questions or send them to the person who can. Do not belittle their previous experience or work or perspectives. As the student gains new lenses, it should be natural for them to compare earlier thinking about organizational or student situations (in a higher education program, for example) and come to appreciate the richness provided by the new perspectives. The moments when those discussions can be broached will become obvious.

Rule #2. Treat the student's ego as though it were as fragile as a robin's egg. When a student risks appearing ignorant by asking questions, or opens themselves to new ideas, they make themselves vulnerable. Offer critique with sufficient support so that the student is left with the self-confidence to proceed. Ask how they feel about the feedback. Remember the way it feels when you give the first draft of a manuscript to a friend to critique. When my dear late colleague Dr. Fred Neubauer gave me a draft chapter of the book we were writing together, he asked "Please, treat it like a robin's egg."

Rule #3. Give feedback generously; do not hesitate to give feedback. Tell the student when they have done well. Tell the student when they need to improve. Be specific. Suggest alternatives that might lead them to more effective or productive approaches. Think about this image: they are traveling down a mountain path at dusk with a flashlight that has a faulty battery and flickers. You have a flashlight with a good battery and have been down the path before. How can you help them "see" the way so that if they stumble, they don't break a leg?

Rule #4. Form a partnership. Mid-career students have experience that is relevant to their studies, and their research. In their previous roles, they may have been "the boss," "in charge," or "the expert." As a result, they have opinions, sometimes strong ones that grow out of those experiences. mid-career students know a lot. So, they are not as easily convinced that "your" idea is the best. They are not as malleable as younger students. Treat them as partners rather than underlings. Choose your position on the Advisor Matrix (figure 8.4). Be honest and consistent with your personal style. Then identify the other faculty, staff, or alumni who can round out the advising support the student may need.

Rule #5. We faculty should dare to share. We are not therapists, but faculty are role models, ipso facto. Offering glimpses into some aspect of professional or personal lives helps to build trust and will help the student listen to and hear feedback more clearly. Share a story about a difficult teaching moment. Perhaps the proper framing of a research question or the most appropriate analytic framework eluded you on an important project. Let them know they are not the only ones who have been challenged to figure out a complex problem. Each advisor has to figure out for him- or herself an appropriate privacy boundary. In my experience, students will respect that. They want a genuine relationship, and that can take many forms.

Rule #6. Celebrate the moments of progress. "Bravo" e-mails, and face-to-face "yippees" mean a lot. Not only did I learn this from my students, but I learned this from my dressage training. When I have sweated for forty minutes to get my horse to move in a certain way and finally there are two or three or four "correct" steps, it really helps to have my instructor jump up and down and yell out "Bravo!" If the student has produced a diagram, or a chapter draft that finally captures the essence of the research or analysis, let them know, even if the material still needs substantial revision.

Rule #7. Be open to new perspectives and new ways of framing research or issues. Student expressions may differ from yours and mine, and from convention. So long as the new framework is rigorous and logical, welcome it. Students will grow and develop from their own strengths; we need to identify those strengths and build on them. Those "different" ideas may well lead to exciting new research directions and findings.

Rule #8. Remember that cognitive styles differ dramatically and can affect communication. An apparent "problem" in communicating ideas may stem from differences in information-processing logics, rather than the person's attitude. Specifically, your student may have a different cognitive style than your own. Those differences are hardwired, but can be overcome. There is wonderful research about differences in the way people process information: deductive vs. inductive thinkers, concrete vs. abstract learners, and so on. I particularly like David Kolb's body of work (1984, 1999). I had used Kolb's simple and powerful Learning Style Inventory to illustrate cognitive differences for years in the executive classroom. As an advisor, I used it to unravel communication challenges with all five of my advisees who were based in the health professions: nurses, optometrists, athletic trainers. Once we uncovered the differences in our personal information processing, we got creative and found effective ways to express ideas.

Rule #9. Try to be flexible (and patient) about the larger timelines. This is a hard rule to live by. Course requirements should be due on time. However, mid-career students carry a lot of responsibility—for jobs, partners, and children. The unexpected can happen to any of us—the flu, a slip on the ice, a death in the family. When two or more individuals are involved, the opportunities for "Murphy" to screw things up expand accordingly.

Students who are parents or spouses must care for children and partners. It's just that simple. A crisis in a job situation cannot be ignored. And students must also care for themselves. About half the students in this study marched right through the program, completing on time, in the four- to five-year time frame. "Life happens," and it did for Polly, Emily, Ben, and Tina. That Olivia gave birth to two children and still managed to finish within her original timeline was absolutely extraordinary. The participants and I all agreed that her example should be left in the "exceptional" category, and should not be used to set a standard for anyone else. Students may need a semester when they take fewer courses than would be ideal. They may need to take an "incomplete" in a course. Such modifications to schedules may set them back a full year. Take a deep breath, and roll with it.

Rule #10. We must be attentive to signs of real distress. Taking fewer courses, or requesting an incomplete might simply reflect good judgment about how much a person can handle. Checking with faculty teaching other courses might yield useful information. However, if the flow of e-mails diminishes dramatically, or stops completely, go on alert. Check in. Ask. Send e-mail, text, or call. When Emily's communication ceased the summer she was registered with me for dissertation work, and when she barely interacted during the following quarter, I sent e-mails and called, finally eliciting the unhappy news that she was going through her divorce. She needed personal time away from the program. Armed with that information, I worked with our student services staff to handle procedures with the graduate school so that her status was not jeopardized. My next conversation with her was simply to ask whether she had found a good therapist and was taking care of herself. A year later, she reengaged at full-steam, even with a new job in a distant location, and completed her dissertation research. Remember how many of the participants in this study said that they contemplated quitting the program!

EXPECTATIONS AND SURPRISES

Often in a dissertation defense a faculty member will ask the candidate, "What were the surprises in your research? And which parts of the project played out as you expected?" So it seems only fair to address those questions briefly here.

Expectations

During the years I spent advising mid-career students I had become aware that finding the time to study and to write was going to be a challenge, and that the workload associated with jobs would vary from month to month. After several students who were working full-time hit plateaus while writing their proposals, I began to advise students that the process would require sustained hours and that working students would need to use vacation to create blocks of time for writing.

Time pressure is typically a consequence of family circumstances. Single students can pretty much set their own schedules around jobs or assistantship responsibilities. Children's priorities often define parental schedules, and finding time for personal work can be challenging. Despite my general appreciation of the challenge, I was surprised when Olivia told me she was getting up at 3:30 AM to write!

The need for a roadmap through the doctoral program and steps involved did not seem particularly unusual for the mid-career students. Perhaps their initial reaction to the rigidity of the university bureaucracy reflected time away from college settings and the student role. My experience with our master's students, however, gave me plenty of evidence that even students moving directly into graduate work from undergraduate degrees need lots of procedural guidance.

Surprises

The big surprises in this study related to the extent of the emotional response that the experience elicited, the transformative nature of the journey, the strength of participant insistence on the differences between advising and mentoring, and the reentry process. For example, these students were not simply committed to their doctoral work, they were passionate about it. The passion led them to rearrange their lives, the lives of their partners, children, and professional situations. For many, the dislocations resulted in strong feelings of guilt and isolation, as well as exhilaration.

Other authors have noted that "most doctoral students enter graduate school fired up with enthusiasm and idealism. Along the way, this passion often seems to disappear. The positive side of this is that romantic ideals of academic life are replaced by more realistic goals. The negative side is that the zeal with which many begin their studies is unnecessarily eroded" (Golde et al., 2009, 64). The passion did not disappear for these students; it was reinforced for many through their dissertation research and encouraged by the supporting cast.

Most of the participants had anticipated that the doctoral work would change them, give them new perspectives and skills. Like them, however, I was surprised by the extent of the personal transformations in identity that resulted. Belief systems were challenged and re-framed, and even those for whom the trajectory remained roughly straightforward, the process seemed deeply transformative.

The discussion about advisors and mentors was one of the biggest surprises for me. I had been generally familiar with the literature on advising and mentoring, but had not found the distinctions terribly enlightening. The participants were crystal clear that there was a difference, and that they could name the dimensions that distinguished mentors from advisors. Surely the basics of a good advising were clear to all of us prior to the discussion. However, the insights about the differences presented in chapter 7 were new to me, and led me to frame them in chapter 8, as figures 8.2 and 8.4. They helped me clarify my years of experience.

The other big surprise was the identification of the period following the doctoral program as "reentry." In fact, I think that discussion was a big "aha" moment for the participants as well. While aware that there were needs for readjustment, until Carole, Olivia, Kathy, and Laura began exploring their sense of that period in each of their lives, it didn't have a name. Nor had folks realized the length of time it might take to reestablish a new normal. Once named, that insight evolved into an understanding that doctoral students are moving through a personal journey with distinct phases, simultaneously and in parallel with their intellectual journey. In my mind's eye, the two journeys intertwine, much as the helix of a DNA molecule.

BAKED ALASKA

When I think about my original idea for this project and compare that to the outcome, my overwhelming sentiment is gratitude—for the years of rich interaction with these talented professionals, for the collaboration on fascinating research, and for teaching me as much as they did. I was already an experienced professional, had been a senior administrator at two universities and taught in executive seminars in Europe for many years when I moved into my faculty role here. However, I had not previously advised doctoral students. So the journey was one of exploration and learning for me as well as for the students, particularly in those first few years with Carole and Kelly.

I can best describe the comparison between my original expectation for this project and the outcome with a metaphor. Imagine that you had organized a potluck dinner, and invited fifteen people. You fully expected they would bring delicious salads, a homemade bread, perhaps some lovely chicken or pasta dishes, and of course, yummy desserts. Instead, to your amazement, they brought caviar, lobster bisque, stuffed mushrooms, homemade bread, filet mignon, moussaka, beef Wellington, stuffed shrimp, roasted pear and pecan salad, and baked Alaska. The dinner turned into a feast! I may have hosted the party, but they brought the ingredients that made it a success.

Appendix

Research Design and Methodology

The purpose of this project was to understand whether and how the experience of mid-career doctoral students differed from other doctoral students. My observations during my years as a faculty member led me to believe that the life of a student for these folks presented challenges that the faculty did not fully understand, and that their knowledge and experience resulted in a different type of engagement with the theory and research they encountered in course work and dissertation research. This appendix outlines the assumptions, approach, research design, methodology, and limitations for the project.

ASSUMPTIONS AND APPROACH

Learning more about the experience of a group of people required a qualitative approach that would offer participants plenty of opportunity to describe the phenomenon as they lived it. So, this is a phenomenological study (Cilesiz, 2010; Moustakas, 1994) based on a constructivist view of reality (Crotty, 1998), a view that asserts that each person constructs reality in context (Lincoln and Guba, 2000). An extended focus group discussion permits collaborative meaning-making and produces both individual statements and a blended version of reality.

The central steps in empirical phenomenological studies are: (1) delineating a focus of investigation by formulating a question; (2) asking participants, who are viewed as core-searchers, to provide descriptive narratives; and (3) reading and scrutinizing the data to reveal "their structure, meaning configuration, coherence, and the circumstances of their occurrence and clustering" (von Eckartsberg, 1986, 27). The primary roles of the researcher involve first capturing and then interpreting their descriptions of that reality (Creswell, 2007; Jones, Torres, and Arminio, 2006). The interpretation is accomplished through a thematic analysis of the data, seeking to recognize patterns that reflect the concepts and meanings in participant comments (Ayres, 2008; Patton, 2002).

As much as possible, I wanted the project to be driven by participant perspectives, so that we would be cocreating the design of the project as well as the content. Two aspects of the design were specifically geared toward that objective: (1) Half of the participants were invited to a set of preliminary conversations; and (2) participants chose the topics for discussion at the primary focus group meeting in August.

SETTING AND PARTICIPANTS

All participants were enrolled in The Ohio State University, in the Higher Education and Student Affairs (HESA) program, one of a half dozen *sections* in the School of Educational Policy and Leadership, which is part of the College of Education and Human Ecology. The HESA program is nationally ranked among the top ten in the country, and admission is competitive. During the years the participants were students, the program typically enrolled sixty or sixty-five master's students and forty doctoral students. All students either worked full-time or were supported through graduate assistantships. The five professors carried an advising load of between fifteen and twenty-five students, with tenured faculty advising the higher number. For several years from 2006 to 2010, the two senior tenure-track faculty, a colleague and myself, each had more than a dozen doctoral advisees.

The School of Educational Policy and Leadership Student Services office is headed by a very energetic and experienced woman. She and her staff reach out to students constantly with course and program information, graduate school and college deadlines, scholarship and fellowship applications, and workshop and orientation meetings. Both the master's and doctoral students in the program regularly use her office as a resource.

The HESA program is cohort based for both master's and doctoral students. There is a two-day orientation in September, as Tina pointed out, and doctoral students take a number of courses together: (a) three core doctoral courses (one each quarter) were taken in the first year with the students from Educational Administration, and (b) four core higher education and student affairs courses were taken during the first and second year, in classes with the master's students. In addition, some students enroll in the same inquiry courses, depending upon their research preferences.

The participants were drawn from the group of doctoral students whom I had advised between 1994 and 2010 and who had successfully completed their degrees. The choice of participants was purposeful. The questions we would explore together would involve reflections on both personal and professional activity and feelings and would require a level of trust that I felt could best be achieved if there were already a relationship upon which to base the sharing. This type of purposeful sample creates limitations, which will be discussed below.

However, one advantage of the sample is that the advising style, program requirements and culture, and school and university settings were kept constant, and added no variation beyond the passage of time. Having said that, between 1994 and 2010 when the last participant graduated, there were many changes: five different school directors, the creation of a "section" combining the HESA program with the program in Educational Administration, and ten years later, the separation of those two programs into two independent sections, departure of three tenured faculty, recruitment of three new tenured faculty, recruitment of five visiting professors and lecturers, and a substantial, college-wide budget cut that, among other changes, resulted in replacing a full-time program support position with a twenty-hour-per-week graduate assistantship.

Sixteen graduates were invited to participate; sixteen agreed. Family circumstances caused one participant to withdraw before the August conference. The characteristics of the participants are presented at the end of the first chapter. Table A.1 presents a summary with participants listed by age at the beginning of their PhD program. Names clearly indicate gender; there were eleven women, and four men.

Table A.1 Participant Characteristics

Name	Age	GA Position	Working F–T	Married or Partnered	Single	Children	No Children
Olivia	26		x	x		x	
Laura	26	x		x			x
Jaime	26	x			x		x
Brian	28		x	x			x
Stephanie	30		x		x		x
Davida	30	x	Year 4+		x	x	
Brad	30	x	In Diss	x			x
Kathy	31	In Diss	x	x			x
Ben	31		x	x		x	
Seth	31	x			x		x
Kelly	35	x		x			x
Carole	41		x	x		x	
Emily	41	x	Year 2+	x Divorced Y4		x	
Polly	42		x	x		x	
Tina	47		x	x		x	

Geographically, seven participants lived within the greater Columbus area. One lived an hour away. The others who traveled for the conference were located in Florida, Maryland, Michigan, Wisconsin, and upstate Vermont. The project contributed $200 toward expenses for each of the three people from Maryland, Wisconsin, and Vermont. Everyone arranged their own accommodations, and those who drove simply came on their own tabs. Seth participated via video link from Washington, D.C., for the full two-day August meeting, and Stephanie participated via audio link from her home in Luxembourg as well.

RESEARCH DESIGN AND DATA COLLECTION

The research design was reviewed and approved by the Institutional Review Board at the university. The design involved several stages: preliminary conversations, reflection papers, a two-day focus group discussion, and for those who could not attend the focus group, a three-hour video conference.

Preliminary Meetings

Consistent with my intent to create a process that invited cocreation, participants who lived nearby were invited to discuss the project idea as the design was developing. Eight graduates met as two different groups of four for about an hour and half to discuss the project; one meeting was held at my home and the other at the university. During the meetings I asked their opinions about the need for the research, for help scoping out the breadth of topics that might be addressed, and about their willingness to participate.

Reflection Papers

One challenge of the project was that participants were being asked to reflect on activity that had occurred between 1995 and 2010. This was both a disadvantage, as memory can be unreliable, and an advantage. Typically, memories associated with strong emotions tend to be the most vivid. To assist with memory and elicit information for the focus group agenda, participants were asked to write short reflection papers before the August focus meeting. We had discussed the question of memory at the preliminary meetings, and those folks suggested using reflection papers to help people recapture their sense of the doctoral experience. However, everyone indicated that the exercise should be of a length that would be manageable for busy professionals. So, rather than seeking the type of reflection that might support a full auto-ethnography (Ellis and Bochner, 2003; Jones, 2009), a series of questions were posed to guide the reflections and begin the conversation (see Table A.2).

Table A.2 Reflection Paper Questions

1. What was it about this project, and these conversations, that you found appealing?

2. What are your strongest memories of your doctoral experience?

3. For those of you who left a full-time position, and entered the PhD program with a GAA appointment: If you were to talk with an incoming mid-career student, what elements of the change from working full-time in a responsible position to becoming a doctoral student would you bring to their attention, (a) as the most exciting, and (b) as the most difficult?

4. For those of you who enrolled in the PhD program while working full-time: If you were to talk with an incoming mid-career student, what aspects of maintaining your current job while engaging in a doctoral program would you bring to their attention, (a) as the most exciting, and (b) as the most difficult?

5. As you reflect, consider whether you might like to comment on some of the following topics here, and please note those you think should be the subject of a longer conversation (e.g., in August, or through video-conference).

a) family obligations	h) knowing how to set priorities
b) loss of income	i) having life experience to relate to theory
c) loss of status	j) finding time to study
d) lack of practice at being in school	k) finding time to write
e) becoming a 'neophyte'	l) impact of the dissertation
f) clarity of goals	m) role of the cohort
g) fear	n) changes in your identity

6. What other topics should we be sure to discuss?

7. Tell me please, whether to include, or remove, your name from the document

Focus Group Meeting

Thirteen graduates participated in the two-day focus group discussion August 21–22, 2010, from 8:30 AM to 6:00 PM on Saturday, and from 9:00 AM to noon on Sunday as shown on the agenda (Table A.3). The entire day was spent as a full group conversation. Everyone had time to speak, and people tended to follow one thought or topic before moving to another. The focus group discussions were recorded on videotape and later transcribed professionally. One person, Olivia, participated only on Saturday, and Carole participated only on Sunday. The project research assistant attended all sessions. Seth participated both days through a video-link from his new home in Washington, D.C. Stephanie participated through an audio link for both days, from her home in Luxembourg. We had hoped to have a video connection with her, but the trans-Atlantic bandwidth did not support video, so we posted a large picture of Stephanie at the front of the room. All but two people went to a group dinner Saturday evening, which I hosted at a local, favorite Chinese restaurant. None of the dinner conversations were recorded.

Table A.3 Focus Group Agenda

Saturday	
8:30–9:00 am	Munch on Bagels, Greet and Chat
9:00–10:15	Welcome and Setting the Stage (Ada)
	Individual Comments (Participants)
	Your name, and date of completion
	Why you are taking the time this weekend . . .
	What struck you about the reflection papers
10:30–noon	Focusing on the Experience
	Reviewing and choosing among Topics
	Topic 1
	Topic 2
Noon to 1:00 pm	Lunch
1:15–3:00	Continuing with Topics
	First, what 'else' do you remember after this morning . . .
	Topic 3
	Topic 4
3:15–5:00	Bringing together current research with your perspectives
	Gleanings from the current research (Ada & Alycia)
	Your reactions and comments
5:15–6:00	Summary comments for the Day
6:30	Dinner at China Dynasty Sunday
Sunday	
8:30–9:00 am	Munch on Bagels, Greet and Chat
9:00–10:15	What is unique about the Mid-Career Experience?
10:30–11:30	Let's talk about output possibilities
	Format . . . article, book
	Who might like to write with Ada
11:30	Afterword (for those able to stay a little longer)

We spent the entire first Saturday session with people introducing themselves, explaining their reasons for participating, and sharing reactions to the reflection papers. While some members of the group knew each other from having been in the same cohort or having taken courses together, others had never met. They might have recognized names by reading previous student's dissertation chapters at my suggestion, or by my having referenced them in conversation, but did not know the others personally.

The second session opened with a discussion of the themes that emerged from the reflection papers and an invitation to create an agenda. We filled a white-board with suggestions, and a flip chart. Ultimately the group settled on a handful of topics, including fear, family, the cohort, the role of the advisor, and the difference between advisor and mentor.

The focus group agenda reveals an important decision that I made regarding the introduction of information from previous research about doctoral students. Consistent with my goal that participant perspectives should drive the discussion, I waited to introduce a summary of previous research until mid-afternoon on Saturday, the fourth session of the day. By that time not only had the participants chosen the topics for discussion (Saturday morning), but we had discussed several of the topics that were most important to them, and they had developed a rapport with each other that supported the sharing of some very personal and heart-felt emotions. By the afternoon I felt new information would not derail the evolution of their conversation and that they would feel free to comment about the points. The research summary given to them appears in chapter 10.

Video-Conference

Three graduates who were unable to attend the August meeting, Brian, Carole, and Davida, participated instead in a three-hour video conference on Sunday afternoon, November 13, 2010. The research assistant also attended this session, which was recorded and later transcribed professionally. The questions that guided the afternoon session were based on the August focus group discussion, and appear in Table A.4.

Table A.4 Agenda for November Video-Conference

a. Why participate in the project? We're a small club, who else can be interested … I want to understand and add insights.

b. What more or else would you like to understand about your experience?

c. What struck you about the papers?

d. In what ways did the content of your dissertation change you? E.g., Tina said she found there was a need for advocacy for this older group of students.

e. In what ways did the process change you?

f. See Davida's reflection p. 3, re DOUBT . . . what is everyone else's version of this? What were your 'turning points'? the critical moments for you? Tina "reclaimed" her courage one evening. What incident or moment allowed or caused you to "claim" your PhD?

g. Who were your role models, or whose story kept you going? Tina mentioned Dolly Parton's biography.

h. What characteristics does a person need to be a successful PhD student?

i. What, if anything, do you miss about the PhD now?

j. How important is professional socialization for a mid-career student by contrast with younger folks who take GAA positions (álà Leaving the Ivory Tower)? How did/does the professional orientation that you came in with, or that is part of your on-going job, affect your change to the new role as a graduate student?

k. How did your family obligations affect you? Spouse, children? [guilt, per Alycia?]

l. How did the changes in the School of Policy & Leadership affect you? And why? E.g., the re-organization and faculty departures (other than your advisor).

VALIDITY, OR QUALITY OF THE DATA

The primary concern in a qualitative project is the validity of the data, which is typically termed *trustworthiness*. Is the data accurate and believable? Like other researchers, I used a variety of strategies to improve the trustworthiness of the data.

Accuracy

The videotapes were transcribed by a professional service because there was so much material and yielded about four hundred pages of transcript. The research assistant and I read through all of it in order to separate out places where the transcript noted words missing or where the typist was unclear. Member checks (Creswell, 2007; Glesne, 2006) consisted of two steps: First, each participant was offered the opportunity to read the entire transcript, which had been posted on the website we used for distributing material. Second, each participant whose comments included missing words was sent an annotated request for clarification. Everyone returned those with corrections.

In addition, five participants read the entire book manuscript prior to publication: Laura, Tina, Carole, Seth, and Davida. Through this process they were able to review and comment on my findings and interpretation of the data (Jones, Torres, and Arminio, 2006).

Trustworthiness

The two primary threats to the validity of the data in this design were: (a) the time that had passed since participants were students, and (b) their relationship with me. To address the first, I sought several ways of prompting participants to reflect on their experiences prior to the focus group meetings. As part of their invitations, the purpose of the project was described for each person in detail. I spoke with each person. Then, everyone was asked to write a reflection paper to help prompt memories. For the eight participants who lived nearby, the preliminary meetings offered another opportunity. And, finally, the length of the two meetings: a combined thirteen hours of focus group discussion, plus another hour and a half for dinner on Saturday, where people were listening to each other and recalling specific incidents, gave them lots of time to reflect and remember.

The second, their relationship to me, was of great concern to me as a researcher, especially after it became clear that a discussion of the role of the advisor and definition of mentors would be a central part of the conversation. The risk was clear: that "my former advisees" might perceive the project as a request for a pat on the back. Evidence that my role was central to their participation appeared during their responses in the introductory session to the question about "Why did you agree to participate?" Virtually everyone said, "Because you asked." Moreover, Sunday morning Tina gave an illustration to be sure I understood their meaning. While her comment was heartwarming, in the context of the project, it was almost alarming.

> On the way up here this morning, I was thinking about all that we talked about yesterday and the advising, advisor discussion. It reminded me of an experience I had some years ago with a young man who was my advisee. He . . . would come and meet with me, and we kept getting these audit sheets from the registrar's office that were not correct, his audit sheet. One day I said to him, "Come on. We're going to the registrar's office together, and we're going to get this straightened out." He looked at me, and he said, "Well you don't have to do that." I said, "Yes I do, because you're one of my people." So for years after he finished the program, he would write me these

notes around Christmas time and he would always sign it "one of your people." [Laughter.] Which I thought was extremely dear, so I'm thinking kind of to summarize all that we said to you yesterday, "We are your people." So you can ask of us what you need.

So we talked about that idea specifically at three different points in the conversation: (1) at the outset of the meeting on Saturday, (2) later that afternoon very explicitly as the discussion began about advisors and mentors, and (3) at the outset of the video conference in November. I voiced my worry. Participants assured me they would try to separate out the personal relationship from their comments about those topics. Several made the point that students talk to one another a lot about faculty, and that many of their comments reflected issues they heard from students in other programs.

The other strategies that researchers can use to assure that the researcher has truly reflected participant feelings and perspectives are triangulation, prolonged engagement, and a search for negative cases (Glesne, 2006; Jones, Torres, and Arminio, 2006). In this project, triangulation was accomplished by comparing comments from different points in time. Comments made during the preliminary meeting and the reflection papers could be compared with the later discussions; comments made during the different focus group sessions within the August meeting, could be compared for consistency, and comments by participants in the August meeting could be compared to those of the participants in the November video conference. My presentation at the annual conference of the National Academic Advising Association in October 2011 offered another opportunity for triangulation, as that audience reacted to the findings about advisors and mentors (Demb, 2011).

Intense, prolonged engagement defined this project: Three hours of preliminary meetings began the process, followed by hours spent reading the reflection papers. The August meetings involved twelve hours of discussion and a dinner. The November session, which involved only three people, consisted of three hours of nonstop conversation. And, of course, while time advising the graduates previously was not formally part of the research process, the sixteen years spent interacting with them while they were students certainly enabled a richer appreciation of their comments.

Searching for negative cases helps the researcher avoid narrow interpretation resulting from appealing themes. It is easy to be seduced into thinking that all the participants in a study agreed with a particular well-articulated perspective. Vigilance is required not only in interpretation, but also in creating a research setting which supports and invites contrary comments. The comfort and rapport the participants felt with each other and me resulted in discussions where people felt free to voice alternative points of view. Particularly in the discussion about guilt and partners, both Tina and Kathy related personal experiences quite different from the others. As we explored the impact of doctoral study on career directions, Stephanie and Polly described their progress along paths that were planned rather than taking radical new directions. And Stephanie gave us a wonderful illustration of a person for whom feedback was simply something to absorb and use, rather than causing undue stress. These situations provide a basis for confidence that the research setting supported the expression of differing perspectives and that the interpretation left room for variation.

Researcher Bias and Ethical Considerations

Researchers are obligated to ask themselves, "Have I interpreted participant comments properly, or are my own experience and bias leading to possible misinterpretation?" Having been advisor to each of these individuals, having interacted with each of them for years, there was clearly the possibility that I might mis-hear or misinterpret comments (Creswell, 2007; Jones,

Torres, and Arminio, 2006). During the discussions, I often paraphrased comments and asked for clarification in order to assure that I had properly understood them. In addition, at several points during the conversations about family, guilt, and the advisor/mentor, the participants anticipated the possibility that I might hear their words differently than intended and several participants would rephrase and explain the points. (Many of the participants had used qualitative methods in their own research and were accustomed to paying attention to these issues.) We used diagrams and charts on the white board to help clarify meanings. Later, my research assistant, Alycia, was invaluable as a sounding board after the conference as we began to discuss the emergent themes.

Perspectives and opinions developed by reviewing previous research or through personal experience can also distort the research process. Both participants and the researcher are at risk. My decision to delay presentation of current research on the topic during the August meeting was one part of a technique called "bracketing" that I used to avoid contaminating participant thoughts (Jones, Torres, and Arminio, 2006, 48). For my own part, the data analysis and writing were both undertaken without reference to previous research until both were completed. While it may be impossible to completely divorce thinking from internalized notions, a self-conscious effort to read and consider interview data with an open and fresh mind allows new ideas to emerge more readily.

Confidentiality and anonymity were considerations only in the context of later use of the data. Participants knew from the outset that they would be meeting each other and many looked forward to it. Toward the end of the sessions when it was clear that there would be at least an article, and possibly a book to be written that would quote them extensively, I asked the participants whether they were comfortable having their names used. Two participants asked for pseudonyms and everyone else said to use their first names. I rechecked with everyone months later, after the book contract had been signed, and asked the five who read the manuscript if they had any concerns about anonymity. All were comfortable having their first names appear.

Only doctoral students who had successfully completed the degree were invited to participate. Structurally, that created a situation where my role had no direct bearing on their professional circumstances. Certainly, several of us might yet collaborate on research, and from time to time, I write references for people. However, they were no longer "my students," and so could interact as independent, experienced professionals as we discussed the topics they chose.

DATA ANALYSIS

A thematic analysis of the reflection papers yielded thirty-two separate topics. Mentioned by half or more of the participants were the following: fear, knowing how to set priorities, finding time to write, role of cohort, having life experience to relate to theory, and changes in identity. Six more were mentioned more than four times: finding time to study, family obligations, becoming a "neophyte," clarity of goals, loss of income, and impact of dissertation. A table showing the distribution of responses by individual was shared, mid-morning on Saturday, with the group of participants attending the August meeting and was sent to Brian, Carole, and Davida prior to the November video conference. It served as the basis for selecting topics the group wished to discuss for the remainder of the session.

The August meeting and November video conference together generated four hundred pages of transcripts, and a half dozen diagrams. I used NVivo9 (QSR International, 2012) to analyze the data from these sessions. Seventy-one codes emerged from those discussions, which were then clustered into nine broader categories or themes. Listed from most frequently to least frequently mentioned, the categories were: (1) emotions, (2) mid-career itself, (3) challenges, (4) advisor-related, (5) support, (6) family, (7) mechanics of dissertation, (8) why the project, and (9) models and theory. The final analysis occurred as the book was written and resulted in the themes that appear in chapter titles and sections. For example, subthemes within both emotions and challenges were identified, and advisor and mentor themes were treated separately.

LIMITATIONS AND TRANSFERABILITY

The structure of the project results in three limitations that should be noted. The first is, as mentioned earlier, that the project was retrospective and relied on the memories of participants.

Second, participants were all students in a higher education and student affairs program, and so we do not know whether their perspectives apply to students in other fields. The reactions of attendees at the NACADA conference indicated that many of the findings related to advising and mentorship might apply more broadly, and the comparison with the literature is strongly suggestive. However, requirements and support within doctoral programs vary widely across fields and so this remains an area for further research.

Third, participants were all advised by the same faculty member. Participants with advisors whose style differs from mine may well have different reactions. They might choose to emphasize different topics than those that were emphasized by this group of participants.

As I discussed in chapter 11, generalization is typically not a goal of qualitative research. Rather, the goal is to illuminate a phenomenon. Transferability, the applicability of findings to another setting, depends upon the reader comparing the research setting to other settings to determine whether the findings might be transferable. I have provided details about the participants, the setting, support services, and the cohort-based program structure in order to offer the "thick description" that might support transferability (Creswell, 2007). I look forward to learning from readers about the findings that resonate with them.

References

Anderson, M. S. (1996). "Collaboration, the doctoral experience, and the departmental environment." *Review of Higher Education* 19(3): 305–26.

Ayres, L. (2008). "Thematic coding and analysis." In L. M. Given (Ed.), *The Sage Encyclopedia of Qualitative Research Methods.* Thousand Oaks, CA: Sage Publications. Retrieved from http://ebooks.ohiolink.edu.proxy.lib.ohio-state.edu/.

Baird, L. L. (1969). "A study of the role relations of graduate students." *Journal of Educational Psychology,* 60(1): 15–21.

———. (1972). "The relation of graduate students' role relations to their stage of academic career, employment and academic success." *Organizational Behavior and Human Performance* 7(3): 428–41.

Bandura, A. (1986). *Social Foundations of Thought and Action: A Social Cognitive Theory.* Englewood Cliffs, NJ: Prentice-Hall.

Blake, R. S., and J. S. Mouton. (1968). *The Managerial Grid: Key Orientations for Achieving Production through People.* Houston, TX: Gulf Publishing Company.

Bridges, W. (1991). *Managing Transitions: Making the Most of Change.* Reading, MA: Addison-Wesley.

———. (2004). *Transitions: Making Sense of Life's Changes.* Cambridge, MA: DaCapo Press.

Calabrese, R. L., and P. A. Smith (Eds.). (2010a). *The Doctoral Students' Advisor and Mentor: Sage Advice from the Experts.* Lanham, MD: Rowman & Littlefield Publishers.

——— (Eds.). (2010b). *The Faculty Mentor's Wisdom: Conceptualizing, Writing and Defending the Dissertation.* Lanham, MD: Rowman & Littlefield Publishers.

Cataldi, E. F., and P. Ho. (2010). *Web Tables: Profiles of Students in Graduate and First-Professional Education: 2007–08.* Washington, DC: U.S. Department of Education, NCES 2010-177.

Chait, R. P., T. P. Holland, and B. E. Taylor. (1991). *The Effective Board of Trustees.* New York: ACE/Macmillan.

Choy, S. P., and T. Weko. (2011). *Stats in Brief: Graduate and First-Professional Students: 2007–08.* Washington, DC: U.S. Department of Education, NCES.

Cilesiz, S. (2010). "A phenomenological approach to experiences with technology: Current state, promise, and future directions for research." *Education Technology Research Development* 59: 487–510.

Clance, P. R., and S. A. Imes. (1978). "The imposter phenomenon in high-achieving women: Dynamics and therapeutic interventions." *Psychotherapy: Theory, Research and Practice* 15(3): 241–47.

Creswell, J. W. (2007). *Qualitative Inquiry and Research Design: Choosing among Five Approaches* (2nd ed.). Thousand Oaks, CA: Sage Publications.

Crotty, M. (1998). *The Foundations of Social Research: Meaning and Perspective in the Research Process.* London, UK: Sage Publications.

Cumming, J. (2009). "The doctoral experience in science: Challenging the current orthodoxy." *British Educational Research Journal* 35(6): 877–90.

Demb, A. (2011). *Beginning Again in Mid-Career.* Presentation at the Annual Conference of the National Academic Advising Association. Denver, October 3.

Demb, A., and F. F. Neubauer. (1992). *The Corporate Board: Confronting the Paradoxes.* New York: Oxford University Press.

de Valero, Y. F. (2001). "Departmental factors affecting time-to-degree and completion rates of doctoral students at one land-grant research institution." *Journal of Higher Education* 72(3): 341–67.

Devenish, R., S. Dyer, T. Jefferson, L. Lord, S. van Leeuwen, and V. Fazakerly. (2009). "Peer to peer support: The disappearing work in the doctoral experience." *Higher Education Research & Development* 28(1): 59–70.

Ehrenberg, R. G., and C. V. Kuh (Eds.). (2009). *Doctoral Education and the Faculty of the Future.* Ithaca, NY: Cornell University Press.

Ehrenberg, R. G., and P. G. Mavros. (1995). "Do doctoral students' financial support patterns affect their times-to-degree and completion probabilities?" *Journal of Human Resources* 30(3): 581–609.

Ehrenberg, R. G., H. Zukerman, J. A. Groen, and S. M. Brucker. (2009). "Changing the education of scholars." In Ehrenberg and Kuh, *Doctoral Education and the Faculty of the Future* (pp. 15–34).

Ellis, C., and A. P. Bochner. (2003). "Autoethnography, personal narrative, and reflexivity: Researcher as subject." In N. K. Denzin and Y. S. Lincoln (Eds.), *Collecting and Interpreting Qualitative Materials* (2nd ed.) (pp. 199–257). Thousand Oaks, CA: Sage Publications.

English, A., and B. Stengel. (2010). "Exploring fear: Rousseau, Dewey, and Friere on fear and learning." *Educational Theory* 60(5): 521–42.

Erikson, E. (1959). *Identity and the Life Cycle.* New York: Norton.

———. (1963). *Childhood and Society.* (2nd ed.). New York: Norton.

Evans, T. (2010). "Supervising part-time doctoral students." In Walker and Thomson, eds., *The Routledge Doctoral Student's Companion* (pp. 131–37).

Fishman, S. M. (2010). *Faculty Emeriti: Retired with Distinction* (Dissertation). The Ohio State University, Columbus, Ohio.

Galvan, J. (2006). *Writing Literature Reviews: A Guide for Students of the Social and Behavioral Sciences* (4th ed.). Glendale, CA: Pyrczak.

Gardner, S. K. (2007). "I heard it through the grapevine: Doctoral student socialization in chemistry and history." *Higher Education: The International Journal of Higher Education and Educational Planning* 54(5): 723–40.

———. (2008). "Fitting the mold of graduate school: A qualitative study of socialization in doctoral education." *Innovative Higher Education* 33(2): 125–38.

———. (2010). "Contrasting the socialization experiences of doctoral students in high- and low-completing departments: A qualitative study of disciplinary contexts at one institution." *Journal of Higher Education* 81(1): 61–81.

Glesne, C. (2006). *Becoming Qualitative Researchers: An Introduction* (3rd ed.). Boston: Pearson.

Golde, C. M. (2000). "Should I stay or should I go? Student descriptions of the doctoral attrition process." *Review of Higher Education* 23(2): 199–227.

———. (2005). "The role of the department and discipline in doctoral student attrition: Lessons from four departments." *Journal of Higher Education* 76(6): 669–700.

Golde, C. M., and T. M. Dore. (2001). *At Cross Purposes: What the Experiences of Today's Doctoral Students Reveal about Doctoral Education.* Washington, DC: The Pew Charitable Trusts.

Golde, C. M., A. D. Bueschel, L. Jones, and G. E. Walker. (2009). "Advocating apprenticeship and intellectual community." In Ehrenberg and Kuh, *Doctoral Education and the Faculty of the Future* (pp. 54–64).

Gravois, J. (2007). "New data offer a rosier picture of Ph.D. completion rates." *Chronicle of Higher Education*, July 17. Retrieved from http://chronicle.com/article/New-Data-Offer-a-Rosier/123433/.

Herman, C. (2010). "Emotions and being a doctoral student." In Thomson and Walker, *The Routledge Doctoral Student's Companion* (pp. 283–94).

Hoffer, T. B., V. Welch, K., Webber, K. Williams, B. Lisek, M. Hess, D. Loew, and I. Guzman-Barron. (2006). *Doctorate Recipients from United States Universities: Summary Report 2005.* Chicago, IL: National Opinion Research Center.

Hornfischer, J. A. (2005). *The Last Stand of the Tin Can Soldiers.* New York: Bantam.

Johnson-Bailey, J., T. Valentine, R. M. Cervero, and T. Bowles. (2009). "Rooted in the soil: The social experiences of black graduate students at a southern research university." *Journal of Higher Education,* 80(2): 178–203.

Jones, S. R. (2009). "Constructing identities at the intersections: An autoethnographic exploration of multiple dimensions of identity." *Journal of College Student Development* 50(3): 287–304.

Jones, S. R., V. Torres, and J. Arminio. (2006). *Negotiating the Complexities of Qualitative Research in Higher Education: Fundamental Elements and Issues.* New York: Routledge.

Kolb, D. A. (1984). *Experiential Learning: Experience as the Source of Learning and Development.* Englewood Cliffs, NJ: Prentice-Hall.

———. (1999). *Learning Style Inventory.* Boston: Hay/McBer Training Resources Group.

Leonard, D., R. Becker, and K. Coate. (2005). "To prove myself at the highest level: The benefits of doctoral study." *Higher Education Research & Development* 24(2): 135–49.

Levinson, D. J. (1978). *The Seasons of a Man's Life.* New York: Ballantine Books.

———. (1986). "A conception of adult development." *American Psychologist* 41: 3–13.

Lewin K. (1975). *Field Theory in Social Science: Selected Theoretical Papers.* Westport, CT: Greenwood Press.

Lincoln, Y. S., and E. G. Guba. (2000). "Paradigmatic controversies, contradictions, and emerging influences." In N. Denzin and Y. S. Lincoln (Eds.), *Handbook of Qualitative Research* (2nd ed.) (pp. 163–88). Thousand Oaks, CA: Sage Publications.

Lovitts, B. E. (2001). *Leaving the Ivory Tower.* Lanham, MD: Rowman & Littlefield.

———. (2005). "Being a good course-taker is not enough: A theoretical perspective on the transition to independent research." *Studies in Higher Education* 30(2): 137–54.

Millett, C. M., and M. T. Nettles. (2006). "Expanding and cultivating the Hispanic STEM doctoral workforce: Research on doctoral student experiences." *Journal of Hispanic Higher Education,* 5(3): 258–87.

———. (2009). "Three ways of winning doctoral education." In Ehrenberg and Kuh, *Doctoral Education and the Faculty of the Future* (pp. 66–79).

Mindtools. (2011). "The Blake Mouton managerial grid: Balancing task and people oriented leadership." Retrieved from www.mindtools.com/pages/article/newLDR_73.htm.

Merriam-Webster OnLine. (n.d.). "Trust." Retrieved from www.merriam-webster.com/dictionary/trust.

Morrison-Saunders, A., S. A. Moore, D. Newsome, and J. Newsome. (2005). "Reflecting on the role of emotions in the PhD process." Presented at 14th Annual Teaching Learning Forum, February 3–4, 2005, Murdoch University, Western Australia.

Moustakas, C. (1994). *Phenomenological Research Methods*. Thousand Oaks, CA: Sage Publications.

Myers and Briggs Foundation. (n.d.). "MBTI Basics." Retrieved from www.myersbriggs.org/my-mbti-personality-type/mbti-basics/.

Nerad, M. (2004). "The Ph.D. in the U.S.: Criticisms, facts, and remedies." *Higher Education Policy* 17: 183–99.

———. (2009). "Confronting common assumptions." In Ehrenberg and Kuh, *Doctoral Education and the Faculty of the Future* (pp. 80–89).

Nettles, M. T. (1990). "Success in doctoral programs: Experiences of minority and white students." *American Journal of Education*, 98(4): 494–522.

Nettles, M. T., and C. M. Millett. (2006). *Three Magic Letters: Getting to PhD*. Baltimore: Johns Hopkins University Press.

Paré, A. (2010). "Making sense of supervision: Deciphering feedback." In Thomson and Walker, *The Routledge Doctoral Student's Companion* (pp. 107–15).

Patton, M. Q. (2002). *Qualitative Research and Evaluation Methods* (3rd ed.). Thousand Oaks, CA: Sage Publications.

———. (2009). "My sister's keeper: A qualitative examination of mentoring experiences among African American women in graduate and professional schools." *Journal of Higher Education* 80(5): 510–37.

Pedersen, P. (1995). *Five Stages of Culture Shock: Critical Incidents Around the World*. Westport, CT: Greenwood Press.

Protivnak, J. J., and L. L. Foss. (2009). "An exploration of themes that influence the counselor education doctoral student experience." *Counselor Education & Supervision* 48(4): 239–56.

QSR International. (2012). *NVivo 9*. Retrieved from www.qsrinternational.com/products_nvivo.aspx.

Redmoon, A., (n.d.). *The Board of Wisdom*. Retrieved from www.boardofwisdom.com/default.asp?topic=1005&listname=Courage.

Senge, P. M. (1990). *The Fifth Discipline: The Art and Practice of the Learning Organization*. New York: Doubleday Currency.

Sheehy, G. (1978). *Passages: Predictable Crises of Adult Life*. New York: Ballantine Books.

———. (1995). *New Passages: Mapping Your Life Across Time*. New York: Ballantine Books.

Solem, M., J. Lee, and B. Schlemper. (2009). "Departmental climate and student experiences in graduate geography programs". *Research in Higher Education* 50(3): 268–92.

Suhre, C. J. M., P. W. A. Jansen, and E. G. Harskamp. (2007). "Impact of degree program satisfaction on the persistence of college students." *Higher Education* 54: 207–26.

Thomson, P., and B. Kamler. (2010). "It's been said before and we'll say it again—research is writing." In Thomson and Walker, *The Routledge Doctoral Student's Companion* (pp. 149–60).

Thomson, P., and M. Walker. (2010a). "Doctoral education in context: The changing nature of the doctorate and doctoral students." In Thomson and Walker, *The Routledge Doctoral Student's Companion* (pp. 9–26).

———. (2010b). *The Routledge Doctoral Student's Companion: Getting to Grips with Research in Education and the Social Sciences* (1st ed.). London: Routledge.

Tinto, V. (1993). *Leaving College: Rethinking the Causes and Cures of Student Attrition* (2nd ed.). Chicago: University of Chicago Press.

Von Eckartsberg, R. (1986). "Fieldwork on the beat." In J. Van Maanen, J. M. Dabbs, and R. R. Faukner (Eds.), *Varieties of Qualitative Research* (pp. 103–51). Beverly Hills, CA: Sage Publications.

Wall, M. (2012). "John Glenn's historic space flight was no sure thing." Retrieved from www.space.com/14628-john-glenn-orbital-spaceflight-risk.html.

Walker, M., and P. Thomson, eds. (2010). *The Routledge Doctoral Supervisor's Companion: Supporting Effective Research in Education and the Social Sciences* (1st ed.). London; New York: Routledge.

Watts, J. H. (2010). "Supervising part-time doctoral students: Issues and challenges." In Walker and Thomson, *The Routledge Doctoral Student's Companion* (pp. 123–29).

Wilson, R. (2012). "A feminist professor's closing chapters." *Chronicle of Higher Education*, April 22. Retrieved from http://chronicle.com/article/Susan-Gubars-Closing chapters/131611/?sid=at&utm_source=at&utm_medium=en.

Yates, L. (2010). "Quality agendas and doctoral work: The tacit, the new agendas, the changing context." In Thomson and Walker, *The Routledge Doctoral Student's Companion* (pp. 299–310).